THE BOOK OF METAPHYSICAL PENETRATIONS

NEAL A. MAXWELL INSTITUTE
FOR RELIGIOUS SCHOLARSHIP

BRIGHAM YOUNG UNIVERSITY

Mullā Ṣadrā

The Book of Metaphysical Penetrations

كتاب المشاعر

A parallel English-Arabic text
translated by
Seyyed Hossein Nasr

Edited, introduced, and annotated by
Ibrahim Kalin

Brigham Young University Press • Provo, Utah • 2014

Library of Congress Cataloging-in-Publication Data is available.

ISBN: 978-0-8425-2839-9 (alk. paper)

PRINTED IN THE UNITED STATES OF AMERICA

1 2 3 4 5 6 7 8 9 18 17 16 15 14

First Edition

For

S. Amir Hossein

Contents

Foreword to the Series

Brigham Young University and its Middle Eastern Texts Initiative are pleased to sponsor and publish the Islamic Translation Series (ITS). Islamic civilization represents nearly fourteen centuries of intense intellectual activity, and believers in Islam comprise approximately one quarter of the world's population. The texts that appear in ITS are among the treasures of this great culture. But they are more than that. They are properly the inheritance of all the peoples of the world.

As an institution of The Church of Jesus Christ of Latter-day Saints, Brigham Young University is honored to assist in making these texts available to many for the first time. In doing so, we hope to serve our fellow human beings of all creeds and cultures. We also follow the admonition of our own tradition, to "seek . . . out of the best books words of wisdom," believing, indeed, that "the glory of God is intelligence."

—Daniel C. Peterson
—D. Morgan Davis

Notes on Conventions

In the English portions of this work, terms of Arabic derivation found in standard English dictionaries are treated as regular English words. Otherwise, Arabic or Persian words and proper names have been transliterated following the Romanization tables established by the American Library Association and the Library of Congress (*ALA-LC Romanization Tables: Transliteration Schemes for Non-Roman Scripts*, compiled and edited by Randall K. Barry [Washington, DC: Library of Congress, 1997]; available online at http://www.loc.gov/catdir/cpso/roman.html).

Translator's Preface

During the long history of Islamic civilization, philosophy has often been taught outside the regular curriculum of the traditional *madrasahs*; and in Persia, which has been and remains the main home of Islamic philosophy, this kind of teaching of this subject has been called *dars-i khārij* (literally, "outside lessons") and has been often held in private homes or other spaces outside formal school buildings. I had the singular blessing to be able to study Islamic philosophy and gnosis (*ᶜirfān*) as *dars-i khārij* for some two decades with some of the foremost traditional masters of the day in Persia: ᶜAllāmah Ṭabāṭabā'ī, Sayyid Muḥammad Kāẓim ᶜAṣṣār, Ayatollah Sayyid Abū al-Ḥasan Qazwīnī, Mahdī Ilāhī Qumsha'ī, and others. They taught through the traditional method, which involved the reading and explication of well-known texts combined with the exposition of the oral tradition that is so crucial for the traditional understanding of the written word in so many of the Islamic intellectual disciplines.

During those years, in addition to gnostic texts, we studied the *Asfār* of Mullā Ṣadrā and the *Sharḥ al-manẓūmah* of Sabziwārī, which is, in a sense, a general introduction to Ṣadrean philosophy, or the *ḥikmat al-mutaᶜāliyah* (the Transcendent Theosophy); but we did not study the *Kitāb al-mashāᶜir*—at least, not directly. Yet, I was taught the Ṣadrean doctrines deeply enough to be able to read and comprehend by myself this late work of Mullā Ṣadrā as it has been understood by traditional authorities of this school. My familiarity with *al-Mashāᶜir* was further enhanced through the fact that Henry Corbin was editing this text critically and translating it into French early in the 1960s. While he was in Tehran each fall season, he would often discuss the text with me; and in fact, we chose together the title *Le Livre des pénétrations métaphysiques* to translate the Arabic title *al-Mashāᶜir.*

In 1979, the hands of destiny cast me far away from Persia to the United States, where, however, I continued to teach Islamic philosophy from the traditional Islamic point of view. After I came to The George Washington University in 1984, a group of advanced and well-qualified students in the field of Islamic philosophy gradually began to assemble around me. And so I decided to perpetuate this time-honored tradition of *dars-i khārij* in the new context of a Western ambience. From the late 1980s through much of the 1990s, I held classes on Islamic philosophy outside the university curriculum and without any formal credits being attached to them. A group of seven or eight advanced students, all of whom are now teachers and scholars of Islamic thought, were invited to attend, the requirements being interest and the necessary intellectual preparation as well as diligence in continuing their attendance in the classes that were held regularly. We started with the *Kitāb al-ḥikmat al-ᶜarshiyyah* of Mullā Ṣadrā and, upon its termination, turned to *Kitāb al-mashāᶜir*. In both cases, we used the best Arabic text available.

In the *dars-i khārij* in Persia, the teacher first reads the text—usually in Arabic, but sometimes in Persian, especially when teaching *ᶜirfān*—and then comments upon it in Persian with subsequent discussions taking place also in that language. In Washington, we had to substitute English for both Arabic and Persian while beginning with the Arabic text. In the case of *al-Ḥikmat al-ᶜarshiyyah*, we already had a good English translation carried out by James Morris. So in the class, I would first read the Arabic text aloud and then the English translation, making certain modifications to it as we went along. Finally, I would provide a commentary in English based on my own long training and familiarity with the oral tradition and the written text. This phase was then followed by questions and discussions.

For *al-Mashāᶜir*, the situation was different since no acceptable translation of the work existed in English. I would first read the Arabic text as established and edited critically by Corbin (although I did make a few corrections in the Arabic as he had established it). Then I would translate it, and this would be followed by discussions of the translation with the students. Once the definitive English translation was established, I would then comment upon it in English. Questions by the students and discussions with them about my commentary followed, the result of these discussions being sometimes incorporated into the final version of the commentary. All of these proceedings were recorded for both *al-Ḥikmat al-ᶜarshiyyah* and *al-Mashāᶜir*, the completion of which took a number of years.

In 1996, the very gifted young Turkish scholar Ibrahim Kalin came to work on his doctorate with me and soon joined our *dars-i khārij*. When my teaching of these texts was completed, the idea came up to publish my translation of and commentary upon *al-Mashāʿir*, considering the special significance of this work in the corpus of Mullā Ṣadrā. I told Dr. Kalin that I would be happy if this were to happen but that I would leave the task of editing the text and the commentary in his hands. The present work constitutes the first part of this major undertaking. He accepted this heavy responsibility. Our hope is that this outstanding Turkish scholar, who is one of the best students I have ever trained in the field of Islamic philosophy and who is already a recognized Islamic philosopher and scholar, will also be able to edit and make available to the public at large the long commentary, now available only on tape, that is the first of its kind in a European language. The commentary will cover hundreds of pages and will require much effort by both of us.

I wish to thank Professor Kalin for all his dedication to this task and hope that our joint endeavor will provide a work that will be a humble contribution to a better understanding not only of the philosophy of Mullā Ṣadrā and the school of *al-ḥikmat al-mutaʿāliyah*, but also of the whole Islamic intellectual tradition. The preservation, continuation, and renewal of this tradition in the present-day context is of the utmost importance for the Islamic world, faced as it is today with so many challenges, for at their heart stands a challenge of an intellectual and philosophical nature.

—Seyyed Hossein Nasr
Bethesda, Maryland
April 2010; Rabīʿ al-thānī 1430

Editor's Introduction: Mullā Ṣadrā and the *Kitāb al-Mashāʿir*

Muḥammad ibn Ibrāhīm ibn Yaḥyā al-Qawāmī al-Shīrāzī, known more commonly as Ṣadr al-Dīn al-Shīrāzī or Mullā Ṣadrā, is one of the most prominent figures of post-Avicennan Islamic philosophy and among the most important philosophers of Safavid Persia (1501–1722). Coming at a later stage of the Islamic intellectual tradition, Mullā Ṣadrā represents the full maturity of Islamic philosophy. His philosophical school, called Transcendent Wisdom, or Theosophy (*al-ḥikmat al-mutaʿāliyah*)—a name used by Ṣadrā himself—signified the new philosophical synthesis that Ṣadrā sought to create from the wide canvas of the Islamic tradition. Transcendent Wisdom, while following the tradition in its broad outlines, introduced a number of new ideas, concepts, and formulations, some of which can be considered revolutionary. Ṣadrā revised the main themes of traditional Islamic philosophy on the basis of his new philosophical vision and gave them a new, fresh life. In light of God's absolute unity (*tawḥīd*) and Islam's robust monotheism, he presented a unified and integrated vision of reality from God to the universe and the human state.

Ṣadrā produced a large amount of work in the major fields of intellectual and religious sciences. But his most important contribution to Islamic philosophy was in the study of existence (*wujūd*) and its application to such areas as cosmology, epistemology, psychology, and eschatology. Ṣadrā represented a paradigm shift from the Aristotelian metaphysics of fixed substances, which had caused the Muslim Peripatetics numerous problems, to the analysis of existence as the ultimate ground and dynamic source of all things. He held that beings derive their reality and truth from their *wujūd* and that a proper philosophical analysis must therefore start and eventually end with it. *Wujūd* is the key concept that links all realms of being and categories of cognition. In paragraph 4 of the *Mashā*ʿ*ir*, Ṣadrā described *wujūd* as the foundation of all principles:

> The problem of *wujūd* is the foundation of philosophical principles, the ground of metaphysical questions, and the axis around which rotates the millstone of the science of unity, the science of eschatology and the science of the resurrection of souls and bodies and many other things, which we have been the only one to demonstrate and the sole person to bring out [their meaning]. Whoever is ignorant of the knowledge of *wujūd*, his ignorance runs though the most important of all subjects and the greatest among them, and he will become mindless of it and the secrets of Divine knowledge and its inner meanings will become lost to him as well as the science of Divine Names and Qualities and prophecy and the science of the soul and its connections [with the whole of cosmology] and its return to the Origin of its origins and its final end [eschatology]. Therefore, we saw to it that we begin with it [the question of *wujūd*].

For Ṣadrā, existence is not a "concept" in the sense of an abstract term, though it has a conceptual mode of existence that we call "mental existence." It is not a "thing" among other things, though it is "all things" at a certain level of existentiation. It is not a substance, accident, or quality—though it is also all of them because, in the final analysis, there is nothing in reality except *wujūd*. It has no counterpart or opposite, because neither *māhiyyah* (essence/quiddity) nor *ʿadam* (nonexistence) can claim to have the same degree of reality as existence.

Ṣadrā defined *wujūd* as a dynamic and multifaceted reality that defies abstraction and conceptualization. To underscore this point, he introduced a key distinction between the concept and reality of existence. The "concept of existence" (*mafhūm al-wujūd*) is a mental representation of existence and reveals something of its conceptual structure. As the human mind works with concepts and general, abstract terms, it turns existence, like everything else, into a concept. It then applies this concept to a multitude of objects and classes. The "reality of existence" (*ḥaqīqat al-wujūd*), however, remains beyond mental constructions and generalizations. Existence is dynamic, continuous, self-renewing, self-effusing. It is also all-embracing in that nothing can be outside it. As Ṣadrā insisted, *wujūd* is not a thing among things, but the reality by which all things come to exist. To use Ṣadrā's ontological language, the "really existing things" (*al-wujūdāt*) are not those things that are composed of matter, but those that transcend matter through intensification in existence.[1] In this sense, there is nothing more comprehensive and all-embracing than *wujūd*. Failing to understand this key distinction between the concept and reality of existence, as Ṣadrā thought Suhrawardī had done,[2] led to all sorts of philosophical errors and fallacious conclusions about the true nature of existence.

While existence is one, it manifests itself through modalities that, in the end, generate what we call multiplicity. In Ṣadrā's words, "the modalities of existence have different degrees: some are intellective, some are related to the soul, and some are dark without any perception."[3] These levels and layers of manifestation are interconnected and hierarchical, moving from the One to the many and back to the One. There is only one single reality in existence, but it travels through the entire "circle of existence" (*dāʾirat al-wujūd*), leaving a different mark at every level. Existence remains the single immutable reality at the root of all things. But it also displays an infinite number of shades, colors, modes, and modalities. This is what Ibn al-ʿArabī called "unity-in-plurality" (*al-waḥdah fī al-kathrah*). This led Ṣadrā to formulate one of the key principles of his epistemology: "It is in the nature of the intellect to unite what is multiple, and it is in the nature of the senses to multiply what is one."[4]

Without denying the use and necessity of mental analysis, Ṣadrā proposed another way of attaining the reality of existence. In strikingly vivid language, he called it "illuminative presence" (*ḥuḍūr ishrāqī*) and "direct witnessing" (*shuhūd ʿaynī*). In paragraph 57 of the *Mashāʿir*, Ṣadrā stated this point as follows:

> The reality of *wujūd* is not in any way actualized in its essence in any of the minds, because *wujūd* is not a universal concept and the *wujūd* of every existent is this existent itself *in concreto*, and that which is *in concreto* cannot be a mental concept. What is represented of *wujūd* as a general mental concept is the *wujūd* which one calls related [*intisābī*] *wujūd*, which is proper to logical judgments. As for knowledge of the reality of *wujūd*, that cannot be other than illuminative presence and real witnessing. Consequently, no doubt remains concerning its identity.

1. Cf. Ṣadrā, *Asfār* 3.1, 304.
2. Cf. ibid., 353.
3. Ibid., 363.
4. Ibid., 380.

In contrast to the Muslim Peripatetics, the theologians, and the Illuminationists before him, Ṣadrā established *wujūd* as the principal reality that precedes and constitutes things. This is known as the "primacy of existence" (*aṣālat al-wujūd*) and is usually contrasted with Suhrawardī's essentialist metaphysics based on the "primacy of essence" (*aṣālat al-māhiyyah*). Suhrawardī held that *existence* is a common term applicable to individual beings. In this sense, existence is nothing more than a "secondary intelligible" (*al-ma*ᶜ*qūl al-thānī*), a universal to be found only in the mind. What gives things their identity is their essence rather than their existence because, Suhrawardī thought, to know that both man and horse *exist* adds nothing to our knowledge of them. *Existence* is thus nothing but a common term between *man* and *horse*. What distinguishes them from one another is their quiddity (*māhiyyah*), which defines the horse as an animal and man as a rational being. Even though Suhrawardī substitutes *light* (*al-nūr*) for *existence* and develops a metaphysics of light, which Ṣadrā largely accepted, the primacy of existence versus quiddity remained a fundamental point of difference between the two philosophers.[5]

This concept of existence is also the main focus of the *Kitāb al-mashā*ᶜ*ir*. Ṣadrā presented in this widely circulated book a dense summary of his ontology with some subthemes in theology, epistemology, and the temporal origination of the world. Existence is the key concept that underlies all other concepts of philosophy and theology. When Ṣadrā discussed knowledge, he defined it as a "mode of existence" (*naḥw al-wujūd*). When he commented on the cosmos or the world of creation, he described it as a manifestation of the all-inclusive reality of existence. When he analyzed God's names and qualities, he again referred back to existence. In this sense, the *Mashā*ᶜ*ir*'s almost exclusive focus on existence and its modalities is in perfect agreement with Ṣadrā's overall concern to ground all philosophy in his gradational ontology.

5. Mullā Ṣadrā's epistemology based on "knowledge by presence" (*al-*ᶜ*ilm al-ḥudūrī*) is largely derived from Suhrawardī. See Kalin, *Knowledge in Later Islamic Philosophy*, 165–73. See also Yazdi, *Principles of Epistemology*; and Ziai, *Knowledge and Illumination*.

Ṣadrā's Life

Mullā Ṣadrā was born in Shiraz in 1571–1572 CE/AH 979–980 into a prominent family. He received his early education in the "transmitted [religious] sciences" (*al-ʿulūm al-naqliyyah*), which included grammar (*naḥw*), Qurʾanic exegesis (*tafsīr*), jurisprudence (*fiqh*), and the science of the traditions of the Prophet (*ʿilm al-ḥadīth*). After completing his early education in Shiraz, Ṣadrā left his hometown for Qazvin, the capital of the Safavid Empire at the time, and then for Isfahan, where he studied the "intellectual sciences" (*al-ʿulūm al-ʿaqliyyah*) with such figures as Sayyid Bāqir Muḥammad Astarābādī, known as Mīr Dāmād (d. 1631/1040), and Bahāʾ al-Dīn Muḥammad al-ʿĀmilī, known more popularly as Shaykh-i Bahāʾī (d. 1622/1031). Some sources add Mīr Abū al-Qāsim Findiriskī (d. ca. 1640–41/1050) to the list of the scholars with whom Ṣadrā studied in Isfahan, but no direct historical connection between the two has been established in any satisfactory manner. This training in both the religious and philosophical sciences must have helped Ṣadrā compose major works in the various branches of the traditional Islamic sciences.

Ṣadrā began his philosophical career in Isfahan when the cultural and religious landscape of Safavid Iran had been shaped to a large extent by the process of establishing Twelve-Imam Shiʿism as the official religious code of Iran, begun in the early 1500s by Shah Ismāʿīl, the founder of the Safavid dynasty.[6] Ṣadrā flourished in a milieu that saw the convergence of various philosophical, intellectual, and religious strands in Persia, and Shah ʿAbbās the Great (1588–1629/996–1038) played a key role in this cultural revival. While Shiʿism gradually became the dominant religious identity of most Persians in the sixteenth and seventeenth centuries, different intellectual currents continued to live within Safavid Shiʿism.[7] Among others, four major schools of the Islamic intellectual tradition influenced scores of thinkers in Persia, including our own Mullā Ṣadrā. The Peripatetic philosophy represented by al-Fārābī and Ibn Sīnā, the School of Illumination (*ishraq*) founded by Shihāb al-Dīn Suhrawardī al-Maqtūl, the Akhbārī school

6. For the intellectual environment of Isfahan in the seventeenth century, see Nasr, "The School of Iṣpahān"; Nasr, "The School of Isfahan Revisited"; and Newman, "Towards a Reconsideration of the Isfahan School of Philosophy."

7. See Nasr, "Spiritual Movements, Philosophy and Theology in the Safavid Period," 656–97.

established by Ibn al-ᶜArabī and his students Ṣadr al-Dīn al-Qūnawī and Dāwūd al-Qayṣarī, and Sunni and Shiᶜite Kalam schools were all instrumental in the creation of a new philosophical synthesis, a synthesis that would find its finest expression in Ṣadrā's Transcendent Wisdom, which culminated in a synthesis and ultimate fruition of all of these currents. Ṣadrā's honorific titles "*Ṣadr al-din*" (meaning the one who is "the bosom of religion") and "*Ṣadr al-mutaʾallihīn*" (meaning "the foremost among those who have become divine-like") attest to his ability to combine these diverse perspectives into a single philosophical vision.

When Ṣadrā was developing as a major philosopher in the early seventeenth century, a major rift had emerged between two schools of thought in Safavid Persia. The famous and somewhat bitter Akhbārī-Uṣūlī dispute within Shiᶜism reached a climax in this period, especially with the revival of Akhbārism by Mullā Muḥammad Amīn Astarābādī (d. 1627). The Akhbārī traditionalism, grounded in a pietistic anti-intellectualism, was opposed to mystical and philosophical interpretations of the Qurʾan and the sayings of the Shiᶜite Imams. Its followers considered it sufficient to rely on the literal authority of the sayings of the Imams, bolstering, in turn, the socioreligious status of rulers and scholars who claimed family descent from the Shiᶜite Imams. The proponents of the Akhbārī movement, who had gained the favor of the Safavid court until the reigns of Shah Ṣafī (1629–1642) and Shah ᶜAbbās II (1642–1666), came to be called by their opponents the "people of the exterior" (*ahl-i ẓāhir*) and the "scholars of the skin or surface" (*ᶜulamā-yi qishrī*).[8]

In his autobiographical essay, Ṣadrā stated that after studying metaphysics and mastering the views of the previous philosophers and "whatever I was able to find in the books of the Greeks,"[9] he was confronted with the adverse attitude of some "simple-minded scholars"—namely, the Akhbārīs, whom Ṣadrā compares to the Sunni Ḥanbalite scholars of Ḥadīth, known in Islamic history for their strict literalism

8. For the Akhbārī-Uṣūlī debate, see Browne, *A Literary History of Persia*, 4:374–76; Morgan, *Medieval Persia, 1040–1797*, 159–61; Halm, *Shiᶜism*, 97–103; Newman, "ᶜAbdallāh al-Samāhījī's 'Munyat al-Mumārisīn,'" 22–51, and "The Conflict Reassessed," 250–61; Babayan, *Mystics, Monarchs, and Messiahs*, 403–12; and Gleave, *Scripturalist Islam*.

9. Ṣadrā, *Asfār*, 1.1 (4).

and anti-intellectualism.[10] He used strong language in condemning the feeblemindedness of such people and admonished them for failing to understand his grand philosophical system, the Transcendent Wisdom.[11] This opposition seems to have been an important factor in Ṣadrā's decision to retreat from the public life of both Isfahan and his hometown, Shiraz, although Ṣadrā felt this move to be in perfect harmony with his quest for spiritual realization. In his autobiographical essay, he described his struggle as follows:

> I restrained my thoughts from dealing with people and mixing with them, and abstained from their companionship and friendship. Then the turning of cycles [the passing of days] and the obstinacy of the people of the present time became easier for me. I released myself from their repudiation and acceptance, and their praise and harm became equal for me. Then I turned my face to the Cause of all causes, and humbled myself before the One Who makes all difficult matters easy. I stayed in this state of secrecy, retreat, obscurity, and withdrawal for a long time. I busied myself with long moments of spiritual exercise as a luminous work, and my heart burned with the desire of attaining more spiritual discipline in a very strong way. Then the lights of the angelic world (*anwār al-malakūt*) began to emanate upon my heart, the secrets of the world of Dominion (*jabarūt*) were unfolded, the light of the One reached it, the Divine subtleties came upon it, and I obtained the secrets of which I was not aware before. The symbols were unveiled to me, and this unveiling (*inkishāf*) was not a result of logical demonstration (*burhan*). On the contrary, with a plenitude of direct witnessing and seeing of the Divine mysteries, I witnessed everything that I had learned before through logical demonstration.[12]

Following the period of his formal education in Isfahan and Shiraz, Ṣadrā retreated to Kahak, a small village near Qom, where he continued his studies in solitude and began to compose some of his major works. After this solitary period, he returned to Shiraz to teach at the Khān *madrasah* built for him by Allāhwirdī Khān. Ṣadrā spent a good part of his later life in the Khan *madrasah*, whose building is still extant

10. Ibid., 1.2 (344). Ṣadrā refers to the Ḥanbalīs together with the Mujassimah as the representatives of this view and criticizes their literalist interpretation of the allegorical verses (*mutashābihāt*) of the Qur'an.

11. Ibid. (6).

12. Ibid., 1.1 (7–8).

in Shiraz. It was here that Ṣadrā completed his major works and trained his choice students. As a devout Muslim philosopher, he went to pilgrimage on foot to Mecca seven times and died in Basra in 1635–36/1045[13] or 1640/1050 on the way back from his seventh pilgrimage.[14]

Mullā Ṣadrā left a deep impact on Persian intellectual and religious circles. His students and followers wrote commentaries on his works, further developed his contributions to Islamic philosophy, and became prominent scholars and intellectuals in their own right. Ṣadrā trained Mullā Muhsḥin Fayḍ Kāshānī (d. 1680) and ᶜAbd al-Razzāq ibn al-Ḥusayn Lāhījī (d. 1662) as his best students. Fayḍ Kāshānī authored *Uṣūl al-maᶜārif* and *Kalimat-i maknūnah*, works of philosophy-cum-theology that further expound Ṣadrā's teachings. Lāhījī, Ṣadrā's second important student, wrote major works of Twelve-Imam Shiᶜite Kalam, among which *Gawhar-i murād* and *Shawāriq al-ilhām* are of particular importance. Both Kāshānī and Lāhījī married Ṣadrā's daughters, carrying their master-disciple relationship to a personal level, and in their turn trained important figures of the school of Mullā Ṣadrā, such as Qāḍī Saᶜīd Qummī.

As Ṣadrā's ideas spread in the Persian and Indian worlds in the post-Safavid era, Ṣadrā came to have many followers from diverse intellectual circles. In the philosophical circles of Iran, one can mention Āqā Muḥammad Bīdābādī (d. 1783), Qāḍī Saᶜīd Qummī (eighteenth century), Mullā ᶜAlī ibn Jamshīd Nūrī (d. 1830), Mullā Muḥammad Ismāᶜīl Iṣfahānī (d. 1860), Mullā ᶜAbdullāh Zunūzī (nineteenth century), Mullā Muḥammad Jaᶜfar Langarūdī Lāhījī (nineteenth century), Mullā Ismāᶜīl Khājūʾī (nineteenth century), Mullā Hādī Sabziwārī (d. 1873), Mullā ᶜAbdullāh Zunūzī's son Āqā ᶜAlī Mudarris Ṭihrānī (d. 1889), Āqā Muḥammad Riḍā Qumshaʾī (d. 1888–1889), Mīrzā Mahdī Āshtiyīnī (nineteenth century), and, most recently, Muḥammad Ḥusayn Ṭabāṭabāʾī (1892–1981). All of these philosophers have contributed to the flourishing of the school of Mullā Ṣadrā with their own glosses and commentaries on Ṣadrā's major works. We should also mention Sayyid Abū al-Ḥasan Qazwīnī and Muḥammad Kāẓim ᶜAṣṣār among the most

13. This date is based on a note by Mullā Ṣadrā's grandson Muḥammad ᶜĀlam al-Huda (d. 1703–4/1115). See Rizvi, *Mullā Ṣadrā Shīrāzī*, 29.

14. For more on Ṣadrā's life, students, works, and influence, see Nasr, *Ṣadr al-Dīn Shīrāzī and His Transcendent Theosophy*; Rizvi, *Mullā Ṣadrā Shīrāzī*; Kalin, "Annotated Bibliography of the Works of Mullā Ṣadrā." See also Muḥammad Khamanei, *Mullā Ṣadrā*; Khwājawī, *Lawāmiʾ al-ᶜārifīn*.

recent scholars and masters of the school of Mullā Ṣadrā. Seyyed Hossein Nasr, whose translation of the *Kitāb al-mashāᶜir* is presented here, studied Mullā Ṣadrā's works with these two figures, and also with ᶜAllāmah Ṭabāṭabāʾī. As I shall discuss below, this attests to the living tradition of the school of Mullā Ṣadrā to this day.

In the religious and theological circles of Iran, Ṣadrā influenced directly or indirectly a number of prominent scholars since the Safavid period. Among these, one can mention Muḥammad Bāqir Majlisī (d. 1699–1700/1111), the famous Shiᶜite theologian and the author of the monumental *Biḥār al-anwār*. Equally important is Mullā Ḥaydar Khwansārī (d. 1688/1099), the author of the *Zubdat al-taṣānīf*; Mullā Ṣāliḥ Māzandarānī (d. 1669/1080); and Shaykh Aḥmad Aḥsāʾī (d. 1826/1241), the founder of a school of thought known as Shaykhism, to whom we shall return below.

Although Ṣadrā's legacy in the subcontinent of India has yet to be studied in full, several figures should be mentioned briefly. Shah Walī Allāh of Delhi (1702–1762), considered to be the greatest Muslim scholar of India in the eighteenth century, composed works in both religious and philosophical sciences and played a key role in the spiritual, social, and political life of the Muslims of India. Like those of Ṣadrā, Shah Walī Allāh's works, and particularly his *Ḥujjat Allāh al-bālighah*, represent an impressive synthesis of religious knowledge, jurisprudence, philosophy, logic, theology, and Sufism.[15] Ashraf ᶜAlī Thanwī (1863–1943), known among Indian Muslims as *ḥakīm al-ummah* (the wise man of the Muslim *ummah*) made extensive use of Ṣadrā's works in his critical treatment of modernism in India. Like his predecessors, ᶜAlī Thanwī was a philosopher, theologian, jurist, and Sufi all at the same time. In his refutation of modern materialism, he refers his readers to his own philosophical work *Dirāyat al-ᶜiṣmah* and to Mullā Ṣadrā's well-known *Sharḥ hidāyat al-ḥikmah*, a commentary on the famous book of formal logic by Athīr al-Dīn Abharī.[16] This commentary is probably the most widely read work of Ṣadrā in the subcontinent of India, though his other works have also been studied, as evidenced by the large number of the manuscripts of Ṣadrā's works in various libraries in India.

15. See Nasr, *Islamic Philosophy from Its Origin to the Present*, 232–33. For the English translation of Shah Walī Allāh of Delhi's *Ḥujjat Allāh al-bālighah*, see *The Conclusive Argument from God*, trans. Hermansen.

16. For Ashraf ᶜAlī Thanwī, see Naeem, "A Traditional Islamic Response to the Rise of Modernism," 79–116.

To the list of prominent figures who have studied the works of Ṣadrā in India, one can also add Muḥammad Iqbal, considered to be the last great Muslim poet and philosopher of India. Iqbal's influence on the intellectual, social, and political life of Indian Muslims has been wide and deep, and he remains one of the intellectual giants for many Muslims both inside and outside India. Although one cannot count Iqbal among the followers of Mullā Ṣadrā, some of his works contain elements from Ṣadrā's teachings. Iqbal's *The Development of Metaphysics in Persia*, while presenting only fragments of Ṣadrā's thought, shows his familiarity with Ṣadrā's ideas and influence. Finally, it should be mentioned that Mawlānā Mawdūdī, the founder of the Jamaᶜat-i Islami of Pakistan and one of the most influential political thinkers of twentieth-century Islam, translated parts of Ṣadrā's *Asfār* into Urdu in his youth.

Ṣadrā's Works

As a prolific author, Ṣadrā produced a sizable corpus in the many different areas of the traditional Islamic sciences. With the exception of his *Si aṣl* and *Dīwān* of poetry, as well as a few letters in Persian, he wrote all of his works in Arabic. His style of writing is one of the most lucid and systematic forms of philosophical writing in Arabic. As a general trait of his philosophy, Ṣadrā wove together the strictly logical discourse of the Peripatetic philosophers with the ecstatic visions of the mystics. After discussing a particular philosophical or cosmological problem in a rigorously analytical manner, he often burst into various aphorisms, exhortations, and ecstatic exclamations in a way comparable to such figures as al-Ghazālī and Ibn al-ᶜArabī.

Ṣadrā represented a culmination of the various philosophical strands of the Islamic intellectual tradition and sought to synthesize them into a coherent philosophical and mystical vision. His writings displayed an impressive synthesis of perspectives, from the logical discussions of substance and accident to poetic and ecstatic discourses on the all-inclusive reality of existence and "unveiling" (*kashf*) as a direct way of knowing the divine mysteries. But Ṣadrā is also an "original" philosopher in the sense that he introduced a number of new ideas, concepts, terms, and formulations into traditional Islamic philosophy. Among Ṣadrā's major contributions, one can mention the "primacy of existence" (*aṣālat al-wujūd*), the idea that "a reality in its simplicity is all things" (*basīt al-ḥaqīqah kull al-ashyāʾ*), "gradation of existence" (*tashkīk al-wujūd*), "unification of the intellect and the intelligible" (*ittiḥād al-ʿāqil wa'l-maʿqūl*), "substantial motion" (*al-ḥarakat al-jawhariyyah*), and the idea that the human soul is "bodily in its origination and spiritual in its subsistence" (*jismāniyyat al-ḥudūth rūḥāniyyat al-baqāʾ*).

Ṣadrā's corpus covers the wide spectrum of traditional philosophy, including metaphysics, cosmology, ontology, epistemology, eschatology, psychology, ethics, and natural philosophy. In addition to philosophical works, Ṣadrā wrote a lengthy yet incomplete commentary on the Qurʾan and several works on the hermeneutics of the Qurʾan and Shiʿite Ḥadīth. His commentary on the Qurʾan is one of the finest examples of philosophical-mystical commentaries in the Islamic tradition. His *Mafātīḥ al-ghayb* (Keys of the Invisible World) and *Mutashābihāt al-Qurʾān* (Allegorical Verses of the Qurʾan) contain an elaborate expression of Ṣadrā's views on Qurʾanic hermeneutics.[17]

Ṣadrā also wrote a mystico-philosophical commentary on the famous Shiʿite book of Ḥadīth *Uṣūl al-kāfī*, compiled by Kulaynī. As in his Qurʾanic commentaries, Ṣadrā dealt in it with the traditions of the Prophet of Islam and the sayings of Shiʿite imams to bring out their philosophical significance, and he discussed such metaphysical issues as the primacy of existence, God's Names and Attributes, the problem of knowledge, and bodily resurrection. In this group of writings, Ṣadrā seems to have been particularly interested in showing the complementary relationship between the transmitted-religious and intellectual-philosophical sciences.

Ṣadrā's magnum opus is *al-Ḥikmat al-mutaʿāliyah fī al-asfār al-ʿaqliyyat al-arbaʿah*, known briefly as the *Asfār*. With the exception of logic and mathematics, the *Asfār* deals with all the major issues of traditional philosophy. The *Asfār* addresses the major problems of traditional philosophy from the point of view of "transcendent wisdom." Ṣadrā structured the *Asfār* according to the four journeys of the soul in the path of spiritual realization. The first journey is "from the world of creation to the Truth" (*min al-khalq ilá al-ḥaqq*), in which Ṣadrā addressed the questions

17. See Nasr, "The Qurʾanic Commentaries of Mullā Ṣadrā," 123–35; Peerwani, "Quranic Hermeneutics," 468–77; Khamanei, *Principles of Interpretation and Quranic Hermeneutics according to Mulla Sadra*. See also Salih, "The Verse of Light." The most important source for Ṣadrā's Qurʾanic hermeneutics is his partial commentary in seven volumes, edited by Khwājawī, as *Tafsīr al-Qurʾān al-karīm*.

of metaphysics and ontology under the rubric of "general principles" (*al-umūr al-ʿāmmah*) or "divine science in its general sense" (*al-ʿilm al-ilāhī bi'l-maʿná al-aʿam*). In it, Ṣadrā laid the ontological foundations of his system and gave his own definitions of philosophy, existence and its primacy (*aṣālah*) over quiddity (*māhiyyah*), gradation of existence (*tashkīk al-wujūd*), unity of existence (*waḥdat al-wujūd*), mental existence (*al-wujūd al-dhihnī*), Platonic forms (*al-muthul al-aflāṭūniyyah*), causality, substantial motion (*al-ḥarakat al-jawhariyyah*), time, the temporal origination of the world (*ḥudūth al-ʿālam*), the intellect and other faculties of knowing, the imaginal world (*ʿālam al-khayāl*), and the unification of the intellect with the intelligible.

The second journey is "from the Truth to the Truth by the Truth" (*min al-ḥaqq ilá al-ḥaqq bi'l-ḥaqq*). Here we find a full account of Ṣadrā's natural philosophy and his critique of the ten Aristotelian categories. The issues discussed include the categories, substance and accidents, how physical entities come to exist, *hylé* and its philosophical significance, matter and form (hylomorphism), natural forms, and the hierarchy of the physical order.

The third journey is "from the Truth to the world of creation with the Truth" (*min al-ḥaqq ilá al-khalq bi'l-ḥaqq*), where Ṣadrā presented his theology and discussed it under the name of "metaphysics" or "divine science in its particular sense" (*al-ʿilm al-ilāhī bi'l-maʿná al-khaṣṣ*). Here the theological dimension of Ṣadrā's thought and his relentless attacks on the theologians (*mutakallimūn*) come into full fruition. Among the issues Ṣadrā addressed are the unity and existence of God and the previous Kalam proofs for it, the ontological simplicity of the Necessary Being, the names and qualities of God, God's knowledge of Himself and the world, His power, divine providence, good and evil (the problem of theodicy), procession of the world of multiplicity from the One, and the unity of philosophy (*ḥikmah*) and Divine law (*Sharīʾah*).

The fourth journey is "from the world of creation to the world of creation with the Truth" (*min al-khalq ilá al-khalq bi'l-ḥaqq*), where the great chain of being is completed with psychology, resurrection, and eschatology. It is also here that Ṣadrā presents a detailed refutation of the belief in the transmigration of souls (*tanāsukh*). This final journey concludes with Ṣadrā's spiritual psychology and his views on the hereafter.

◆

Ṣadrā's other philosophical works include the following:

al-Ḥikmat al-ʿarshiyyah, a major work of theology dealing with such issues as the human soul and eschatology

Risālat al-ḥashr, a philosophical commentary on the question of resurrection

Ḥudūth al-ʿālam, an extensive discussion of the temporal creation of the world

Iksīr al-ʿārifīn, a philosophical and mystical treatise on knowledge and the soul adapted from Afḍal al-Dīn Kāshānī's (d. 1214) Persian work *Jāwidān-nāmah*

Kasr aṣnām al-jāhiliyyah, a critique of what Ṣadrā considered to be the pretensions of the Sufis and ascetics of the Safavid period

al-Mabdaʾ wa'l-maʿād, a major work on philosophical theology that presents Ṣadrā's ideas on a number of key issues in traditional philosophy and theology and that follows the main outline of Ibn Sīnā's work with the same title

Mafātīḥ al-ghayb, containing important discussions of the principles of Qurʾanic exegesis and presenting a detailed analysis of Ṣadrā's views on such issues as the creation of the universe, its purpose, man's quest for spiritual realization, knowledge as a way of attaining perfection, God and His Names and Qualities, angels, and the hereafter

Majmūʿa-yi rasāʾil-i falsafī-yi Ṣadr al-Mutaʾallihīn, containing a number of short and long treatises on various themes of classical philosophy

Kitāb al-mashāʿir, a condensed summary of Ṣadrā's ontology and theology, the translation and a fuller discussion of which are provided below

al-Maẓāhir al-ilāhiyyah fī asrār al-ʿulūm al-kamāliyyah, a mystico-philosophical work dealing with philosophy as spiritual perfection

Sharḥ-i ilāhiyyāt-i shifāʾ, a major commentary on the *Metaphysics* of Ibn Sīnā's *Shifāʾ*

al-Shawāhid al-rubūbiyyah, a collection of reflections on various philosophical and spiritual issues, including existence, knowledge, the human soul, revelation, and political philosophy

Sharḥ al-hidayat al-athīriyyah, a commentary, widely read in Iran and India, on the famous logico-philosophical treatise of Athīr al-Dīn Faḍl ibn ʿUmar al-Abharī al-Samarqandī (d. 1264)

Tafsīr al-Qurʾān al-karīm, an unfinished commentary on the Qurʾan; one of the finest examples of philosophico-mystical commentary in the Islamic tradition, showing Ṣadrā's full repertoire of religious and intellectual expositions

Si aṣl, Ṣadrā's only treatise written in Persian and one of his important works on spiritual ethics, of particular importance in showing his critical attitude toward the Shiʿite literalists of his day; it also contains some autobiographical remarks

Īqāẓ al-Nāʾimīn, a Sufi work that combines Ṣadrā's ontology and epistemology as he analyzes the traditional themes of philosophy to show their relevance for spiritual wayfaring

Sharḥ uṣūl al-kāfī, an unfinished commentary on the Shiʿite Ḥadīth collection *Uṣūl al-kāfī*

Various editions of these works and others not listed above constitute Ṣadrā's enduring intellectual legacy and continue to be studied by students of philosophy all over the world.[18]

Kitāb al-Mashāʿir

Given the number of commentaries and glosses written on it, *Kitāb al-mashāʿir* can be considered one of the most widely read and circulated works of Mullā Ṣadrā. This is partly due to the fact that the *Mashāʿir* is a dense summary of Ṣadrā's metaphysics of existence and theology, to which later commentators turned for a quick overview of Ṣadrā's

18. For manuscript and publication details of Ṣadrā's works, see Rizvi, *Mullā Ṣadrā Shīrāzī*; Kalin, "An Annotated Bibliography of the Works of Mullā Ṣadrā," 21–62.

ontology.[19] The Persian translation of the *Mashāʿir* by the Qajar prince-philosopher Badīʾ al-Mulk Mīrzā ʿImād al-Dawlah, whose father, Fatḥ ʿAlī Shah Qajar, ruled Persia from 1797 until 1834, may also have encouraged the Persian-speaking students of traditional metaphysics and philosophy in Iran and elsewhere to study Ṣadrā's thought. Also, the completion of *Mashāʿir* is dated to January 14, 1628, when Ṣadrā was about fifty-eight years old.[20] On the basis of this date, we may consider the *Mashāʿir* to be one of Ṣadrā's most mature works.

The *Mashāʿir* concentrates on two issues: ontology and theology. In the section on ontology, Ṣadrā provided an extensive analysis of *wujūd*, its modalities, and how it generates the world of multiplicity and change while itself remaining one and unchanging. Since Ṣadrā used existence as the main frame of reference for all problems of philosophy, he analyzed existence not as a topic of philosophy among others but as the underlying and all-comprehensive principle or reality that encapsulates everything. It is therefore not surprising to see Ṣadrā devoting two-thirds of the *Mashāʿir* to existence.

This long section on existence is followed by a discussion of certain theological issues that include God's existence, His unity, and His act in the world of creation. Ṣadrā goes over the traditional proofs for the existence of God and explains how God must be the Necessary Being and why there cannot be more than one such being. But unlike the previous Kalam and Peripatetic proofs for the existence of God based mostly on logical inferences, Ṣadrā based his analysis again on existence and its full actuality, perfection, and plenitude. Unlike the Peripatetics, who used the same arguments to prove the existence of God but ran into many difficulties as they tried to explain how this God fit into their self-regulated, Aristotelian cosmology, Ṣadrā defended both the existence and constant presence of God in His creation. While it is clear that Ṣadrā paid due attention to the Qurʾanic description of God as all-powerful, omnipresent, and omniscient, he also made full use of his gradational and dynamic ontology, which enabled him to reinterpret the world of creation into a "structure of events" and utterly dependent order. This may explain in part why Ṣadrā ended the *Mashāʿir* with a

19. An English translation of this work by Morewedge, entitled *The Metaphysics of Mullā Ṣadrā*, attempts to translate Ṣadrā in terms of analytic philosophy but is marred by various translation and conceptual problems.

20. Rizvi, *Mullā Ṣadrā Shīrāzī*, 66.

condensed section on the temporal origination of the world (*ḥudūth al-ᶜālam*), a subject to which he devoted a number of works.[21]

The book ends with a series of philosophical exhortations and spiritual intimations concerning the meaning of philosophy and spiritual wayfaring. After stating that "the paths to God, transcendent is He, are multiple, because He possesses countless virtues and aspects" (paragraph 142), Ṣadrā contrasted his path to God with that of "the majority of the philosophers . . . the philosophers of nature (*al-ṭabīʾiyyūn*) . . . [and] the theologians (*al-mutakallimūn*)," all of whom sought to reach God by looking in the wrong place—that is, by examining things other than God Himself. By contrast, "the sages of the Lord (*rabbāniyyūn*)," with whom Ṣadrā identified himself, took a radically different approach. They "first of all look at the reality of *wujūd*. Then they realize it and come to know that it is the principle of all things and that it is, according to the truth, the Necessary Being." As elsewhere, Ṣadrā began and ended his exposition of theology with existence.

While the two themes of ontology and theology clearly stand out as the main focus of the book, the plan of the *Mashāᶜir* presents several problems. Ṣadrā proposed an outline in the second part of paragraph 4 but did not follow it. He said that he "composed this treatise on the basis of an introduction and two stations, each one of which consists of metaphysical penetrations (*mashāᶜir*)." But these two stations do not appear in the plan of the book. What we have instead is an introduction without a title, an opening (*al-fātiḥah*), eight penetrations (*mashᶜar*), and three paths (*manhaj*). Both "penetrations" and "paths" have unequal numbers of subdivisions, also called "penetrations." But they are not divided as "two stations." One way of explaining this is to say that the "two stations" to which Ṣadrā referred in his introduction could be a reference to the first part of the book, which consists of the main "eight penetrations," and the "three paths," which make up the final parts of the book.

In a broad sense, Ṣadrā devotes the main "eight penetrations" to ontology and the "two paths" to theology. In the ontology section, he discusses the concept and reality of existence, how it is above definitions, how it encapsulates all things, questions and doubts concerning the concrete reality of existence, the precise nature of the qualification of the

21. See, for example, Ṣadrā, *al-Risalah fī al-ḥudūth*. For Ṣadrā's concept of the temporal origination of the world, see Kalin, "Will, Necessity, and Creation as Monistic Theophany." See also Jambet, *Mort et résurrection en islam*.

quiddity (*māhiyyah*) by existence, the particularization of existence, the problem of "instauration" (*jaʿl*), and the relation between instauration (or secondary causation) and the "effusion" (*ifāḍah*) of the world of multiplicity from the One. At the end of the Eighth Penetration, Ṣadrā introduces God's existence and unity. He devotes the First and Second Paths to the relation between God and the world of creation, why and how God is the source and end of all things, how God "intellects" Himself and other things, God's names and qualities and why they are not different from His essence, how God knows all things, and God's attribute of speech and its meaning for creation. In the Third Path, Ṣadrā continues to elaborate on several theological issues and sums up his discussion with a short description of the temporal origination of the world.

In terms of the paragraphs and paragraph numbers assigned by the Henry Corbin edition and adopted by us in this translation, the actual order of the book is as follows:

Introduction	Paragraphs 1–4
First Penetration	Paragraphs 5–11
Second Penetration	Paragraphs 12–14
Third Penetration	Paragraphs 15–37
Fourth Penetration	Paragraphs 38–68
Fifth Penetration	Paragraphs 69–80
Sixth Penetration	Paragraphs 81–88
Seventh Penetration	Paragraphs 89–101
Eighth Penetration	Paragraphs 102–103
First Path	Paragraphs 104–117
Second Path	Paragraphs 118–122
Third Path	Paragraphs 123–141
"The Seal of the Treatise"	Paragraphs 142–150

Some of these chapters have further subchapters and short explanatory passages.

In addition to this problem of organization, there is also the issue of what Ṣadrā promised to discuss and what he actually ended up discussing. In paragraph 4, he presents a long list of issues that he says he will discuss in the book. These include "the principles of *wujūd* . . . the science of the soul and its resurrection to the spirits and [subtle] bodies; the science of prophecy and sanctity (*walāyah*); the secret of the descent of revelation and the verses; the science of the angels and their inspirations and signs; the demons and their temptations and doubts; the proof of the world of the grave and the intermediate states. [Then we shall discuss] the manner in which God knows both universals and particulars; the knowledge of divine predetermination [pre-eternal decree] (*qaḍāʾ*) and destiny (*qadar*) and the Pen and the Guarded Tablet; the proof of the luminous Platonic ideas; the question of the unity of the intellect and the intelligibles; the unity of sense and the sensibles; and the problem of a simple reality (*basīṭ*), such as the intellect and all the beings above it, being all things." But Ṣadrā discusses only some of these issues, and he does so in a very summary manner and mostly by way of allusion. He spends most of his time elaborating on existence and approaching it from various angles. On other issues, he refers his readers to his other books.

How can one explain this? Could it be that Ṣadrā started out to write the *Mashāʿir* as he planned but then decided to cut it short? After explaining existence and its modalities, did he feel that he had explained the essential issue(s) and that the rest should be left to the reader to follow up? Or could it be that Ṣadrā, as Corbin suggested, simply forgot the original plan of the book? Like Corbin, we can only speculate about these possibilities.[22] Despite these structural problems, the *Mashāʿir* remains a first-rate work of metaphysics and one of the most important statements of Ṣadrā's ontology and theology.

Commentaries on the *Mashāʿir*

I have already referred to *Mashāʿir*'s popularity in posterity. Generations of scholars and masters of Islamic philosophy have taught the *Mashāʿir* as a textbook in their advanced courses, while Ṣadrā's other works, including the *Asfār*, have also been widely read and taught. Around a dozen known commentaries and glosses have been written on the *Mashāʿir* over the last two centuries. While Ṣadrā's immediate students and followers knew and studied most of Ṣadrā's major works, the

22. For Corbin's edition and translation, see Ṣadr al-Dīn Shirāzī, *Le Livre des pénétrations métaphysiques*, 44.

Mashā^cir, together with the *Asfār*, has received the lion's share in terms of commentaries and glosses.

The prominent commentators of the *Mashā^cir* include Badī^ᵓ al-Mulk Mīrzā ^cImād al-Dawlah, referred to above; Shaykh Aḥmad Aḥsā^ᵓī (d. 1826); Mullā ^cAlī Nūrī (d. 1830); Mullā Muḥammad Langarūdī Lāhījī (d. circa mid-nineteenth century); Mullā Ismā^cīl Iṣfahānī (d. 1860); Mīrzā Aḥmad Ardakānī Shīrāzī (d. in the second half of the nineteenth century); Mullā Zayn al-^cĀbidīn ibn Muḥammad Jawād Nūrī (d. in the second half of the nineteenth century); Mīrzā Abū al-Ḥasan Jilwah (d. 1896); and several others. The Persian translation and commentary of the *Mashā^cir*, entitled *^cImad al-ḥikmah*, by the Qajar prince-philosopher Badī^ᵓ al-Mulk Mīrzā ^cImād al-Dawlah, must have played an important role in its wider circulation and study among the Persian-speaking students of philosophy.[23]

Of these commentators, Shaykh Aḥmad Aḥsā^ᵓī, the founder of the school of Shaykhism, has received particular attention in later scholarship for several reasons. First of all, Aḥsā^ᵓī wrote commentaries on the *Mashā^cir* and *al-Ḥikmat al-^carshiyyah* in which he criticized the two key ideas of Mullā Ṣadrā: the primacy of being (*aṣālat al-wujūd*) and the idea that "a reality in its simplicity is all things" (*basīṭ al-ḥaqīqah kull al-ashyā^ᵓ*). While this attests to Aḥsā^ᵓī's independence of mind, he is important for a historical, if not philosophical, connection that he is alleged to have provided between Ṣadrā's teachings and the rise of Babism and, later, Baha^ᵓism. As a controversial and heterodox movement within Shi^cism, Babism branched out from Shaykhism when Sayyid ^cAlī Muḥammad of Shiraz, the founder of Babism, claimed in 1844 that he was the "*bāb*" (the gate) through which the Hidden Imam spoke to his followers. Mīrzā Ḥusayn ^cAlī Nūrī Bahā^ᵓullāh (d. 1892), a devout follower of Sayyid ^cAlī Muḥammad al-Bāb, established Baha^ᵓism by declaring himself to be Bāb's successor and later claiming to be a prophet—a claim rejected by both Sunni and Shi^cite Islam.

The fact that Sayyid ^cAlī Muḥammad Bāb, the founder of Babism, was a follower of Shaykh Aḥmad Aḥsā^ᵓī, who had studied Ṣadrā's teachings and had written commentaries on his works, has been interpreted by some to suggest a link between Ṣadrā's ideas and the rise of Babism and

23. For more on these commentators, see ibid., 46–54.

Baha'ism. Muḥammad Iqbal,[24] E. G. Browne,[25] and Carl Brockelmann[26] have all claimed or alluded to a philosophical continuity between Ṣadrā and Baha'ism. Corbin rejects any direct link but argues that "Mullā Ṣadrā has furnished the Shaykhī school with an occasion to formulate and clarify its proper positions."[27] None of these suggestions, however, is sufficient to establish a link between Ṣadrā and the schools of Shaykhism, Babism, and Baha'ism as already established by Seyyed Hossein Nasr.

In preparing the notes to the present translation, I consulted Mullā Muḥammad Langarūdī Lāhījī's commentary on *Mashāʿir.* Lāhījī wrote in a clear and fluid manner and added considerable depth to Ṣadrā's text with his own glosses. I have translated some passages from Lāhījī's commentary to clarify a point but also to allow the English reader to have a taste of a nineteenth-century commentary on a seventeenth-century text. Lāhījī's commentary has been prepared by the late Sayyid Jalāl al-Dīn Āshtiyānī, with his own glosses in Arabic and Persian.

Translating the *Mashāʿir*

The task of translating Islamic philosophical texts into modern European languages poses challenges to students of Islamic philosophy in several ways. While the language of classical philosophy itself presents difficulties to contemporary students and translators of Islamic philosophical texts, the situation is further complicated by the absence of an accumulated body of reliable and authoritative translations. Some excellent translations have been produced in recent years, and they are an encouraging sign for the improved quality of Islamic philosophical studies. Yet, we are still far away from having a coherent and consistent vocabulary for the translation of Arabic philosophical texts in English and other European languages. There are several issues to be considered here.

First of all, all translations of texts from the classical languages—whether Arabic, Hebrew, Greek, or Sanskrit—face the problem of losing etymological connections that exist in the original language. This

24. Iqbal, *The Development of Metaphysics in Persia*, 175, where Iqbal says that the "philosophy of Ṣadrā is the source of the metaphysics of early Babism."

25. Browne, *A Literary History of Persia*, 4:430, quotes Iqbal on this issue.

26. Brockelmann, *Geschichte der arabischen Literatur* Supliment, 2:588: "an seine [i.e., Ṣadrā's] Metaphysik knupfte der Grunder der Saihisekte, Saih A. Ahsa'i, seine Lehre an, und auf dieser fusste wieder die Theosophie des Bab."

27. Corbin, *Le Livre des pénétrations*, 20.

is especially true for Arabic, where many key concepts are derived from a single root and often have several layers of meaning. It is difficult to convey meaning and maintain etymology at the same time when translating related concepts with different shades of connotation. A case in point is the root verb *wa-ja-da/aw-ja-da* (meaning "to find" and "to be found") and its derivations. The three well-known words *wujūd* (existence), *wajd* (ecstasy), and *wijdān* (consciousness) all derive from the same root but mean different things while maintaining a conceptual-etymological connection. These terms all share a common field of meaning in the sense that "existence," "state of ecstasy," and "cognition based on direct perception" are all related to the act of "finding" and "being found." But this etymology is lost in translation into English.

In some cases, a straight, literal translation of an Arabic word into conventional English creates problems. A typical example is the rendering of *ᶜaql* and *maᶜqūl* as "reason" and "rational." In certain contexts, *ᶜaql* can be translated as "reason" in the sense of the faculty of cognition. But the word *reason* does not cover all of the fields of meaning that *ᶜaql* has in Arabic. Thus, use of the word *intellect* becomes necessary, despite the fact that Arabic does not have the reason/intellect bifurcation that exists in English. For instance, it does not make sense to translate *ᶜuqūl mujarradah* as "abstract reasons." The same applies to the word *maᶜqūl*. Literally, it can be translated as "reasoned," "rational," or "reasonable." But none of these renderings capture the intended meaning of *maᶜqūl*, which connotes something "intellected" or, more properly, "intelligible." Furthermore, such words as *reason*, *reasonable*, and *rational* are loaded with modern connotations virtually impossible to separate from the history of Western philosophy since the seventeenth century.

In addition, there is the problem of finding appropriate equivalents to Arabic words and concepts. Such key words of Ṣadrā's philosophical vocabulary as *wujūd, jaᶜl, tajawhur, ᶜurūḍ, mashᶜar, tashkīk, aṣālah*, and *kawn*, among others, have no direct equivalents in English. To render them properly, one has no choice but to use several words or combinations of words and occasionally resort to neologisms.

In light of the considerations above, we have decided in this work to keep the term *wujūd* in its original Arabic form rather than translating it, since there is no single equivalent for it in English. *Wujūd* can correspond to Being, being, Existence, or existence, depending on the particular way and context in which it is used. It can mean "Being" in the sense of

Absolute Being, or the Being of God, and the *esse* of medieval philosophy. It can connote "being" in the ordinary sense of the term, such as the being of a tree or a human. It can mean "Existence," not as the supreme ontological principle, but in the sense of the ontological principle of the domain of cosmic existence, equated in later Islamic thought with the term "*al-fayḍ al-muqaddas*," or the "Sacred Effusion." *Wujūd* can also mean "existence" as opposed to essence or quiddity (*māhiyyah*). Ṣadrā uses *wujūd* in all of the meanings mentioned above. Instead of constantly shifting between variations of being and existence for *wujūd*, it makes more sense to keep the word in the original.

Following Corbin's French translation, we rendered the word *mashᶜar*, the singular form of *mashāᶜir*, as "[metaphysical] penetration." *Mashᶜar* is derived from *sh-ᶜ-r*, meaning "to perceive" and "to have the consciousness of something." Its nominal form *shuᶜūr* means "consciousness." *Shuᶜr bi-dhātihi*, for instance, means "self-consciousness." Lane's *Lexicon* translates *mashᶜar* as *maᶜlam*, or "a place where a thing is known to be." This is also closely related to the juridical meaning of *mashᶜar* as "the place where a religious ritual is performed." In this last sense, *mashᶜar* refers to the signposts of Islamic pilgrimage that the pilgrims visit in performing the Ḥajj. Ṣadrā seems to imply that each stop at these signposts represents a new state of consciousness and a higher station of realization. In paragraph 4, he explains why he has chosen the word *mashāᶜir* as its title: "I have composed this treatise on the basis of an introduction and two stations, each one of which consists of metaphysical penetrations (*mashāᶜir*). I have called them such because of the relationship between the apparent and the manifested, the open and the secret." According to Corbin's interpretation, in such moments of cognition, the five senses, which perceive the external world, penetrate into consciousness.[28]

We rendered *māhiyyah* as "quiddity" to distinguish it from "essence," which would translate *dhāt* and its derivatives. *Māhiyyah* has two meanings in Arabic philosophical vocabulary. "*Māhiyyah* in the particular sense" (*māhiyyah bi'l-maᶜná al-akhaṣṣ*) refers to the particular reality of something.[29] "*Māhiyyah* in the general sense" (*māhiyyah bi'l-maᶜná al-ᶜāmm*) is that "by which a thing is what it is" (*mā bihi al-shayᵓ huwa huwa*). This second *māhiyyah* corresponds to what we call "essence" in English in a general sense. But in Ṣadrean metaphysics, this is ultimately nothing

28. Ibid., 43.

29. Cf. Avicenna, *Shifāᵓ: Ilāhiyyāt*, 31.

other than existence, because all things derive their reality from the latter. It is usually clear in Arabic which of the two meanings of *māhiyyah* is meant in a particular context. Therefore, we have kept this distinction by using "quiddity" for *māhiyyah* in the particular, limited sense discussed above and "essence" for *māhiyyah* in a general, comprehensive sense.[30]

The word *ʿurūḍ* is another difficult word to translate. It comes from the same root as the word *ʿaraḍ*, rendered as "accident." In using the word *ʿurūḍ* and its derivatives, Ṣadrā makes full use of the etymological richness of the root *ʿ-r-ḍ*, meaning "to happen to something," "to occur," and "to come to happen." In this sense, if *ʿaraḍ* can be translated as "accident," *ʿurūḍ* might best be rendered as the transitive verb "accidenting," meaning something occurring or happening to something else as an accident. English contains no such word—hence the necessity of using such phrases as "occurring to," "happening to," "coming to be an accident of," and so on.

Another term that is notoriously difficult to translate is *jaʿl*. Ṣadrā uses *jaʿl* and its variations *jāʿil* and *majʿūl* in the sense of the ontological generation of things. In a general sense, *jaʿl* designates a form of "ontological production-cum-causation"; but it should not be confused with causation itself, because causation does not necessarily bring about change in the essential constitution of things, whereas *jaʿl* signifies a substantive production and generation. That is why Fazlur Rahman's rendering of *jaʿl* as "causation" is misleading. Following Corbin, we have translated *jaʿl* as "instauration." Though not a very common word in English, it connotes the meaning of "ontological causation and constitution," which incorporates the sense of what makes things what they are after they have been created. Another French scholar of Ṣadrā—a student of Corbin—uses "instauration" to translate the Arabic word *ibdāʿ* because it refers to "the act of immediate, sudden, instantaneous production of being."[31] We, however, believe that the use of "instauration" should be reserved for *jaʿl*.

Finally, we have the expressions *fī al-khārij* and *fī al-ʿayn*. They can be translated as "external" and "in reality," but this rendering runs the risk of connoting something such as "out there," as opposed to "being inside" and "in the mind." In Ṣadrā's philosophical vocabulary, both terms refer to a mode of reality rather than a place or substratum. In a similar way,

30. Izutsu follows this translation; see his *Concept and Reality of Existence*, 75.
31. Cf. Jambet, *The Act of Being*, 427, n. 8.

the word *makān*, translated usually as "space," denotes a modality of existence whereby corporeal beings possess certain qualities and "effects." That is why we have rendered *fī al-khārij* as "*in concreto*." In paragraph 22 of the *Mashāʿir*, Ṣadrā clarifies this point as follows:

> It is evident and clear that when we say "*in concreto*" and "in the mind" in our statements "this exists *in concreto*" and "that exists in the mind," we do not mean the categories of receptacles or places or substratum. Rather, the meaning of something being *in concreto* is that it possesses *wujūd* from which issue effects and [existential] conditions; and by its being in the mind, the reverse of this. And if there were not to be for *wujūd* a reality other than simply the actualization of the quiddity, then there would never be any difference between *in concreto* and in the mind [or external and mental]. This is impossible since quiddity might be actualized in the mind without having to be actualized *in concreto*.

Fī al-ʿayn denotes a mode of existence by which things have certain effects—namely, existential qualities. As Ṣadrā's commentator Lāhījī points out, "the 'external' is not like a place; rather, what is meant by it is something that is non-conceptual."[32] In the *Asfār*, Ṣadrā puts it as follows:

> What we mean by actual [i.e., external] existence (*al-wujūd al-ʿaynī*) is that the concomitants (*lawāzim*) of an [actual] essence follow from it. When blackness is found in the external world, its proper nature is to cause absence of sight. The proper effect of hotness is to cause hotness. But when they occur in the soul, these concomitants do not follow from them. We call the former actual [external] existence and the latter mental existence.[33]

Other terms that present certain difficulties in translation have been explained in the text. The examples above attest to the subtleties and challenges of translating Ṣadrā's philosophical vocabulary into English. The nuances and shades of meaning that accompany classical philosophical Arabic are important for a proper understanding of Ṣadrā's thought, as well as that of other traditional thinkers. As Ṣadrā never tired of reminding us, however, the goal of philosophical analysis is not to imprison the mind in words and concepts, but to bring it to the limits of human language and enable it to transcend the conceptual

32. Lāhījī, *Sharḥ risālat al-mashāʿir*, 43.

33. Ṣadrā, *Asfār*, 1.33 (12). This paragraph, which Ṣadrā quotes without reference, is taken verbatim from al-Rāzī, *al-Mabāḥith al-mashriqiyyah*, 1:459.

domain and attain realized knowledge. This means one thing only: philosophy must be self-transcending. Once we have gazed upon the infinite horizon of truth, we all need to kick away the ladder of philosophy beneath our feet.

◆

I cannot end this introduction without expressing my deep gratitude to Professor Seyyed Hossein Nasr. Dr. Nasr's lucid translation of the *Mashāʿir* was completed over some period of time in a *dars-i khārij* (extracurricular class) held in its traditional format. Dr. Nasr began this class with a group of his choice students at The George Washington University in the early 1990s. I joined the group in the mid-1990s when I began my doctoral studies under Dr. Nasr's supervision. As a typical example of Dr. Nasr's remarkable discipline of mind and work ethic, the classes were held on a fairly regular basis despite his many engagements, classes, and travels. We thank Joseph Lumbard, Waleed al-Ansary, David Dakake, and Caner Dagli for their contributions to the recording and editing of the original translations. Likewise, for their diligent efforts in the publication of this book in the Islamic Translation Series, we thank D. Morgan Davis and many others on the editorial team at the Middle Eastern Texts Initiative: Muḥammad Eissa, Joseph Bonyata, Don Brugger, Andrew Heiss, and Elizabeth Watkins.

We hope that the present volume will be accepted as a modest contribution to the study of Mullā Ṣadrā in the English language. Our *Mashāʿir* classes under Dr. Nasr at The George Washington University, out of which the present translation came, are a testimony to its continuing *barakah*, which has never dried out over the four centuries since it was composed.

—IBRAHIM KALIN

بسم الله الرحمن الرحيم

[Preface]

In the Name of God, the All-Good, the Infinitely Merciful

(1) We give thanks to God and ask for His Help through His Power, by which subsist the spiritual principles of earth and heaven. We ask His Help through His Word, by means of which He fashioned the two abodes of existence: the other world and this world. We ask His Help to purify our faculties so as to have the potentiality for perfection and the correction of the passive intellects—passive to the meanings and the states concerning their union with the Active Intellect. We ask His Help to cast away, through the lights of demonstration, the demons of illusion that cause one to be lost in the darkness, and to hurl the enemies of wisdom and certitude into the deep abyss of those who have distanced themselves from religion and into the domicile of those who are proud. May our praise be upon Muḥammad, he who has been sent with the Book of God, and upon His Light, which has descended upon all creatures through him. And praise be upon his family and children, who are kept pure, through the lights of the truth and certitude, from impurities of nature and from the darkness of illusion. May God bless him, them, and all who follow their path—their partisans who are God-fearing.

بســـم الله الرحمن الرحيم

(١) نحمد الله ونستعين بقُـوَّته التي أقام بها ملكوت الأرض والسماء، وبكلمته التي أنشأ بها نشأتي الآخرة والأولى على تهذيب القوى القابلة للاستكمال وإصلاح العقول المنفعلة عن المعاني والأحوال للاتّصال بالعقل الفعّال، وطرد شياطين الأوهام المضلّة بأنوار البراهين، وقمع أعداء الحكمة واليقين إلى مهوى المبعدين ومثوى المتكبّرين . ونصلّي على محمّد المبعوث بكتاب الله ونوره المنزل على كافّة الخلق أجمعين، وآله وأولاده المطهّرين عن أرجاس الطبيعة المقدّسين عن ظلمات الوهم بأنوار الحقّ واليقين. اللَهمّ صلّ وسلِّم عليه وعليهم وعلى جميع من سلك سبيلهم، واقتفى دليلهم من شيعتهم المتّقين.

(2) And then: The least of God's creation in stature and in body, and the most among them in errors and sin, Muḥammad known as Ṣadr al-Dīn al-Shīrāzī, says: O brothers who are journeying to God by means of the light of gnosis:[1] Listen, through the instrument of hearing of your heart, to my discourse, in order to have the light of my wisdom penetrate into the inner levels of your being. Obey my word, and take from me the virtuous practices[2] of my path, which comprises faith in God and the Last Day—a faith that is true faith, produced in souls that have gained in-depth knowledge by means of demonstrations that are certain and of divine verses and portents, to which allusion was made by Him—praise be upon Him—in His saying "Believers all believe in God and His angels and His books and His messengers" ("al-Baqarah," Q. 2:285), and "Whosoever disbelieves God and His angels and His books and His messengers and the Last Day has verily gone far astray into error" ("al-Nisaʾ," Q. 4:136).

This knowledge is the wisdom to which are welcome those who are suitable for it and which is forbidden to other than those who are made for it. And this is, in its essence, the knowledge of God with respect to His Essence, to which allusion has been made in His Word: "Is it not enough [for them to know] that thy Sustainer is witness unto everything?" ("Fuṣṣilat," Q. 41:53). And the knowledge of it is, from one point of view, the knowledge of the horizons and the selves to which allusion has been made in His Word: "We shall make them fully understand Our messages in the utmost horizons and within themselves, so that it will become clear unto them that this [revelation] is indeed the truth" ("Fuṣṣilat," Q. 41:53). The divine sciences [metaphysics] are exactly the same as the faith in God and His Qualities. Moreover, the sciences of the horizons [cosmology] and of the souls [psychology] are from the signs of knowledge of God, His Dominion, and His books and His prophets, the witnessing of knowledge of the Last Day and its conditions [that is, eschatology], the grave and resurrection and the questioning [of the soul at the time of death by the angels], the Tablet [upon which our actions are written], the reckoning, the path [between heaven and hell], and awareness of what is between the Hands of God and paradise

(٢) أمّا بعد: فأقّل الخلائق قدرًا وجِرْمًا وأكثرهم خطأ وجُرْمًا محّمد المشتهر بصدر الدين الشيرازي يقول: أيّها الإخوان السالكون إلى الله بنور العرفان! استمعوا باستماع قلوبكم مقالتي، لينفذ في بواطنكم نور حكمتي وأطيعوا كلمتي، وخذوا عنّي مناسك طريقتي من الإيمان بالله واليوم الآخر إيمانًا حقيقيًا حاصلاً للأنفس العلامة بالبراهين اليقينيّة والآيات الإلهيّة كما أشار إليه سبحانه في قوله ‹وَالْمُؤْمِنُونَ كُلٌّ آمَنَ بِاللّهِ وَمَلآئِكَتِهِ وَكُتُبِهِ وَرُسُلِهِ› وقوله ‹وَمَن يَكْفُرْ بِاللَّهِ وَمَلائِكَتِهِ وَكُتُبِهِ وَرُسُلِهِ وَالْيَوْمِ الآخِرِ فَقَدْ ضَلَّ ضَلالاً بَعِيدًا.› وهذه هي الحكمة الممنون بها على أهلها والمضنون بها على غير أهلها، وهى بعينها العلم بالله من جهة ذاته، المشار إليه بقوله ‹أَوَلَمْ يَكْفِ بِرَبِّكَ أَنَّهُ عَلَى كُلِّ شَيْءٍ شَهِيدٌ.› والعلم به من جهة العلم بالآفاق والأنفس المشار إليه بقوله ‹سَنُرِيهِمْ آيَاتِنَا فِي الآفَاقِ وَفِي أَنفُسِهِمْ حَتَّى يَتَبَيَّنَ لَهُمْ أَنَّهُ الْحَقُّ.» فالعلوم الإلهيّة هي عين الإيمان بالله وصفاته، والعلوم الآفاقيّة والأنفسيّة من آيات العلم بالله وملكوته وكتبه ورسله، وشواهد العلم باليوم الآخر وأحواله والقبر والبعث والسؤال والكتاب والحساب والصراط والوقوف بين يدي الله والجنّة والنار.

and hell. Furthermore, this wisdom does not issue from theological disputations, nor from popular imitations, nor from blameworthy investigative philosophy, nor from Sufi imaginings. Rather, it is a result of learning lessons from contemplation of the message of the verses of God and from meditation upon the dominion of His heavens and His earth, with a strong aversion to that to which the nature of the people of disputation and the majority are drawn and a complete rejection of what the hearts of ordinary people have accepted as beautiful.

(3) I have presented to you, O brothers, in my books and treatises, some of the lights of wisdom, subtleties of divine gifts, perfume of spirits, ornaments of intellects, and introductory principles concerning the very essence of virtues. These are the steps of the spiritual path toward the stations of guidance and of ascension to the very peak of the highest nobility of the sciences of the Qurʾan and hermeneutic interpretation, and the meanings of revelation and its descent, coming from what the Supreme Pen wrote upon the Noble Tablet. And this is what was read by the person [the Prophet] to whom God sent inspiration, to whom God spoke His Words and to whom He taught His indubitable verses, from what the Trusted Spirit [the archangel Gabriel] made to descend upon the heart of him whom God chose and guided, and whom God placed as the first viceregent in the earthly world and the ornament for the lower dominion. Then He placed him as a member of His higher world and as an angel in His heavenly dominion. Everyone the house of whose heart is illuminated by these lights has his spirit elevated to this abode. And he who disputes and denies it verily falls into the abode of the evil ones, the abyss of the devils and the perfidious, and the dwelling of the proud and the people of fire.

(4) Since the problem of *wujūd* is the foundation of philosophical principles, the ground of metaphysical questions, and the pole around which rotates the millstone of the science of unity, the science of eschatology, the science of the resurrection of souls and bodies, and many other things that we have been the only one to demonstrate and the sole person to bring out [their meaning], whoever is ignorant of the knowledge of *wujūd*,[3] his ignorance runs through the most important of all subjects and the greatest among them; and he will become mindless of it and of

وهى ليست من المجادلات الكلاميّة، ولا من التقليدات العامية، ولا من الفلسفة البحثيّة المذمومة، ولا من التخيّلات الصوفيّة، بل هي من نتائج التدبّر في آيات الله والتفكّر في ملكوت سماواته وأرضه مع انقطاع شديد عمّا أكبّ عليه طباع أهل المجادلة والجماهير، ورفض تامّ لما استحسنته قلوب المشاهير.

(٣) ولقد قدّمتُ إليكم، يا إخواني، في كتبي ورسائلي من أنوار الحكم ولطائف النعم وبزهر الأرواح وزينة العقول مقدّمات ذوات فضائل جمّة هي مناهج السلوك إلى منازل الهدى ومعارج الارتقاء إلى الشرف الأعلى من علوم القرآن والتأويل ومعاني الوحي والتنزيل ممّا خطّة القلم العظيم في اللوح الكريم، وقرأه من ألهمه الله قراءته، وكلّمه بكلماته، وعلّمه محكم آياته ممّا نزل به الروح الأمين على قلب من اصطفاه الله وهداه، فجعله أول خليفة في العالم الأرضيّ وزينة للملكوت السفلى . ثمّ جعله أهلاً لعالمه العلوي و ملكًا في ملكوته السماويّ . فكلّ من تنور بيت قلبه بهذه الأنوار، ارتقى روحه إلى تلك الدار. ومن جحدها أو كفرها، فقد أهوى إلى مهبط الأشرار ومهوى الشياطين والفجّار ومثوى المتكبّرين وأصحاب النار.

(٤) ولمّا كانت مسألة الوجود أُسّ القواعد الحكميّة، ومبنى المسائل الإلهيّة، والقطب الذي يدور عليه رحى علم التوحيد وعلم المعاد وحشر الأرواح والأجساد، وكثير مما تفردنا باستنباطه، وتوحدنا باستخراجه، فمن جهل بمعرفة الوجود يسري جهله في أمّهات المطالب ومعظماتها، وبالذهول عنها فاتت عنه خفيّات المعارف وخبيئاتها، وعلم الربوبيّات،

the secrets of divine knowledge; and its inner meanings will become lost to him, as well as the science of Divine Names and Qualities, prophecy, and the science of the soul and its connections [with the whole of cosmology] and its return to the Origin of its origins and its final end. Therefore, we saw to it that we begin with [the question of *wujūd*]. The discourse in this treatise concerns, thereby, the principle of the truths of faith and the principles of philosophy and gnosis.

We shall enter first of all into the discussion of the principles of *wujūd* and the proof that it is the immutable principle within every existent; that it is both the truth and the reality; and that that which is other than it is like a reflection, a shadow, and an apparition. Then we shall mention here the subtle principles and noble discussions that were bestowed upon us through divine grace and inspiration, upon which depend knowledge of the Origin and the end; the science of the soul and its resurrection to the spirits and [subtle] bodies; the science of prophecy and sanctity; the secret of the descent of revelation and the verses; the science of the angels and their inspirations and signs; the demons and their temptations and doubts; and the proof of the world of the grave and the intermediate states. [Then we shall discuss] the manner in which God knows both universals and particulars; the knowledge of divine predetermination and destiny and the Pen and the Guarded Tablet; the proof of the luminous Platonic ideas; the question of the unity of the intellect and the intelligibles; the unity of sense and the sensibles; and

ونبواتها ومعرفة النفس واتّصالاتها ورجوعها إلى مبدأ مبادئها وغاياتها، فرأينا أن نفتح بها الكلام في هذه الرسالة المعمولة في أصول حقائق الإيمان وقواعد الحكمة والعرفان. فنورد فيها أوّلاً مباحث الوجود وإثبات أنّه الأصل الثابت في كل موجود، وهو الحقيقة؛ وما عداه كعكس وظلّ وشبح. ثمّ نذكر هنا قواعد لطيفة ومباحث شريفة سنحت لنا بفضل الله وإلهامه ممّا يتوقف عليه معرفة المبدأ والمعاد، وعلم النفس وحشرها إلى الأرواح والأجساد، وعلم النبوّات والولايات، وسرّ نزول الوحي والآيات، وعلم الملائكة وإلهاماتها وعلاماتها، والشياطين ووساوسها وشبهاتها، وإثبات عالم القبر والبرزخ، وكيفية علم الله تعالى بالكليات والجزئيّات، ومعرفة القضاء والقدر، والقلم واللوح، وإثبات المثل النوريّة الأفلاطونيّة، ومسألة اتّحاد العقل بالمعقولات، واتّحاد الحسّ بالمحسوسات، ومسألة أنّ البسيط

the problem of a simple reality, such as the intellect and all the beings above it, all beings. [Then we shall address] the problem that all of *wujūd*—despite the differences of the species and the individual quiddities belonging to it, the differences of its genera, and its specific differences in their logical definitions—is in truth a single substance having a single identity, while possessing stations and high and low degrees. [Finally, we shall address] other problems that we have been unique in bringing out and that we have been alone in being able to prove—problems that we have articulated in various books and treatises for the sake of approaching closer to God and in order to gain access to the Origin of all origins and the Beginning of all beginnings.

Moreover, our knowledge of these [matters] is not of the kind that you find in theological disputations, nor in popular imitations, nor in the views of discursive philosophy, nor [in those] of sophistic fallacy, nor in Sufi imaginings. Rather, it issues from demonstration discovered through unveiling,[4] to whose truth bear witness the Book of God, the prophetic *Sunnah*, and the sayings of the people of prophethood, sanctity, and wisdom—may God's peace be upon him and upon all of them. I have composed this treatise on the basis of an introduction and two stations, each one of which consists of metaphysical penetrations (*mashāʿir*). I have called them such because of the relationship between the apparent and the manifested, the open and the secret. I say this, asking God's aid and support from the people of His dominion.

كالعقل وما فوقه كل الموجودات، وأنّ الوجود كله مع تباين أنواعه وأفراد ماهيته وتخالف أجناسه وفصوله حدّا وحقيقة جوهر واحد له هويّة واحدة ذات مقامات ودرجات عالية ونازلة، إلى غير ذلك من المسائل التي توحّدنا باستخراجها وتفرّدنا باستنباطها ممّا فرقناها في الكتب والرسائل تقرّباً إلى الله وتوسّلاً إلى مبدأ المبادئ وأوّل الأوائل، وعلومنا هذه ليست من المجادلات الكلاميّة، ولا من التقليدات العامية، ولا من الأنظار الحكميّة البحثيّة والمغالطات السفسطيّة، ولا من التخيّلات الصوفيّة، بل هي من البراهين الكشفيّة التي شهد بصحّتها كتاب الله وسنّة نبيّه وأحاديث أهل بيت النبوّة والولاية والحكمة — سلام الله عليه وعليهم أجمعين. — و جعلتُ الرسالة منطوية على فاتحة وموقفين، وكلّ منهما مشتمل على مشاعر؛ وسمّيتها بها لمناسبة بين الفحوى والظاهر، والعلن والسرّ . فنقول مستعيناً بالله مستمدّا من أهل ملكوته:

The Opening

Concerning research into the concept of wujūd, *its conditions, the proof of its reality, and its states*

There are several penetrations.

[The] First Penetration

Concerning the explanation that it is free of the need to be defined

(5) The reality of *wujūd* is the most manifest of all things through presence and unveiling,[5] and its quiddity is the most hidden among things conceptually and in its inner reality. Of all things, its concept is the least in need of definition because of its manifestness and clarity and its being the most general among all concepts in its comprehensiveness. Its identity is the most particular of all particular things, in both

الفاتحة

في تحقيق مفهوم الوجود وأحكامه و إثبات
حقيقته وأحواله

وفيه مشاعر

المشعر الأوّل

في بيان أنّه غنيّ عن التعريف

(٥) أنّيّة الوجود أجلى الأشياء حضورًا وكشفًا وماهيّته أخفاها تصوّرًا واكتناهًا؛ ومفهومه أغنى الأشياء عن التعريف ظهورًا ووضوحًا وأعمّها شمولاً وهويّته أخصّ

its determination and concreteness, because through it is made concrete all that is concrete, is realized all that is realized, and is determined all that is determined and particularized. As you will learn, it is particularized through its own essence and is determined through itself, as you will know.

(6) As for the fact that it cannot be defined, the reason is that a definition is by means of either logical definition or description. It [*wujūd*] cannot be made known through definition because it has no genus and no specific difference. Thus, it has no [logical] definition. It cannot be described either, because it cannot be conceived through anything that is more manifest or better known than it, nor through a form that is equal to it.[6]

(7) Consequently, whoever seeks to define it is mistaken because it would need to be known by something more obscure than it. However, one can seek to awaken the person [who wants to define *wujūd*] and to provoke in him a remembrance. But at the end, [even] this would be only a verbal definition.[7]

(8) I say that the conceptualization of something in a general way consists of the actualization of its meaning in the soul as corresponding to what exists in the external world.[8] And this holds true for things other than *wujūd*, [such as] meanings and universal quiddities that are found either through real objective existence or through shadowy mental existence, while its essence is preserved in both of these modes of existence. Moreover, pure *wujūd* has no other *wujūd* into which it could be permutated while preserving its meaning externally and mentally.

(9) Every existential reality has one single manner of actualization. Furthermore, *wujūd* does not possess mental existence; and what does not possess mental existence is neither universal nor particular, neither general nor specific.

الخواصّ تعيّنًا وتشخّصًا، إذ به يتشخّص كل متشخّص، و يتحصّل كل متحصل، و يتعيّن كلّ متعيّن ومتخصّص، وهو متشخّص بذاته ومتعيّن بنفسه كما ستعلم.

(٦) وأمّا أنّه لا يمكن تعريفه، فلأن التعريف إمّا أن يكون بحدٍّ أو برسمٍ. ولا يمكن تعريفه بالحدّ، حيث لا جنس له ولا فصل له؛ فلا حدّ له. ولا بالرسم إذ لا يمكن إدراكه بما هو أظهر منه وأشهر، ولا بصورة مساوية له.

(٧) فمن رام تعريفه، فقد أخطأ، إذ قد عرّفه بما هو أخفى منه. اللّهم إلا أن يريد تنبيهًا وإخطارًا بالبال وبالجملة تعريفًا لفظيّاً .

(٨) ولأنّي أقول إنّ تصوّر الشيء مطلقاًعبارة عن حصول معناه في النفس مطابقاً لما في العين. وهذا يجري فيما عدا الوجود من المعاني والماهيّات الكلّية التي توجد تارةً بوجود عينيّ أصيل وتارةً بوجد ذهنيّ ظلّيّ مع انحفاظ ذاتها في كلا الوجودين، وليس للوجود وجود آخر يتبدّل عليه مع انحفاظ معناه خارجاً وذهناً.

(٩) فليس لكلّ حقيقة وجوديّة إلا نحو واحد من الحصول. فليس للوجود وجود ذهنيّ، وما ليس له وجود ذهنيّ، فليس بكلّيّ ولا جزئيّ ولا عامّ ولا خاصّ.

(10) It [*wujūd*] is, in essence, a simple reality, distinguished by its essence without having a genus or specific difference. Also, it is not the genus for other things and has no specific difference, no species, no general accident, and no specific accident. As for what is said concerning its being an accident for existents, from the point of view of abstract mental meaning, that is not the reality of *wujūd*. Rather, it is the mental meaning of it, which is derived from secondary intelligibles such as thing-ness, possibility, substantiality, accidentality, humanity, blackness, and other infinitive (*masdari*)[9] abstract words by which one gives an account of real or unreal things. Our discourse is not [solely] about this [meaning of *wujūd*], but [it] gives an account of it and [explains] that it is a single, simple reality that does not at all need, in its realization or actualization, anything to be added to it—any condition of specific difference or accident, whether it be of a class or [of] an individual.[10]

(11) Rather, it necessitates these things with respect to what is actualized by it and what is found from among the meanings and quiddities. That is because all *wujūd*—except the first, simple *wujūd*, which is the Light of lights—necessitates having universal possible quiddity and is qualified by these qualifications according to their actualization in the mind.[11] And they become genus or specific difference, essentiality or accidentality, definition or description, or other things from among the qualities of universal concepts, conditioning *wujūd* only through accidentality.

(١٠) فهو في ذاته أمر بسيط متشخّص بذاته لا جنس له ولا فصل له؛ ولا هو أيضًا جنس لشيء ولا فصل له ولا نوع ولا عرض عامّ ولا خاصّ. وأمّا الذي يقال له عرضيّ للموجودات من المعنى الانتزاعيّ الذهني، فليس هو حقيقة الوجود، بل هو معنى ذهنيّ من المعقولات الثانية كالشيئيّة والممكنيّة والجوهريّة والعرضيّة والإنسانيّة والسواديّة وسائر الانتزاعيّات المصدريّة التي يقع بها الحكاية عن الأشياء الحقيقيّة أو غير الحقيقيّة . وكلامنا ليس فيه بل المحكي عنه، وهو حقيقة واحدة بسيطة، لا يفتقر أصلاً في تحقّقه وتحصّله إلى ضميمة قيد فصليّ أو عرضيّ صنفيّ أو شخصيّ.

(١١) بل قد يلزمه هذه الأشياء بحسب ما يتحصّل به ويوجد من المعاني والماهيّات، إذ كّل وجود سوى الوجود الأوّل البسيط — الذي هو نور الأنوار — يلزمه ماهيّة كلّيّة إمكانيّة تتّصف بهذه الأوصاف باعتبار حصولها في الأذهان، فيصير جنسًا أو فصلاً أو ذاتيًا أو عرضيًا أو حدًا أو رسمًا أو غير ذلك من صفات المفهومات الكلّيّة دون الوجود إلا بالعرض.

The Second Penetration

Concerning the manner in which wujūd *comprises*[12] *things*

(12) The reality of *wujūd* being comprised of existing things is not like a universal concept being comprised of particulars and its holding valid for them. As we have already informed you, the reality of *wujūd* is not a genus, nor a species, nor an accident, since it is not a natural universal (*kulli tabiᶜi*).[13] Rather, its comprising is of another kind, which is not known except by the gnostics, those who are "firm in knowledge" ("Āl ᶜImrān," Q. 3:18). It is interpreted sometimes as the "Breath of the Compassionate"; sometimes as the Compassion "which embraces all things" ("Aᶜrāf," Q. 7:156) or as the "reality by which things are created," according to a group of gnostics; and [sometimes] as the expansion of the light of *wujūd* upon the temples of contingent beings and the receptivity of the quiddities, and its descent into the stations of ipseities.[14]

(13) You will know the meaning of this proposition that *wujūd*—while being in itself an individual reality, individualized by its essence and determined by itself—individualizes all of the universal quiddities that exist through it. [You will understand] how they are united by it, how in the domain of external reality they are corroborated by it, and how in the mind and in rational analysis its concept occurs to them.

المشعر الثاني

في كيفية شموله للأشياء

(١٢) شمول حقيقة الوجود الأشياء الموجودة ليس كشمول المعنى الكليّ للجزئيّات، وصدقه عليها — كما نبّهناك عليه — من أنّ حقيقة الوجود ليست جنسًا ولا نوعًا ولا عرضًا إذ ليست كليّاً طبيعيّاً، بل شموله ضرب آخر من الشمول لا يعرفه إلا العرفاء «وَالرَّاسِخُونَ فِي الْعِلْمِ».وقد عبّروا عنه تارة بـ «النفس الرحمانيّ» وتارةً بالرحمة التي «وَسِعَتْ كُلَّ شَيْءٍ»، أو بـ «الحقّ المخلوق به» عند طائفة من العرفاء، وبانبساط نور الوجود على هياكل الممكنات وقوابل الماهيّات ونزوله في منازل الهويّات.

(١٣) وستعلم معنى هذا الكلام من أنّ الوجود مع كونه أمرًا شخصيّاً متشخّصًا بذاته، متعيّناً بنفسه، مشخّصًا لما يوجد به من ذوات الماهيّات الكلّيّة، كيف يتّحد بها وتصدق هي عليه في الخارج ويعرض مفهومه عليها عروضًا في الذهن بحسب التحليل العقليّ.

(14) It will become apparent to you also in what way it is true to say that the reality of *wujūd*, while being individualized by itself, is differentiated according to the differentiation of contingent quiddities, each of which is united with one of its degrees and one of its stages. The only exception is the first real *Wujūd*, which has no quiddity because it is pure *wujūd*, of which there is none more complete, more intense, or more perfect.[15] Neither generality nor particularity is mixed with it [*wujūd*]; no definition defines it, nor does any name or description render it precise; and no knowledge comprehends it. "And all faces will be humbled before the Ever-Living, the Self-Subsistent" ["Ṭaha," Q. 20:111].

(١٤) ويظهر لك أيضًا أنّه كيف يصدق القول بكون حقيقة الوجود مع كونها متشخّصة بذاتها أنّها مختلفة الحقائق بحسب اختلاف الماهّيات الإمكانيّة المتّحدة كل منها بدرجة من درجاته ومرتبة من مراتبه، سوى الوجود الحقّ الأوّل الذي لا ماهيّة له، لأنّه صريح الوجود الذي لا أتّم منه ولا أشدّ قوّةً وكمالاً، ولا يشوبه عموم وخصوص، ولا يحده حد، ولا يضبطه اسم ورسم، ولا يحيط به علم «وعنت الوجوه للحي القيّوم».

[The] Third Penetration

Concerning the verification of wujūd *objectively*

(15) Know—may God help thee by His light—that *wujūd* is the most appropriate of all things to possess an existent reality. And concerning this matter, there are decisive testimonies.

The first witness

(16) The reality of everything is its *wujūd*, through which its effects on it and its [existential] conditions result.[16] *Wujūd* is, therefore, the most appropriate of all things to possess reality because everything else becomes the possessor of reality through it; it is the reality of all that possesses reality, and it does not need, in its possessing reality, another reality. It is by itself in the external world, and other things—by which I mean the quiddities—exist in the external world through it, not by themselves.

(17) What we mean by it is that, for all concepts—as, for example, human—when we say that it possesses a reality or *wujūd*, it means that there exists in the external world something about which we say and verify that it is a human being. The same holds true for horse, sky, water, fire, and other titles. The concepts that possess external individuals are titles verifying them. The meaning of the assertion that these concepts are real, or that their essence is real, signifies that the concepts hold true for something in its essence. Premises formulated in this way, such as "This is a man" or "That is a horse," are essential necessities. The same

المشعر الثالث

في تحقيق الوجود عينًا

(١٥) اعلم — أيّدك الله تعالى بنوره — أنّ الوجود أحقّ الأشياء بأن يكون ذا حقيقة موجودة، وعليه شواهد قطعيّة.

الشاهد الأوّل

(١٦) إنّ حقيقة كل شيءٍ هو وجوده الذي يترتّب عليه آثاره وأحكامه. فالوجود إذن أحقّ الأشياء بأن يكون ذا حقيقة، إذ غيره به يصير ذا حقيقة، فهو حقيقة كلّ ذي حقيقة، ولا يحتاج هو في أن يكون ذا حقيقة إلى حقيقة أخرى. فهو بنفسه في الأعيان، وغيره — أعني الماهيّات — به في الأعيان لا بنفسها .

(١٧) نريد به أنّ كل مفهوم — كالإنسان مثلا — إذا قلنا إنّه ذو حقيقة أو ذو وجود، كان معناه أنّ في الخارج شيئًا يقال عليه ويصدق عليه أنّه إنسان. وكذا الفرس والفلك والماء والنار وسائر العناوين. والمفهومات التي لها أفراد خارجيّة هي عنوانات صادقة عليها. ومعنى كونها متحقّقة أو ذات حقيقة، أنّ مفهوماتها صادقة على شيءٍ صدقًا بالذات، والقضايا المعقودة — كهذا إنسان، وذاك فرس — ضروريّات ذاتيّة. فهكذا حكم مفهوم

holds true for the concept of reality. *Wujūd* and its synonyms must have their title corroborate something in order [for us] to be able to say that this reality is such-and-such through essential corroboration. The premise formulated in this way is an essential necessity, or a pre-eternal necessity.[17]

(18) I do not say that the concept of reality or *wujūd*, which is a self-evident concept, can be said to have reality or *wujūd* through common predication, because the corroboration of every title by itself does not require that it be through common predication. Rather, it is through primary predication, which is different from common [predication].[18]

(19) Rather, I say that the thing that is included in the quiddity, or its consideration through [the quiddity] in such a way that [the thing] has a real essence, requires that the concept of being real or being existent holds true for it. *Wujūd* requires something to which it is attributed externally [*in concreto*], and this essential title is predicated through common predication. Each title holds true for something in the external world; this something is an individual instance of it, and this title is realized in it. There exists for the concept of *wujūd* an individual instance *in concreto*. It therefore possesses a real and external form independent of all considerations of the intellect and intervention of the mind. And *wujūd* exists in reality, and its existentiality *in concreto* is through its own essence existing in reality *in concreto*. For example, Zayd is a human being in reality, and his being human in reality consists of the fact that he is an existent. In the same way, the fact that this *wujūd* exists in reality means that *wujūd* exists by itself and that other things exist through it, not that there is for *wujūd* another *wujūd* that is external to it and an accident for it, through some kind of accidentality—even hypothetically, as in the case of analytical accidents [meaning genus and differentia] in contrast to [a real] quiddity, such as human being. Hence, the meaning of [human being] existing is that something *in concreto* is human, not that something *in concreto* is *wujūd*. The meaning of *wujūd* existing is that something *in concreto* is *wujūd*, and it is real[ity] (*haqiqah*).[19]

(20) Know that every existent *in concreto* is other than *wujūd*; and there is in it a blemish of composition, even if it be only rationally, in contrast to pure *wujūd*. And because of this, the philosophers have said: All contingent beings—that is, all things that possess quiddity—are a compound pair, and there is nothing among the quiddities that is a simple reality. To summarize, wujūd exists by its own essence, not by something else. And through this, the obstacles mentioned concerning *wujūd*

الحقيقة. والوجود ومرادفاته لا بدّ أن يكون عنوانه صادقًا على شيءٍ، حتّى يقال على شيءٍ أنّ هذا حقيقة كذا صدقًا بالذات، وتكون القضيّة المعقودة هنا ضروريّة ذاتيّة أو ضروريّة أزليّة.

(١٨) لستُ أقول إنّ مفهوم الحقيقة أو الوجود — الذي هو بديهيّ التصوّر — يصدق عليه أنّه حقيقة أو وجود حملاً متعارفًا، إذ صدق كلّ عنوان إلى نفسه لا يلزم أن يكون بطريق الحمل المتعارف، بل حملاً أوليّاً غير متعارف.

(١٩) بل إنّما أقول إنّ الشيء الذي يكون انضمامه مع الماهيّة أو اعتباره معها، مناط كونها ذات حقيقة، يجب أن يصدق عليه مفهوم الحقيقة أو الموجوديّة. فالوجود يجب أن يكون له مصداق في الخارج، يحمل عليه هذا العنوان بالذات حملًا شائعًا متعارفًا. وكلّ عنوان يصدق على شيء في الخارج، فذلك الشيء فرده، وذلك العنوان متحقّق فيه. فيكون لمفهوم الوجود فرد في الخارج، فله صورة عينيّة خارجيّة مع قطع النظر عن اعتبار العقل وملاحظة الذهن. فيكون الوجود موجودًا في الواقع، وموجوديّته في الخارج أنه بنفسه واقع في الخارج، كما أنّ زيدًا مثلًا إنسان في الواقع، وكون زيد إنسانًا في الواقع عبارة عن موجوديته. فكذا كون هذا الوجود في الواقع عبارة عن كونه بنفسه موجودًا وكون غيره به موجودًا، لا أنّ للوجود وجودًا آخر زائدًا عليه عارضاً له بنحو من العروض ولو بالاعتبار، كما في العوارض التحليليّة، بخلاف الماهيّة كالإنسان. فإنّ معنى كونه موجودًا، أنّ شيئًا في الخارج هو إنسان، لا أنّ شيئًا في الخارج هو وجود. ومعنى الوجود موجودًا أنّ شيئًا في الخارج هو وجود وهو حقيقة.

(٢٠) واعلم أنّ كل موجود في الخارج غير الوجود، ففيه شوب تركيب ولو عقلاً بخلاف صرف الوجود. ولأجل هذا قال الحكماء: كل ممكن — أي كل ذي ماهيّة — زوج تركيبي، فليس شيء من الماهيّات بسيط الحقيقة. وبالجملة الوجود موجود بذاته لا بغيره.

being existent are overcome. As for the matter of the abstract and intelligible concept of *wujūd*, it is like other general matters and mental concepts (such as thing-ness, quiddity, possibility, and their likes), except that there exist, corresponding to this concept, things that have their roots in realization and existential permanence, in contrast to thing-ness, quiddity, or other concepts.

(21) Know that all existing beings have external realities, yet their names are unknown. In order to explain these names, we say "the existence of this" or "the existence of that." All of these must lead to a general concept in the mind. [In contrast,] the names and properties of the [constitutive] parts of the thing and the quiddity are known. However, it is not possible to express the real *wujūd* of everything through a name or description, because the positing of names and descriptions is in correspondence to concepts and universal meanings [used in logic], not in correspondence to existential identities and external/concrete forms.[20]

The second witness

(22) It is evident and clear that when we say "*in concreto*" and "in the mind" in our statements "This exists *in concreto*" and "That exists in the mind," we do not mean the categories of receptacles, places, or substrata. Rather, the meaning of something being *in concreto* is that it possesses *wujūd*, from which issue effects and [existential] conditions; and [the meaning of] its being in the mind is the reverse of this. And if there were not to be for *wujūd* a reality other than simply the actualization of the quiddity, then there would never be any difference between *in concreto* and in the mind, [or external and mental]. This is impossible since quiddity might be actualized in the mind without having to be actualized *in concreto.*

وبهذا تدفع المحظورات المذكورة في كون الوجود موجودًا. وأمّا الأمر الانتزاعيّ العقليّ من الوجود، فهو كسائر الأمور العامّة والمفهومات الذهنيّة — كالشيئيّة والماهّية والممكنيّة ونظائرها — إلا أنّ ما بإزاء هذا المفهوم أمور متأصّلة في التحقّق والثبوت، بخلاف الشيئيّة والماهيّة وغيرها من المفهومات.

(٢١) واعلم أنّ للوجودات حقائق خارجيّة، لكنّها مجهولة الأسامي. شرح أسمائها إنّها وجود كذا ووجود كذا. ثمّ يلزم الجميع في الذهن الأمر العام. وأقسام الشيء والماهيّة معلومة الأسامي والخواصّ. والوجود الحقيقي لكل شيء من الأشياء لا يمكن التعبير عنه بإسم ونعت، إذ وضع الأسماء والنعوت إنّما يكون بإزاء المفهومات والمعاني الكليّة، لا بإزاء الهويّات الوجوديّة والصور العينيّة.

الشاهد الثاني

(٢٢) إنّ من البيّن الواضح أنّ المراد بالخارج والذهن في قولنا «هذا موجود في الخارج» و«ذاك موجود في الذهن» ليسا من قبيل الظروف والأمكنة ولا المحال، بل المعنى يكون الشيء في الخارج أنّ له وجودًا يترتّب عليه آثاره وأحكامه، وبكونه في الذهن أنّه بخلاف ذلك. فلو لم يكن للوجود حقيقة إلا مجرّد تحصّل الماهيّة، لم يكن حينئذ فرق بين الخارج والذهن، وهو محال، إذ الماهيّة قد تكون متحصّلة ذهنًا وليست بموجودة في الخارج.

The third witness

(23) If the existentiality of things were dependent upon their quiddities and not upon something else, then it would be impossible to attribute some of them to others and to attribute something to something else, such as when we say, "Zayd is a living being" and "Man is a being who walks," because the meaning of predication and its verification is the unification of two different concepts in existence. In the same way, the judgment of something [pertaining] to something else [that is, to pronounce judgment for something holding true for something else] consists of their unification in existence and difference in concept and quiddity. Furthermore, what causes difference among them is different from what brings about unification;[21] and to this refers the saying that predication necessitates unification *in concreto* and difference in the mind. If *wujūd* were not different from the quiddity, the aspect of unification would not be different from the aspect of difference. The consequent is false, according to what has been said; the antecedent must, therefore, also be false.

As for the question of consequence, the soundness of verification depends upon some kind of unification and some kind of difference because, if there were pure unity, there would be no predication in the first place. If there were [only] pure multiplicity, there would also be no predication. If, therefore, *wujūd* were only a conceptual abstraction [and not a reality], its unity and plurality would be subject to the unity of that to which it is related, and its plurality would issue forth from [abstract] meanings and quiddities. If this were the case, it would never be possible to have a common predication between things except for the primary essential predication, and [all] predication would be limited to essential predication, which depends upon unification with regard to meaning.

الشاهد الثالث

(٢٣) إنه لو كانت موجوديّة الأشياء بنفس ماهيّاتها لا بأمر آخر، لإمتنع حمل بعضها على بعض، والحكم بشيءٍ منها على شيءٍ كقولنا زيد حيوان والإنسان ماشٍ، لأنّ مفاد الحمل ومصداقه هو الاتّحاد بين مفهومين متغايرين في الوجود؛ وكذا الحكم بشيء على شيء عبارة عن اتّحادهما وجودًا وتغايرهما مفهومًا وماهيّة، وما به المغايرة غير ما به الاتّحاد. وإلى هذا يرجع ما قيل إنّ الحمل يقتضي الاتّحاد في الخارج والمغايرة في الذهن. فلو لم يكن الوجود شيئًا غير الماهيّة، لم يكن جهة الاتّحاد مخالفة لجهة المغايرة. واللازم باطل كما مّر، فالملزوم مثله. بيان الملازمة أنّ صحّة الحمل مبناه على وحدة ما وتغاير ما، إذ لو كان هناك وحدة محضة، لم يكن حمل؛ ولو كان كثرة محضة، لم يكن حمل. فلو كان الوجود أمرًا انتزاعيًا، يكون وحدته وتعدّده تابعين لوحدة ما أضيف إليه وتعدّده من المعاني والماهيّات. وإذا كان كذلك، لم يتحقّق حمل متعارف بين الأشياء سوى الحمل الأوّليّ الذاتيّ ، فكان الحمل منحصرًا في الحمل الذاتيّ الذي مبناه الاتّحاد بحسب المعنى.

The fourth witness

(24) If *wujūd* were not existent, nothing would exist. The falsity of the consequent necessitates the falsity of the antecedent. The explanation of the consequent is as follows: If the quiddity is considered by itself, independent of *wujūd*, then it is nonexistent. Likewise, if it is considered by itself, irrespective of existence and nonexistence, through this consideration it would be neither existent nor nonexistent. And if *wujūd* were not to exist in itself, nothing would be established for something else, because affirming something for something else—or its attachment to another thing, or its consideration with it—is secondary to the existence of that which is firmly established or requires its existence.[22] If, then, *wujūd* were not to exist in itself, and also [if] quiddity were not to exist in itself, then how could anything ever be existent? Quiddity does not exist [by itself]. Whoever refers to his consciousness will note with certitude that if quiddity were not one with *wujūd* (as we claim), or [if it] did not receive *wujūd* as an accident (as is [the] famous [view] among the Peripatetics), or if it were an accident of [*wujūd*] (as is held by a group of the Sufis), [outside of these cases] it would be impossible to think that quiddity could exist, from a certain point of view.[23] The reason is that attaching a nonexisting thing to a nonexisting thing is irrational. Similarly, attaching a concept to another concept without one of them existing—or one being an accident for the other, or both existing, or both being accidents for a third—is completely false; and the intellect confirms the impossibility of this matter.

(25) What is said [by certain people] concerning [the idea] that the existentiality of things depends upon their attachment to the Necessary Being does not lead to anything, because *wujūd* in relation to quiddity is not like filiation in the case of children. [This is] because in the latter case they receive such a qualification because of their attachment to a single person. In this case, the actualization of the relationship is posterior to the existence of those in this relationship, whereas the attachment of the quiddities to existence is nothing other than their very existence.[24]

(26) Bahmanyār has said in his book *al-Taḥṣīl*: "When we say that something exists, we mean by it two things: The first is that it possesses a certain *wujūd*, such as when we say, 'Zayd is in a relation,'" and this is to speak in a metaphorical manner. And the second is that it exists in the real sense of the term. The existent is *wujūd*, as 'in relation to' is, in reality, the relation itself."

الشاهد الرابع

(٢٤) لو لم يكن الوجود موجودًا، لم يوجد شيء من الأشياء، وبطلان التالي يوجب بطلان المقدّم. بيان الملازمة أنّ الماهيّة إذا اعتبرت بذاتها مجرّدة عن الوجود، فهي معدومة وكذا إذا اعتبرت بذاتها مع قطع النظر عن الوجود والعدم؛ فهي بذلك الاعتبار لا موجودة ولا معدومة. فلو لم يكن الوجود موجودًا في ذاته، لم يمكن ثبوت أحدهما للآخر. فإنّ ثبوت شيءٍ لشيءٍ أو انضمامه إليه أو اعتباره معه متفرّع على وجود المثبت له أو مستلزم لوجوده. فإذا لم يكن الوجود في ذاته موجودًا ولا الماهيّة في ذاتها موجودة، فكيف يتحقّق ههنا موجود؟ فلا تكون الماهيّة موجودة. وكلّ من راجع وجدانه يعلم يقينًا أنّه اذا لم تكن الماهيّة متّحدة بالوجود— كما هو عندنا —ولا معروضة له— كما اشتهر بين المشّائين —ولا عارضة له— كما عليه طائفة من الصوفيّة —فلم يصحّ كونها موجودة بوجهٍ، فإنّ انضمام معدوم بمعدومٍ غير معقول؛ وأيضًا انضمام مفهوم بمفهوم من غير وجود أحدهما، أو عروضه للآخر، أو وجودهما، أو عروضهما لثالثٍ، غير صحيح أصلاً، فإنّ العقل يحكم بامتناع ذلك.

(٢٥) وما قيل من أنّ موجوديّة الأشياء بانتسابها إلى واجب الوجود، فكلام لا تحصيل فيه، لأنّ الوجود للماهيّة ليس كالبنوّة للأولاد حيث يتّصفون بها لأجل انتسابهم إلى شخص واحد. وذلك لأنّ حصول النسبة بعد وجود المنتسبين، واتّصافها بالوجود ليس إلا نفس وجودها.

(٢٦) وقال بهمنيار في «التحصيل» إنّا إذا قلنا كذا موجود، فإنا نعني أمرين: أحدهما أنّه ذو وجود كما يقال «إنّ زيدًا مضاف» وهذا كلام مجازي. والثاني أنّه بالحقيقة، أنّ الموجود هو الوجود كما أنّ المضاف بالحقيقة هو الإضافةّ.

The fifth witness

(27) Verily, if *wujūd* were not to have a form in the objective world, there would never be realized in the species an actual particular that would be an individual of the species. This is because the very essence of the quiddity does not refrain from being shared by multiple things and by the occurrence of universality to it with regard to the mind, even if it is particularized by a thousand particularizations as a result of multiple concepts added to it. Therefore, it is necessary that there be, for a particular thing *in concreto*, something above and beyond common nature and that this extra thing itself be particularized. Furthermore, it is inconceivable that it would occur in multiplicity. And we do not mean by *wujūd* anything other than this. If this something were not to have a reality in the members of the species, no member of the species would exist *in concreto*. And this is a contradiction.[25]

(28) As for the argument that particularization comes from the relation to the real *wujūd* particularized by itself, the fallacy of this view is known by the example given above [in paragraph 25], because the relationship of one thing to another relies upon the particularization of both.

(29) Relation *qua* relation is itself an intelligible and universal thing. The addition of universal to universal does not of necessity lead to particularity.

(30) If what is considered here has the condition of a relationship inasmuch as it is a concept among other concepts, then, from this point of view, it is not a relationship—that is, a meaning that is not independent [of other meanings]. But if one considers it in its condition of being a quiddity, then it is not judged to have any relationship with something other than itself, and nothing happens to it. It is through this "being" that it becomes related to its instaurer.[26] And we do not mean by *wujūd* anything other than this "being." It is impossible to intellect and conceive this [truth] except through presential witnessing, as its explanation will become clear later.

الشاهد الخامس

(٢٧) إنّه لو لم يكن للوجود صورة في الأعيان، لم يتحقّق في الأنواع جزئيّ حقيقيّ هو شخص من نوع. وذلك لأن نفس الماهيّة لا تأبى عن الشركة بين كثيرين وعن عروض الكلّيّة لها بحسب الذهن، و إن تخصّصت بألف تخصيص من ضمّ مفهومات كثيرة كلّيّة إليها. فإذن لا بدّ وأن يكون للشخص زيادة على الطبيعة المشتركة تكون تلك الزيادة أمرًا متشخّصًا لذاته غير متصوّر الوقوع للكثرة. ولا نعني بالوجود إلا ذلك الأمر. فلو لم يكن متحقّقًا في أفراد النوع ، لم يكن شيء منها متحقّقًا في الخارج. هذا خلف.

(٢٨) وأمّا قول إنّ التشخّص من جهة الإضافة إلى الوجود الحقّ المتشخّص بذاته، فقد علم فساده بمثل ما مّر ، فإنّ إضافة الشيء إلى شيء بعد تشخّصها جميعًا.

(٢٩) ثم النسبة بما هي نسبة أيضًا أمر عقليّ كليّ، وانضمام الكلّيّ إلى الكّليّ لا يوجب الشخصيّة.

(٣٠) هذا إذا كان المنظور إليه حال النسبة بما هي مفهوم من المفهومات، وليست هي بذلك الاعتبار نسبة، أي معنى غير مستقل. وأمّا إذا كان المنظور إليه حال الماهيّة بالذات، فليست هي بحسب نفسها محكومًا عليها بالانتساب إلى غيرها ما لم يكن لها كون هي تكون بذلك الكون منسوبةً إلى مكوّنها وجاعلها. ولا نعنى بالوجود إلا ذلك الكون، ولا يمكن تعقّله و إدراكه إلا بالشهود الحضوريّ، كما سيتّضح بيانه.

The sixth witness

(31) Know that there are two kinds of things that are accidental: that which is accidental upon *wujūd* and that which is accidental upon *māhiyyah*. The first is like the accidentality[27] of whiteness for a body, or aboveness for the sky *in concreto*, and like the accidentality of universality and species for man and genus for animal. The second is like the accidentality of specific difference for genus and particularization for species.

(32) According to the language of the accomplished [philosophers][28] from among the people of wisdom, the qualification of quiddity by *wujūd* and *wujūd*'s occurrence to quiddity is neither an external qualification nor an accidentality by incarnation in such a way that the qualified [that is, the quiddity] would already have a degree of reality [before *wujūd*]. Yet existence at this stage is not mixed by the qualification of this attribute. Rather, it is totally separated from it and from its having accidentality [imposed] upon it, whether this attribute be concrete and objective inclusion [meaning predication], as when we say, "Zayd is white"; or [whether it be] abstract and mental, as when we say, "The sky is above us"; or whether it be based upon a negation, as when we say, "Zayd is blind."

Verily, the qualification of quiddity by *wujūd* is an intellective qualification and an accidentality based on mental analysis. In this kind of accidentality, it is not possible for the substratum that receives the accident to have any degree of existence and any ontological reality, either *in concreto* or in the mind; and [such a being] is not named [identified] according to the imposition of this accident. When specific difference, for example, is said to occur to a genus as an accident, that does not mean that the genus has *in concreto* existential reality, whether it be external or mental, without the specific difference. Rather, it means that the concept of specific difference is outside the concept of genus [but] related to it in meaning, even if united with it existentially. And accidentality belongs to the quiddity from the point of view of analysis while united with it [*in concreto*]. The same holds true for quiddity and *wujūd* when it is said that *wujūd* is one of the accidents of quiddity.

الشاهد السادس

(٣١) اعلم أنّ العارض على ضربين: عارض الوجود، وعارض الماهيّة. والأوّل كعروض البياض للجسم أوالفوقيّة للسماء في الخارج، وكعروض الكلّيّة والنوعيّة للإنسان والجنسيّة للحيوان. والثانّي كعروض الفصل للجنس والتشخّص للنوع.

(٣٢) وقد أطبقت ألسنة المحصّلين من أهل الحكمة بأنّ اتّصاف الماهيّة بالوجود وعروضه لها ليس اتّصافًا خارجيًا وعروضًا حلوليًا، بأن يكون للموصوف مرتبة من التحقّق. والكون ليس في تلك المرتبة مخلوطًا بالاتّصاف بتلك الصفة، بل مجردا عنها وعن عروضها، سواء كانت الصفة انّضماميّة خارجيّة، كقولنا: زيد أبيض — أو انتزاعيّة عقليّة، كقولنا: السماء فوقنا — أو سلبيّة، كزيد أعمى. و إنّما اتّصاف الماهيّة بالوجود اتصاف عقلي وعروض تحليليّ ، وهذا النحو من العروض لا يمكن أن يكون لمعروضة مرتبة من الكون ولا تحصّل وجوديّ — لا خارجًا ولا ذهنًا — لا يكون المسمّى بذلك العارض. فإنّ الفصل مثلاً إذا قيل إنّه عارض للجنس، ليس المراد أنّ للجنس تحصّلاً وجوديًا في الخارج أو في الذهن بدون الفصل، بل معناه أنّ مفهوم الفصل خارج عن مفهوم الجنس لاحق به معنىً، و إن كان متّحدًا معه وجودًا. فالعروض بحسب الماهيّة في اعتبار التحليل مع الاتّحاد، فهكذا حال الماهيّة والوجود إذا قيل إنّ الوجود من عوارضها.

(33) Now that this discourse has been established, we say: If there were not for *wujūd* a form *in concreto*, its being an accident for the quiddity would not be in the way we have described it.[29] Rather, it would be like other [mental] abstractions that we attach to the quiddity after the latter is confirmed and established. Therefore, it is necessary that *wujūd* be exactly that something by which the quiddity is made to exist and with which the quiddity is united *in concreto*, despite its being different from *wujūd* both in meaning and in concept through mental analysis. Contemplate this matter.

The seventh witness

(34) Among the witnesses proving this issue is the one related to the saying of [the philosophers] that the existence of accidents in themselves is precisely their existence in their substratum. That is, the existence of an accident in its reality is its entering into its substratum. There is no doubt that the entering of the accident into its substratum is an external [concrete] matter that is added to its quiddity. Likewise, the substratum is not [included] within the quiddity of the accident and the latter's definition; nevertheless, it is implicated in its existence, which is its very accidentality and its entering into this substratum. This is the meaning of the sayings of the philosophers, in [sections of logic called] *The Book of Demonstration*, that the substratum is implicated in the definitions of accidents. They have confirmed also that it is there, in this ensemble of substrata, in which definition possesses something over and beyond the object defined—as, for example, the implication of the circle in the definition of the arc, or the implication of the mason in the definition of building. Therefore, it has become known that the accidentality of the accident, such as [the accident] black, [means that] its existence is added to its quiddity.

(35) If *wujūd* were not real *in concreto* but were, rather, something abstracted—by which I mean the infinitive of existence [in the form of the copula]—then the existence of the color black would simply be its own blackness and not its entering into a body. And since the existence of accidents—which is their accidentality and their entering into a substratum—is something added to their universal quiddities, then this would also be true of substances. Therefore, we would not speak of any difference [between them].

(٣٣) فإذا تقرّر هذا الكلام، فنقول: لو لم يكن للوجود صورة في الأعيان، لم يكن عروض للماهيّة هذا النحو الذي ذكرناه، بل كان كسائر الانتزاعيّات التي تلحق الماهيّة بعد ثبوتها وتقرّرها. فإذن يجب أن يكون الوجود شيئًا توجد به الماهيّة وتتّحد معه وجودًا مع مغايرتها إيّاه معنىً ومفهومًا في ظرف التحليل. تأمّل فيه.

الشاهد السابع

(٣٤) من الشواهد الدالّة على هذا المطلب أنّهم قالوا: إنّ وجود الأعراض في أنفسها وجوداتها لموضوعاتها، أي وجود العرض بعينه حلوله في موضوعه. ولا شكّ أنّ حلول العرض في موضوعه أمر خارجي زائد على ماهيّته. وكذا الموضوع غير داخل في ماهيّة العرض وحدها، وهو داخل في وجوده الذي هو نفس عرضيّته وحلوله في ذلك الموضوع. وهذا معنى قول الحكماء في كتاب البرهان، إنّ الموضوع مأخوذ في حدود الأعراض. وحكموا أيضًا بأنّ هذا من جملة المواضع التي تقع للحدّ زيادة على المحدود، كأخذ الدائرة في حدّ القوس وأخذ البنّاء في حدّ البناء. فقد علم أنّ عرضيّة العرض — كالسواد — أي وجوده زائد على ماهيّته.

(٣٥) فلو لم يكن الوجود أمرًا حقيقيًا، بل كان أمرًا انتزاعيًّا، أعني الكون المصدريّ، لكان وجود السواد نفس سوداويتّه لا حلوله في الجسم. وإذا كان وجود الأعراض، وهو عرضيّتها وحلولها في الموضوعات، أمرًا زائدًا على ماهيتّها الكليّة، فكذلك حكم الجواهر. ولهذا لا قائل بالفرق.

The eighth witness

(36) What is unveiled concerning this matter and what illuminates the path is [the fact] that the degrees of intensity and weakness in things that possess a scale of intensity and weakness constitute, according to [the philosophers], specific differences differentiated by logical differentiae. And in qualitative intensification, such as in the color black, intensification that is a qualitative movement would be required by [the philosophers].[30] If *wujūd* were only a certain way of intellectual consideration, then different species without constraint would be limited within two limits, [which is illogical]. That the consequent follows and that the consequent is false is what would be understood by anyone who reflects upon and observes [the fact] that, for each of the definitions of a more intense or a more feeble degree, if they be quiddities of species, there would be quiddities differentiated according to meaning and reality [in the same way] as assuming infinite definitions. If, therefore, *wujūd* were a relational and intellective thing, its multiplication would be through the multiplication of distinct meanings with different quiddities. The consequence would therefore be what we have said.

(37) Certainly, if for the whole there be a single *wujūd* and a single form that is continuous—as is true in the case of continuous quantities, whether they be fixed or mobile—the definitions being then [only] potential, there would not result from that any harm, since the *wujūd* of these species that correspond to the definitions and the divisions would be a *wujūd* that is potential and not actual. Since the whole exists through a unique and continuous *wujūd*, its unity is actual, while its multiplicity is potential. And if *wujūd* were not to have an objective form,[31] the consequence would be inevitable and the difficulties would persist.

الشاهد الثامن

(٣٦) إنّ ما يكشف عن وجه هذا المطلب و ينوّر طريقه، أنّ مراتب الشديد والضعيف فيما يقبل الأشدّ والأضعف—أنواع متخالفة بالفصول المنطقيّة عندهم. ففي الاشتداد الكيفيّ—مثلاً في السواد—وهو حركة كيفية، يلزم عليهم، لو كان الوجود اعتباريًا عقليًّا، أن يتحقّق أنواعًا بلا نهاية محصورة بين حاصرَين. وثبوت الملازمة كبطلان اللازم معلوم لمن تدبّر واستبصر أنّ بإزاء كلّ حدّ من حدود الأشدّ والأضعف، إذا كان ماهيّة نوعيّة، كانت هناك ماهيّات متباينة بحسب المعنى والحقّيقة حسب انفراد الحدود غير المتناهية. فلو كان الوجود أمرًا عقليًّا نسبيًا، كان تعدّده بتعدّد المعاني المتمايزة المتخالفة الماهيّات، فيلزم ما ذكرناه.

(٣٧) نعم، إذا كان للجميع وجود واحد وصورة واحدة اتصاليّة، كما هو شأن المتّصلات الكميّة القارّة أو غير القارّة، وكانت الحدود فيها بالقوة، لم يلزم محذورًا أصلاً، إذ وجود تلك الأنواع التي هي بإزاء الحدود أو الأقسام، وجود بالقوّة لا بالفعل، إذ الكلّ موجود بوجود واحد اتصاليّ وحدته بالفعل وكثرته بالقوّة. فإذا لم يكن للوجود صورة عينيّة، كان الخلف لازمًا والإشكال قائماً.

The Fourth Penetration

In responding to doubts that have been brought against the objectivity of wujūd

(38) Verily, for those who are veiled from the witnessing of the light of *wujūd*, which shines upon all contingent beings that exist, and for those who dispute the lights of the sun of the Truth that manifests itself in all quiddities that are contingent, there are imaginary veils and strong arguments, which we have cast aside. We dispersed their darkness and untied their knots, and we solved the difficulties by permission of God, the Wise. And here they are:

(39) Question: "If *wujūd* were to be actualized *in concreto*, it would be an existent. It would then have an existence. And then, for that existing thing, there would have to be another *wujūd*, and so on, *ad infinitum*."

(40) Answer: If one means by existent that by which *wujūd* subsists, that is impossible because there is nothing in the world that is existent according to this meaning—neither quiddity nor *wujūd*.[32] As for the quiddity, we have indicated that it is not possible for *wujūd* to subsist by it. As for *wujūd* itself, since a thing cannot subsist by itself, the consequent is false, just as the antecedent is false. Rather, we say that if we mean by existent this meaning, that it is that by which *wujūd* subsists, it is necessary that *wujūd* be nonexistent, according to this meaning. [In fact,] a thing does not subsist by itself. For example, whiteness is not something that possesses white color. In fact, that which possesses white

المشعر الرابع

في دفع شكوك أوردت على عينيّة الوجود

(٣٨) إنّ للمحجوبين عن مشاهدة نور الوجود الفائض على كلّ ممكن موجود، والجاحدين لأضواء شمس الحقيقة المنبسطة على كلّ ماهيّة إمكانيّة حجبًا وهمية وحجبًا قويّة كشفناها، وأزحنا ظلمتها، وفككنا عقدتها، وحللنا أشكالها، بإذن الله الحكيم؛ وهي هذه:

(٣٩) سؤال: إنّ الوجود لو كان حاصلاً في الأعيان، لكان موجودًا، فله أيضًا وجود، ولوجوده وجود آخر إلى غير النهاية.

(٤٠) جواب: إنّه إن أريد بالموجود ما يقوم به الوجود، فهو ممتنع، إذ لا شيء في العالم موجود بهذا المعنى، لا الماهيّة ولا الوجود. أما الماهيّة، فلِما أشرنا إليه من أنه لا قيام للوجود بها. وأما الوجود فلإمْتناع أن يقوم الشيء بنفسه. واللازم باطل، فكذا الملزوم. بل نقول: إن أريد بالموجود هذا المعنى، أي ما يقوم به الوجود، يلزم أن يكون الوجود معدومًا بهذا المعنى. فإنّ الشيء لا يقوم بنفسه، كما أنّ البياض ليس بذي بياض. إنّما الذي هو ذو بياض

color is something else, such as a body or matter. And being nonexistent according to this meaning does not necessitate qualifying a thing by its opposite, because that which is contradictory to *wujūd* is nothingness or nonexistence, not a thing that has become nonexistent. Now one considers [in what is logically called contradiction] the unity of predication in which the predicate is predicated of the subject by univocality or by derivation.

And if one means by [*wujūd*] the simple meaning that is stated in Persian as *hast* ["is"] and its equivalents, it is existent. Its existent-ness is its actualization by itself *in concreto*; and its being existent is the same as its being a *wujūd*, not that something is added to its essence. Whatever is actualized for other than *wujūd* through *wujūd* is actualized for *wujūd* in itself in its very essence, just as to become actualized in space and in time is to be so in their essence and for others through them. And the same is true for temporal and spatial precedents and antecedents; they take place for their parts by themselves and for others through their mediation. This is also the case in the meaning of conjunction (*ittiṣāl*), which is unchanging in mathematical quantity by itself and accidental through it for other things. And [this is also the case of] the known for the form of knowledge by its essence and for something else by accident.

(41) Question: "But, then, each *wujūd* is a necessary *wujūd* by its essence, since there is no meaning to 'necessary being' except that its existence be necessary. And the affirmation of something for itself is necessary."

(42) Answer: One can solve this through three considerations: anteriority and posteriority, perfection and deficiency, richness and indigence. This objection does not distinguish between essential necessity and pre-eternal necessity.[33] Now, the Necessary Being is anterior to everything and is not caused by anything. It is perfect; there is nothing more intense than It, as far as the potency of *wujūd* is concerned; and there is no imperfection in It in any way whatsoever. Furthermore, It is sufficient unto itself and not related to any existents, because Its *wujūd* is necessary through pre-eternal necessity and is not limited by the duration of Its essence nor conditioned by the duration of any qualification. Contingent existences are essences that are not sufficient unto themselves to exist, being dependent ipseities when considered independent of their instaurer. From this point of view, they are illusory and impossible since the act is constituted by the agent in the same way that

شيء آخر، كالجسم أو المادّة. وكونه معدومًا بهذا المعنى لا يوجب اتّصاف الشيء بنقيضه، لأنّ نقيض الوجود هو العدم أو اللاوجود، لا المعدوم أو اللاموجود. وقد اعتبرت في التناقض وحدة الحمل مواطأة أو اشتقاقًا. وإن أريد به المعنى البسيط المعبّر عنه بالفارسيّة بـ«هست» ومرادفاته، فهو موجود، وموجوديّته هو كونه في الأعيان بنفسه، وكونه موجودًا هو بعينه كونه وجودًا، لا أنّ له أمرًا زائدًا على ذاته، والذي يكون لغيره منه، يكون له في ذاته، كما أنّ الكون في المكان وفي الزمان لهما بالذات ولغيرهما بواسطتهما، وكما في التقدّم والتأخّر الزمانّيين والمكانييّن، فإنّهما لأجزائهما بالذات ولغيرهما بواسطتهما، وكما في معنى الاتّصال، فإنه ثابت للمقدار التعليمي بالذات ولغيره بسببه، وكالمعلوميّة للصورة العلميّة بالذات وللأمر الخارجي بالعرض.

(٤١) سؤال: فيكون كلّ وجود واجبًا بالذات، إذ لا معنى لواجب الوجود إلا ما يكون وجوده ضروريًّا وثبوت الشيء لنفسه ضروريٌّ.

(٤٢) جواب: هذا مندفع بثلاثة أمور: التقدّم والتأخّر، والتمام والنقص، والغنى والحاجة. وهذا المورود لم يفرّق بين الضرورة الذاتيّة والضرورة الأزليّة. فواجب الوجود يكون مقدّماً على الكلّ غير معلول لشيءٍ، وتامًّا لا أشدّ منه في قوّة الوجود، ولا نقصان فيه بوجه من الوجود، وغنيًّا لا تعلّق له بشيء من الموجودات، إذ وجوده واجب بالضرورة الأزليّة من غير تقييده بما دام الذات، ولا اشتراطه بما دام الوصف. والوجودات الإمكانيّة مفتقرات الذوات متعلّقات الهويّات، إذ قطع النظر عن جاعلها، فهي بذلك الاعتبار باطلة مستحيلة، إذ الفعل يتقوّم بالفاعل، كما أنّ ماهيّة النوع المركّب يتقوّم بفصله. فمعنى كون

the quiddity of composite species is constituted by its specific difference. The meaning of "*wujūd* being necessary" is that its essence is existent by itself without having need of any instaurer that would bestow existence upon it, nor of a receptacle that would receive it. And the meaning of "*wujūd* being existent" is that when it is actualized, either by itself or by an agent, it has no need, in order to be realized, of another existence that would make it realized, in contrast to non-*wujūd*, because of its need in becoming existent through the consideration of *wujūd* and its adjoining.[34]

(43) Question: "If it is understood that for *wujūd* to be existent signifies existence itself, while for something else to be existent signifies that it is a thing that possesses *wujūd*, then *wujūd* is not predicated of everything with the same meaning. And yet it was proven that the employment of *wujūd* for all existents is according to a common meaning. One must therefore take the proposition that *wujūd* is existent as having the same meaning as what [it possesses] in other things among existents—that is to say, a thing possessing *wujūd*. However, existence is not existent because of the necessity of a chain *ad infinitum*, because one would have to begin once again with the *wujūd* of the *wujūd*, and so forth."

(44) Answer: This difference between the existentiality of things and the existentiality of *wujūd* does not necessitate a difference in employing the concept of *wujūd* as one that is derived and common among all things, because either [the existent] is taken in its simple meaning, as we have indicated before, or it is taken in the most general sense as signifying something whose *wujūd* one affirms. [This is the case] whether it involves the affirmation of a thing in itself, which comes back to saying that it is impossible for a thing to be separate from itself, or it involves affirming something else for it—as, for example, the concept of whiteness, relation, and others. Therefore, the concept of whiteness is what possesses whiteness, whether [whiteness] be this thing itself or something else.

(45) To permit the use of a part of the meaning of a term does not exclude its use in terms of [its] truth. That white encompasses something added to whiteness results from the particularity of some of the individuals and not from the concept of white. [This is] in the same way that the existent encompassing something that is added to *wujūd*—for example, the quiddity—results from the particularities of contingent individuals and not from the concept that is common among them.

الوجود واجبًا أنّ ذاته بذاته موجود من غير حاجة إلى جاعل يجعله، ولا قابل يقبله. ومعنى كون الوجود موجودًا أنّه إذا حصل إمّا بذاته أو بفاعل، لم يفتقر في كونه متحقّقًا إلى وجود آخر يحصل له، بخلاف غير الوجود لافتقاره في كونه موجودًا إلى اعتبار الوجود وانضمامه.

(٤٣) سؤال: إذا أُخذ كون الوجود موجودًا أنّه عبارة عن نفس الوجود، وكون غيره من الأشياء موجودًا أنّه شيء له الوجود، فلم يكن حمل الوجود على الجميع بمعنى واحد. وقد ثبت أنّ إطلاق الوجود على جميع الموجودات بمعنى مشترك. فلا بدّ من أخذ الوجود بالمعنى الذي أُخذ في غيره من الموجودات، وهو أنّه شيء له الوجود. فلم يكن الوجود موجودًا، لاستلزامه التسلسل عند عود الكلام إلى وجود الوجود جذعًا.

(٤٤) جواب: هذا الاختلاف بين موجوديّة الأشياء وبين موجوديّة الوجود ليس يوجب الاختلاف في إطلاق مفهوم الوجود المشتقّ المشترك بين الجميع، لأنّه إمّا معنى بسيط كما مرّت الإشارة، وإمّا عبارة عمّا ثبت له الوجود بالمعنى الأعمّ، سواء كان من باب ثبوت الشيء لنفسه الذي مرجعه عدم انفكاكه عن نفسه، أو من باب ثبوت الغير له، كمفهوم الأبيض والمضاف وغيرهما. فإنّ مفهوم الأبيض ما له البياض سواء كان عينه أو غيره.

(٤٥) والتجوّز في جزء معنى اللفظ لا ينافي كون إطلاقه بحسب الحقيقة. وكون الأبيض مشتملاً على أمر زائد على البياض إنّما لزم من خصوصيّة بعض الأفراد، لا من نفس المفهوم؛ فكذلك كون الموجود مشتملاً على أمر زائد على الوجود — كالماهيّة — إنّما ينشأ من خصوصيّات الأفراد الممكنة، لا من نفس المفهوم المشترك.

(46) Similar to this is what Ibn Sīnā has said in the *Metaphysics* of the *Shifāʾ*: "The Necessary Being can be understood to be the Necessary Being Itself. In the same way, the one can be understood to be the one itself. One comprehends from this that a quiddity, whatever it may be—such as man or another substance—is the necessary being, just as one can understand by the one that it is water or man, and that this [water or man] is one." He [Ibn Sīnā] has also said: "There is thus a difference between a quiddity to which has been added the one or the existent, and the one and the existent inasmuch as they are one and existent."

(47) And he [Ibn Sīnā] has also said in the *Taʿliqat*: "If it is asked: 'Does *wujūd* exist?' the answer is that it exists in the sense that it is the very reality of *wujūd* to exist, for *wujūd* is existing."

(48) The words of Sayyid Sharif al-Jurjani in his *Hawashi* (Glosses) on *al-Mataliʿ* [by Urmawi] really astonished me: "It is not the concept of a thing that is considered in the concept of the derived form as such—for example, 'rational'; otherwise, general accident would enter into specific difference. [And inversely,] if that to which a thing is attributed were to be considered in the derived form, the matter of particular possibility would become necessary. In fact, the thing to which one attributes 'laughing' is 'man,' and the affirmation of something for itself is necessary. And the mention of a thing in the explanation of derived forms is an explanation of how the pronoun in them [the derived forms] returns to it." End of his words.

(49) And this is close to what has been mentioned by some of the outstanding figures among those who have come later [namely, Jalal al-Dīn Dawani] in *al-Hashiyat al-qadimah* in order to prove the unification of the accident and the accidental.

(50) It is, then, understood that that to which the derived form is attributed and that to which it corresponds is a simple thing that does not necessitate any composition between qualified and quality. Furthermore, a thing is not taken into notional consideration in the qualification itself, whether it be in a general or particular manner.

(51) Question: "If *wujūd* were *in concreto* a qualification existing for a quiddity that is a receptacle for it, and since the *wujūd* of the receptacle is anterior to the *wujūd* of that which it receives, then *wujūd* would have to be anterior to *wujūd* [itself]."

(٤٦) نظير ذلك ما قال الشيخ الرئيس في إلهيات الشفاء «إنّ واجب الوجود قد يعقل نفس واجب الوجود، كما أنّ الواحد قد يعقل نفس الواحد؛ وقد يعقل من ذلك أنّ ماهيّة مّا—إنسان أو جوهر آخر—هو واجب الوجود كما أنّه يعقل من الواحد أنّه ماء أو إنسان، وهو واحد.» قال «ففرق إذًا بين ماهيّة يعرض لها الواحد أو الموجود، وبين الواحد والموجود من حيث هو واحد وموجود.»

(٤٧) وقال أيضًا في التعليقات «إذا سئل: هل الوجود موجود؟ فالجواب أنّه موجود بمعنى أنّ الوجود حقيقته أنّه موجود. فإنّ الوجود هو الموجوديّة.

(٤٨) ولقد أعجبني كلام السيّد الشريف في حواشي المطالع وهو «إن مفهوم الشيء لا يعتبر في مفهوم المشتقّ كالناطق، وإلا لكان العرض العام داخلاً في الفصل. ولو اعتبر في المشتق ما صدق عليه الشيء، انقلبت مادّة الإمكان الخاصّ ضروريّة. فإن الشيء الذي له الضحك هو الإنسان، وثبوت الشيء لنفسه ضروريّ. فذكر الشيء في تفسير المشتقّات بيان لما رجع إليه الضمير الذي فيها.» انتهى كلامه.

(٤٩) وهو قريب بما ذكره بعض أجلّة المتأخّرين في الحاشية القديمة لإثبات اتّحاد العرض والعرضيّ.

(٥٠) فعلم أنّ مصداق المشتقّ وما يطابقه أمر بسيط ليس يجب فيه تركيب بين الموصوف والصفة، ولا الشيء معتبر في الصفة لا عامًا ولا خاصًّا.

(٥١) سؤال: إن كان الوجود في الأعيان صفة موجودة للماهيّة، فهي قابلة له؛ والقابل وجوده قبل وجود المقبول؛ فيتقدّم الوجود على الموجود.

(52) Answer: That *wujūd* is realized *in concreto* in that which possesses a quiddity does not imply that the quiddity plays the role of a receptacle for it, because the relation between the two is one of unification and not connectedness. The qualification of quiddity by *wujūd* is through mental analysis, since *wujūd* is one of the analytical accidents of the quiddity, as we have already explained and as we shall explain further later.

(53) Question: "If *wujūd* were to be existent, then either it would be anterior to quiddity or posterior to quiddity, or the two would be simultaneous. The consequence of the first alternative is the actualization of *wujūd* independent of quiddity. It follows that qualification is anterior to the thing qualified and is realized independent of it. The second alternative implies that quiddity exists before *wujūd*, from which would follow *regressio ad infinitum*. The third alternative implies that quiddity is existent [at the same time] as *wujūd* but not by it. It therefore must derive its *wujūd* from elsewhere and would have the same consequence as the preceding case. The consequences being essentially false, the antecedent must [also] be false."

(54) Answer: It has been said before that the qualification of quiddity by *wujūd* is a mental abstraction and is not like the qualification of a thing by external accidents—such as a body by whiteness—which would require that each of the two have a positive reality apart from the other, so that one could imagine between them these three alternatives of anteriority, posteriority, and simultaneity. Consequently, there is no anteriority and there is no posteriority for either of the two concerning the other, and also there is no simultaneity, because a thing is not anterior to itself, is not posterior to itself, and also is not simultaneous with itself.[35]

(55) The accidentality of *wujūd* for quiddity is that the intellect is able to consider the quiddity as it is and separate from *wujūd*. Thus, [the intellect] finds *wujūd* to be external to the quiddity. If one comes back to the question concerning the relation between the two, when they are disengaged by the mind, it will be said that these two [*māhiyyah* and *wujūd*], inasmuch as they are considered through mental analysis, exist simultaneously. By this is meant that *wujūd* exists by itself or by its

(٥٢) جواب: كون الوجود متحققًا في الأعيان فيما له ماهيّة، لا يقتضي قابليّة الماهيّة له، إذ النسبة بينهما اتّحاديّة لا ارتباطيّة، واتّصاف الماهيّة بالوجود إنّما يكون في ظرف التحليل، إذ الوجود من العوارض التحليليّة للماهيّة، كما سبق وسيجيء زيادة إيضاح.

(٥٣) سؤال: إن كان الوجود موجودًا، فإمّا أن يتقدّم على الماهيّة، أو يتأخّر، أو يكونا معًا. فعلى الأوّل، يلزم حصوله مستقلاً دون الماهيّة، فيلزم تقدّم الصفة على موصوفها وتحقّقه بدونها. وعلى الثاني، يلزم أن تكون الماهيّة موجودة قبله ويلزم التسلسل. وعلى الثالث يلزم أن تكون الماهيّة موجودة معه لا به. فلها وجود آخر، فيلزم ما مرّ. فبطلان التوالي بأسرها مستلزم لبطلان المقدّم.

(٥٤) جواب: قد مرّ أنّ اتّصاف الماهيّة بالوجود أمر عقليّ، ليس كاتّصاف الشيء بالعوارض الخارجيّة كالجسم بالبياض، حتّى يكون لكلّ منهما ثبوت آخر، ليتصوّر بينهما هذه الشقوق الثلاثة من التقدّم والتأخّر والمعيّة. فلا تقدّم ولا تأخّر لأحدهما على الآخر، ولا معيّة أيضًا، إذ الشيء لا يتقدّم على نفسه، ولا يتأخر، ولا يكون أيضًا معه.

(٥٥) وعارضيّة الوجود للماهيّة أنّ للعقل أن يلاحظ الماهيّة من حيث هي مجّردة عن الوجود. فحينئذ يجد الوجود خارجًا عنه. فلو أعيد السؤال في النسبة بينهما عند التجريد بحسب الذهن، يقال: هما بحسب التحليل معان في الوجود، بمعنى أنّ الوجود بنفسه أو بجاعله موجود، والماهيّة بحسب نفسها واعتبار تجريد العقل إيّاها عن كافة الوجودات، لها نحو من الثبوت كما سيجيء بيانه. والحاصل أنّ كونهما معًا في الواقع عبارة عن كون

instaurer, and quiddity—considered in and of itself and as disengaged by the intellect from all existences—possesses a kind of positive reality, as will be explained further on. As a result, when one speaks of the simultaneity of quiddity and *wujūd* in reality, it means that *wujūd* is existent by itself, and quiddity is united with it and is existent through it [*wujūd*] and not through something else.

When the agent has bestowed existence on a quiddity, it has bestowed its *wujūd*. And when it has bestowed *wujūd*, it has bestowed this *wujūd* by itself. Therefore, the *wujūd* of everything is in its essence the subject that receives in predication the quiddity of this thing. Furthermore, neither quiddity nor *wujūd* possesses antecedence or precedence in relation to the other. When one of the verifiers[36] says that *wujūd* is anterior to quiddity, he means by it that the principal [reality] for emanation and realization *in concreto* is *wujūd*. That is to say that *wujūd* is in its essence the subject of the verification of universal concepts called quiddities and essentialities in the same way that, by the intermediary of another *wujūd* that occurs to it as an accident, it becomes the subject of other concepts that one calls accidentalities. The anteriority of *wujūd* to quiddity is not the same as the anteriority of cause to effect, nor is it the same as the anteriority of the receptacle to the thing received. Rather, it is like the anteriority of the essential to the accidental, or the anteriority of the real to the metaphorical.[37]

(56) Question: "We can conceive *wujūd* while doubting whether it exists. Therefore, it needs an added *wujūd* for it to exist. And the same reasoning could be repeated apropos of the *wujūd* of the *wujūd*, and there would be a *regressio ad infinitum*. There is no refuge except to say that *wujūd* is nothing but a mental consideration."

(57) Answer: The reality of *wujūd* is not in any way actualized in its essence in any of the minds, because *wujūd* is not a universal concept, and the *wujūd* of every existent is this existent itself *in concreto*, and that which is *in concreto* cannot be a mental concept. What is represented of *wujūd* as a general mental concept is the *wujūd* that one calls related *wujūd*, which is proper to logical judgments. As for knowledge of the reality of *wujūd*, that cannot be other than illuminative presence and real witnessing.[38] Consequently, no doubt remains concerning its identity.[39]

الوجود بذاته موجودًا، والماهيّة متّحدة به وموجودة بنفسه لا بغيره. فالفاعل إذا أفاد الماهيّة، أفاد وجودها، وإذا أفاد الوجود أفاد بنفسه. فوجود كلّ شيء هو في ذاته مصداق لحمل ماهيّة ذلك الشيء عليه. فلا تقدم ولا تأخّر لأحدهما على الآخر. وما قال بعض المحققين من أنّ الوجود متقدّم على الماهيّة، أراد به أنّ الأصل في الصدور والتحقّق هو الوجود، وهو بذاته مصداق لصدق بعض المعاني الكلّيّة المسمّاة بالماهيّة والذاتيّات عليه، كما أنّه بواسطة وجود آخر عارض عليه مصداق لمعانٍ أُخر تسمّى بالعرضيّات. وليس تقدّم الوجود على الماهيّة كتقدّم العلّة على المعلول، وتقدّم القابل على المقبول، بل كتقدّم ما بالذات على ما بالعرض، وما بالحقيقة على ما بالمجاز.

(٥٦) سؤال: نحن قد نتصوّر الوجود ونشكك في كونه موجودًا أم لا؛ فيكون له وجود زائد. وكذا الكلام في وجود الوجود، ويتسلسل. فلا محيص إلا بأن يكون الوجود اعتباريًا محضًا.

(٥٧) جواب: حقيقة الوجود لا تحصل بكنهها في ذهن من الأذهان، إذ ليس الوجود أمرًا كلّيًا، ووجود كلّ موجود هو عينه الخارجيّ، والخارجيّ لا يمكن أن يكون ذهنيًا. والذي يتصوّر من الوجود هو مفهوم عام ذهني يقال له الوجود الانتسابيّ الذي يكون في القضايا. والعلم بحقيقة الوجود لا يكون إلا حضورًا إشراقيًا وشهودًا عينيًا، وحينئذ لا يبقى التشكك في هويّته.

(58) The best way to respond to this question is [demonstration] by force to whoever claims that *wujūd* is added to quiddity and says that we can intellectually conceive the quiddity while doubting its existence or neglecting it. What one conceives intellectually is other than what one doubts; therefore, *wujūd* is added to quiddity. However, what we verified in principle is that *wujūd* is not added to quiddity, and also that the way in which it is an "accident of" quiddity is not that of an accident—neither *in concreto* nor conceptually—except from the point of view of mental analysis, as we have already indicated. Thus, the two bases [of the objection] are destroyed.

(59) Question: "If *wujūd* were in the external world and not a substance, then it would be a quality, for the definition of 'quality' is applicable to it. From that would follow, first of all, the absurdity that was mentioned before—that is, that the subject would exist before its own existence, implying a vicious circle and infinite regression. The existence of quality is the most general of all things, while the existence of substance as a quality is through itself. The same holds true for quantity and other [predicates]."

(60) Answer: Substance, quality, and other [predicates] that are the same as [the logical categories] belong to the category of quiddity, and they are the universal concepts of genus, species, essentiality, and accidentality. But existential realities are concrete ipseities and particular entities, not contained under an essential or accidental universal. Substance, for example, is a universal quiddity whose reality in concrete existence is that it is not in a substratum. Quality is a universal quiddity whose reality in concrete existence is not to accept either divisibility or relationality. The same holds true for the other categories. Therefore, [the objection] that *wujūd* would be substance, quality, quantity, or another one of the accidents falls by the wayside.

(61) And it has also been mentioned that *wujūd* has no genus, no specific difference, and no quiddity; and it is not a genus, a specific difference, or a species for anything. It is neither general nor particular accident, because all these matters belong to the category of universals.

(62) What belongs to general accidents and generic concepts is the meaning of "infinitive existence"[40] and not the actual reality of *wujūd*.

(٥٨) والأولى بهذا السؤال أن يورد إلزامًا على من قال بزيادة الوجود على الماهيّة، مستدلاً بما ذكر من أنّا نعقل الماهيّة ونشكّ في وجودها، أو نغفل عنه والمعقول غير المشكوك فيه أو المغفول عنه، فالوجود زائد على الماهيّة، وليس عروضه لها عروضًا خارجيًا ولا ذهنيًا، إلا بحسب التحليل، كما أشرنا إليه. فانهدم الأساسان.

(٥٩) سؤال: لو كان الوجود في الأعيان وليس بجوهر، فيكون كيفًا لصدق تعريف الكيف عليه. فيلزم مع ما مّر من تقدّم الموضوعٍ عليه المستلزم للدور أو التسلسل، كون الكيف أعمّ الأشياء مطلقًا وكون الجوهر كيفًا بالذات، وكذا الكمّ وغيرهما.

(٦٠) جواب: الجوهر والكيف وغيرهما من المقولات من أقسام الماهيّة، وهي معانٍ كلّيّة تكون جنسًا ونوعًا وذاتّية وعرضيّة. والحقائق الوجوديّة هويّات عينيّة وذوات شخصيّة غير مندرجة تحت كلّيّ ذاتيّ أو عرضيّ. فالجوهر مثلاً ماهيّة كلّيّة حقّها في الوجود الخارجيّ أن لا تكون في موضوع. والكيف ماهيّة كلّيّة حقّها في الوجود الخارجيّ أن لا تقبل القسمة ولا النسبة. وهكذا في سائر المقولات. فسقط كون الوجود جوهرًا أو كيفًا أو كمًّا أو عرضًا آخر من الأعراض.

(٦١) وقد مرّ أيضًا أنّ الوجود لا جنس له ولا فصل له ولا ماهيّة له، ولا هو جنس وفصل ونوع لشيء ولا عرض عامّ وخاصّ، لأنّ هذه الأمور من أقسام الكلّيّات.

(٦٢) وما هو من الأعراض العامّة والمفهومات الشاملة هو معنى الموجوديّة المصدريّة، لا حقيقة الوجود.

(63) Whoever says that *wujūd* is an accident means by that the general intelligible concept. As for its being an accident, it is an external [quality] predicated of quiddities.

(64) Also, *wujūd* is opposed to accidents because the *wujūd* of accidents in themselves is their *wujūd* for their substratum, whereas *wujūd* itself is the *wujūd* of the substratum and not the *wujūd* of an accident in the substratum.

(65) In order to become actualized, accidents are in need of a substratum; and *wujūd* does not need a substratum for its actualization. Rather, it is the substratum that needs *wujūd* in order to become actualized.

(66) The truth of the matter is that the *wujūd* of substance is substance through the substantiality of this substance and not by another substantiality; and the *wujūd* of the accident is accident through the accidentality of this accident and not by another accidentality, in the same way that you learned the state [of affairs] between quiddity and *wujūd*.[41]

(67) Question: "If *wujūd* exists for quiddity, then it has a relationship to it; and there is also a *wujūd* for this relationship. Furthermore, the existence of this relationship would have a relation to relation. The same argument can be made concerning the *wujūd* of that relationship of the relationship, leading to a *regressio ad infinitum*."

(68) Answer: The preceding explanations suffice to remove this objection because *wujūd* is quiddity itself *in concreto* and is different from quiddity only conceptually. There is, therefore, no relation between the two, except as considered in thought. Under this consideration, the relationship does possess a certain existence, which is essentially this relationship itself and which is different insofar as its external existence is concerned. This kind of infinite regression is broken as soon as rational consideration is removed. You will come to know later how the two [*wujūd* and *māhiyyah*] are connected according to their condition under conceptual analysis.[42]

(٦٣) ومن قال إنّ الوجود، أراد به المفهوم العامّ العقليّ، وكونه عرضًا أنّه الخارج المحمول على الماهيّات.

(٦٤) وأيضًا الوجود مخالف للأعراض، لأنّ وجودها في نفسها وجودها لموضوعها، وأما الوجود، فهو بعينه وجود الموضوع، لا وجود عرض في الموضوع.

(٦٥) والأعراض مفتقرة في تحقّقها إلى الموضوع، والوجود لا يفتقر في تحقّقه إلى الموضوع، بل الموضوع يفتقر في تحقّقه إلى وجوده.

(٦٦) والحقّ أنّ وجود الجوهر جوهر بعين جوهريّة ذلك الجوهر، لا بجوهريّة أخرى. ووجود العرض عرض بعين عرضيّة ذلك العرض، لا بعرضية أُخرى، كما علمت الحال بين الماهية والوجود.

(٦٧) سؤال: إذا كان الوجود موجودًا للماهيّة، فله نسبة إليها وللنسبة أيضًا وجود حينئذ، فلوجود النسبة نسبة إلى النسبة، وهكذا الكلام في وجود نسبة النسبة فيتسلسل.

(٦٨) جواب: ما مّر من الكلام يكفي لاندفاعه، إذ الوجود عين الماهيّة خارجًا وغيرها في الذهن، فلا نسبة بينهما إلا بحسب الاعتبار العقليّ، وعند الاعتبار يكون للنسبة وجود هو عينها بالذات وغيرها بحسب الخارج، ومثل هذا التسلسل ينقطع بانقطاع الاعتبار العقليّ. وستعلم كيفيّة الارتباط بينها بحسب حالهما عند التحليل.

The Fifth Penetration

Concerning the manner in which quiddity is qualified by wujūd

(69) Perhaps you will return and say: "If there were to be for *wujūd* individuations in quiddities other than portions, then the affirmation of all individuation of *wujūd* for quiddity would presuppose the positive reality of the quiddity, according to the well-known principle.[43] Consequently, quiddity would already have to possess a certain positive reality before its own positive reality, as was mentioned."

(70) Know that the allegation of this objection does not concern the concrete reality of *wujūd*. Rather, when it pertains to the problem of *wujūd* as an abstract concept, then difficulties arise, because *wujūd* is the same as quiddity in point of concrete reality. Properly speaking, there is no real qualification between the two; and the same view applies to other cases. [*Wujūd*] thus becomes a qualification for [quiddity]. It is the modality of this qualification that causes difficulty[44] because if one speaks of the qualification of quiddity by *wujūd*, depending on what one means by infinitive existence, then the subject that receives the predicate is the actualization of the quiddity. And quiddity, in whatever aspect one considers it, possesses being, expressed by the infinitive verb. But then, it is inconceivable that, from the point of view of being in the absolute sense, quiddity be anterior to this Absolute Being. The situation is different if it is *wujūd* that is the real thing *in concreto*, while quiddity possesses a conceptual actuality outside its *wujūd*.

المشعر الخامس

في كيفيّة اتّصاف الماهيّة بالوجود

(٦٩) ولعلّك تعود وتقول: لو كانت للوجود أفراد في الماهيّات سوى الحصص، لكان ثبوت فرد منه للماهيّة فرعًا على ثبوتها بناء على القاعدة المشهورة. فيكون لها ثبوت قبل ثبوتها كما مرّ.

(٧٠) فاعلم أنّه لا خصوصيّة لورود هذا الكلام على عينيّة الوجود. بل وروده على انتزاعيّة الوجود أشكال، لأنّ الوجود عين الماهيّة على تقدير العينيّة، فلم يكن بينهما اتّصاف بالحقيقة وغيرها على هذا التقدير، فيكون وصفاً لها. فيشكل كيفيّة الإتّصاف، لأنّ اتّصاف الماهيّة بالوجود على تقدير أن يراد به الكون المصدريّ، مصداقها حصول الماهيّة. والماهيّة — بأيّ اعتبار أُخذت — كان لها كون مصدريّ، فلا يتصّور تقدّمها بحسب مطلق الكون على مطلق الكون ، بخلاف ما إذا كان الوجود أمرًا حقيقيّاً وللماهيّة تحصّلاً عقليًّا غير وجودها.

(71) However, the truth that merits being verified is that *wujūd*, whether it be concrete or conceptual, is the very affirmation of the quiddity and its *wujūd*. It is not the affirmation of something or [of] the *wujūd* of something belonging to this quiddity. Between these two meanings there is an obvious difference. That to which the already-mentioned rule [the principle of derivation] applies is that the affirmation of something for another thing is not the affirmation of something by itself alone. Thus, our proposition "Zayd is existent" comes to the same thing as "Zayd is Zayd." Therefore, the derivative rule does not apply here.[45]

The majority of the philosophers, since they were inattentive to this subtle distinction, fell into perplexity and commotion and became divided into followers of different paths. Sometimes they applied the general principle of derivation to cases other than the qualification of *wujūd*. Sometimes they fled from this principle and proceeded to substitute [the principle of] derivation. And yet, at other times, they rejected completely the positive idea of *wujūd*, conceptually as well as *in concreto*, maintaining that *wujūd* is purely and simply an interpretation and the creation of a false fantasy. [According to them,] the reason is that a derivative concept is affirmed through its unification with something, whereby the principle of derivation does not subsist by itself because the concept of the derived form—for example, "writer" or "white"—is a simple thing expressed [in Persian] as *dabir* and *safid*. Thus, for a thing to be existent consists in its being united with the concept of existent and not in *wujūd*'s subsistence by it, whether concretely or abstractly. Therefore, in principle, it does not need *wujūd*.

(72) Moreover, for the proponent of this view, the Necessary Being is exactly the same as the concept of existent, not the reality of *wujūd* itself; and the same holds true for the contingent existent. Likewise, the same holds true for all of the qualifications of concepts. For him, the difference between the essential and the accidental, as far as the derived forms are concerned, does not happen through unification in *wujūd*—unification that, according to us, is the basis of predicative judgment, essential in the case of essentialities and accidental in the case of accidentalities—since there is no *wujūd* in his view. According to him, the difference is that the essential concept is that which is given in response to the question, "What is it?" whereas the accident is that which is not given in such a response. All of these are aberrations [from the truth].

(٧١) لكنّ الحقّ الحقيق بالتحقيق أنّ الوجود—سواء كان عينيًّا أو عقليًا—نفس ثبوت الماهيّة ووجودها، لا ثبوت شيء أو وجوده لها. وبين المعنيين فرق واضح. والذي تجرى فيه القاعدة المذكورة، وهو ثبوت شيء لشيء لا ثبوت شيء في نفسه فقط. فقولنا زيد موجود كقولنا زيد زيد. فلا تجري فيه القاعدة الفرعيّة. والجمهور حيث غفلوا عن هذه الدقيقة، ووقعوا فيما وقعوا من الاضطراب، وتشعّبوا في الأبواب. فتارة خصّصوا القاعدة الكلّيّة القائلة بالفرعيّة بما سوى صفة الوجود. وتارة هربوا عنها وانتقلوا إلى الاستلزام بدل الفرعيّة. وتارة أنكروا ثبوت الوجود أصلاً لا ذهنًا ولا عينًا، قائلين أنّه مجرّد اعتبار الوهم الكاذب واختراعه، لأنّ مناط الصدق المشتقّ كالكاتب والأبيض، أمر بسيط يعبّر عنه بـ «دبير» و «سفيد» فكون الشيء موجودًا عبارة عن اتّحاده مع مفهوم الموجود، لا قيام الوجود به قيامًا حقيقيًّا أو انتزاعيًّا، ولا يحتاج إلى وجود أصلاً.

(٧٢) فالواجب عند هذا القائل عين مفهوم الوجود، لاعين الوجود. وكذا الممكن الموجود. وكذا في جميع الاتّصافات بالمفهومات. والفرق بين الذاتيّ والعرضيّ من المشتقّ عنده ليس بكون الاتحاد في الوجود—الذي هو مناط الحمل عندنا في الذاتيّات بالذات وفي العرضيّات بالعرض—إذ لا وجود عنده، بل إنّ المفهوم الذاتي هو الذي يقع في جواب «ما هو؟» والعرضيّ هو الذي لم يقع فيه. وهذا كلّه من التعسّفات.

(73) *An illumination of wisdom*: The *wujūd* of all contingent existents is their very quiddity *in concreto* and is united with it in some kind of unification. This is so based on what was confirmed and established concerning our explanation that the real *wujūd* is something actual *in concreto*.[46] It is the principle of effects [on things] and the source of [existential] states; and through it, quiddity becomes existent and nonexistence is removed from it. And if the *wujūd* of each quiddity were not *in concreto* and were not unified with it, the following [dilemma] would ensue: either *wujūd* is a part of quiddity, or it is added to it as an accident. Both of these are false because the *wujūd* of the part would be anterior to the *wujūd* of the whole, and the *wujūd* of the qualification would be posterior to the *wujūd* of the subject qualified. [In this case,] it would be necessary that the quiddity have an existence actualized before itself and that *wujūd* would be anterior to itself. Both of these are impossible. It would also be necessary that a certain mode of *wujūd* of a single thing be repeated, or it would lead to a *regressio ad infinitum* in the ordered assembly of the individual members of *wujūd*. Now, besides the impossibility of this infinite regression by reason of established proofs, and because this would imply an infinity in act contained between two limits—that is, *wujūd* and quiddity—besides all that, this infinite regression would imply a proof contrary to our thesis, which is that *wujūd* is quiddity itself *in concreto*, because the subsistence of the totality of all existing things in such a way that no accidental existence would lie outside of it implies, for these quiddities, a *wujūd* that would not be an accident; otherwise, that which was supposed to be the totality would not be the totality, but a part of the totality.

(74) Once it is established that the *wujūd* of every contingent being is its very quiddity *in concreto*, then [one of two alternatives] follows: either there exists between quiddity and *wujūd* a difference in meaning and in concept, or there is no difference. The second hypothesis is false. Otherwise *man* and *wujūd*, for example, would be two synonymous terms, and there would be no benefit in saying, "Man is existent." In the same way, to say that "Man is existent" and to say that "Man is man" would

(٧٣) إشراق حكميّ وجود كلّ ممكن عين ماهيّته خارجًا ومتّحد بها نحواً من الاتّحاد. وذلك لأنّه لما ثبت وتحقّق ممّا بيّنّا أنّ الوجود الحقيقيّ، الذي هو مبدأ الآثار ومنشأ الأحكام، وبه تكون الماهيّة موجودة، وبه يطرد العدم عنها، أمر عينيّ. فلو لم يكن وجود كلّ ماهيّة عينها ومتّحدًا بها، فلا يخلو: إما أن يكون جزءًا منها أو زائدًا عليها عارضًا لها. وكلاهما باطلان، لأنّ وجود الجزء قبل وجود الكلّ، ووجود الصفة بعد وجود الموصوف. فتكون الماهيّة حاصلة الوجود قبل نفسها، ويكون الوجود متقدّماً على نفسه. وكلاهما ممتنعان. ويلزم أيضا تكرير نحو وجود شيءٍ واحد من جهة واحدة، أو التسلسل في المترتّبات المجتمعة من أفراد الوجود. وهذا التسلسل مع استحالته بالبراهين واستلزامه لانحصار ما لا يتناهى بين حاصرَين — أي الوجود والماهيّة — يستلزم المدّعي بالخلف، وهو كون الوجود عين الماهيّة في الخارج، لأنّ قيام جميع الوجودات بحيث لا يشذّ عنها وجود عارض يستلزم وجودًا لها غير عارض، وإلا لم يكن المفروض جميعًا بل بعضًا من الجميع.

(٧٤) فإذا ثبت كون وجود كلّ ممكن عين ماهيّته في العين، فلا يخلو: إمّا أن يكون بينهما مغايرة في المعنى والمفهوم، أو لا يكون. والثاني باطل، وإلا لكان الإنسان مثلاً والوجود لفظَين مترادفَين، ولم يكن لقولنا « الإنسان موجود» فائدة ، ولكان مفاد قولنا «الإنسان موجود» وقولنا «الإنسان إنسان» واحدًا، ولما أمكن تصّور أحدهما مع الغفلة

amount to saying the same thing. But in reality, we can conceive one of them while disregarding the other. [These false assumptions] would lead to other absurd consequences mentioned in common books. Furthermore, the absurdity of each of these consequences postulates the absurdity of the antecedent. Therefore, there remains the first alternative—that is, that quiddity and *wujūd* are different from each other in their meaning when they are analyzed by the mind, while they form one single unity essentially and in their ipseity *in concreto.*

(75) There remains [for us] an argument to explain the manner in which quiddity is qualified by *wujūd* considering the difference in qualification with regard to mental analysis, which itself is also a certain mode of *wujūd* of the thing itself without [something else] making or generating [it].[47] This difficulty pertains to the fact that each subject qualified by a qualification, or each subject to which there inheres an accident, must of necessity have a certain degree of existence in function of which, before this qualification or this accident, it is neither a subject qualified by this qualification nor a subject in which this accident inheres. Consequently, either *wujūd* happens to a quiddity that exists, or it happens to a quiddity that does not exist, or it happens to a quiddity that altogether neither exists nor does not exist. The first hypothesis involves *petitio principi* and *regressio ad infinitum.* The second hypothesis implies contradiction; and the third hypothesis, the canceling of two contradictions.

(76) To make the excuse that canceling two contradictions [that belong to] the same level [of reality] is possible and is, in fact, the case is not useful here, because the level at which the removal of the two contradictions is possible is, in fact, one of the degrees of the same reality. Therefore, this level must have a certain reality preceding the two contradictions, similar to the level of the quiddity with respect to accidents. In reality, the quiddity has an existence irrespective of the accident and its counterpart—like the body, for example, with respect to whiteness

عن الآخر، إلى غير ذلك من اللوازم المذكورة في المتداولات من التوالي الباطلة. وبطلان كلّ من هذه التوالي مستلزم لبطلان المقدّم. فتعيّن الشقّ الأوّل، وهو كون كلّ منهما غير الآخر بحسب المعنى عند التحليل الذهنيّ مع اتّحادهما ذاتًا وهويةً في نفس الأمر.

(٧٥) بقي الكلام في كيفيّة اتّصاف الماهيّة بالوجود بحسب اعتبار المغايرة الاتّصافيّة في ظرف التحليل العقليّ، الذي هو أيضًا نحو من أنحاء وجود الشيء في نفس الأمر بلا تعمّل واختراع. وذلك لأنّ كل موصوف بصفة أو معروض لعارض، فلا بدّ له من مرتبة من الوجود يكون متقدّمًا بحسبه على تلك الصفة أو ذلك العارض غير موصوف به ولا معروض له. فعروض الوجود إمّا للماهيّة الموجودة، أو غير الموجودة، أو لا الموجودة ولا المعدومة جميعًا: فالأوّل يستلزم الدور أو التسلسل؛ والثاني يوجب التناقض؛ والثالث يقتضي ارتفاع النقيضين.

(٧٦) والاعتذار بأنّ ارتفاع النقيضين عن المرتبة جائز، بل واقع غير نافع هيهنا، لأنّ المرتبة التي يجوز خلو النقيضين عنها هي ما تكون من مراتب نفس الأمر، ولا بد من أن يكون لها تحقّق ما في الجملة سابقًا على النقيضين، كمرتبة الماهيّة بالقياس إلى العوارض. فإنّ للماهيّة وجودًا مع قطع النظر عن العارض ومقابلة — كالجسم بالقياس على البياض — ونقيضه. وليس لها مرتبة وجود مع قطع النظر عن وجودها. فقياس عروض

and its opposite [nonwhiteness]. But the quiddity does not possess any degree of *wujūd* when one considers it independent of its *wujūd*. Therefore, it is a lame argument to compare the occurrence of *wujūd* to quiddity with the occurrence of whiteness to a body and to compare the state where the quiddity is deprived of existence and nonexistence with the deprivation of a body in its level of existence of whiteness and nonwhiteness. This is so because the subsistence of whiteness and its opposite in a body is secondary to its *wujūd*, whereas the subsistence of *wujūd* by quiddity is not secondary to its *wujūd* precisely because quiddity does not possess *wujūd* except through *wujūd* itself.[48]

(77) The verification of this station leads us, based on what we have indicated, to say that the accident of the quiddity consists of something that is the quiddity itself in *wujūd* and that is different in rational analysis: it is in the nature of the intellect to analyze the existent into a quiddity and *wujūd*. In this analysis, the mind disengages each of these two from the other and concludes the anteriority of one over the other and its qualification by the other. As for that which is *in concreto*, the principle and the existent is *wujūd* because it is essentially what proceeds from the instaurer. Quiddity is united with *wujūd* and is predicated of it, but not in the manner in which the attached accidents are. Rather, [quiddity's] predication of [*wujūd*] and its unification with it is in regard to its own ipseity and essence. As for the order in the mind, what is anterior is the quiddity, because it is a universal concept in the mind that is obtained with its very essence in the mind.[49] What is obtained from *wujūd* is its general concept. Therefore, quiddity is the principle in mental judgments and not in the judgments related to the external world. This anteriority is anteriority by meaning and quiddity and not by *wujūd*. And this anteriority lies outside of the five famous categories [the five universals].[50]

(78) And if you say: "The abstraction of quiddity from *wujūd* through mental analysis is also a sort of *wujūd* for quiddity; then how can the principle of derivation be maintained in the qualification of the quiddity by the undetermined [absolute] *wujūd*, even though this abstraction is a kind of undetermined *wujūd*?" We can say [in response] that although this abstraction constitutes a mode of undetermined *wujūd*, nevertheless the intellect need not consider this abstraction itself in its

الوجود للماهية بعروض البياض للجسم، وقياس خلوّها عن الوجود والعدم بخلوّ الجسم في مرتبة وجوده عن البياض واللا بياض، قياس بلا جامع ، إذ قيام البياض والمقابلة بالجسم فرع على وجوده وليس قيام الوجود بالماهيّة فرعًا على وجودها إذ لا وجود لها إلا بالوجود.

(٧٧) فالتحقيق في هذا المقام أن يقال بعدما أشرنا إليه أنّ عارض الماهيّة عن شيء يكون عين الماهيّة في الوجود وغيره في التحليل العقليّ: إنّ للعقل أن يحلل الموجود إلى ماهيّة ووجود، وفي هذا التحليل يجرّد كلا منهما عن صاحبه ويحكم بتقدم أحدهما على الآخر واتّصافه به: أما بحسب الخارج فالأصل الموجود هو الوجود لأنّه الصادر عن الجاعل بالذات، والماهيّة متّحدة به محمولة عليه، لا كحمل العرضيّات اللاحقة، بل حملها عليه واتّحادها به بحسب نفس هويّته وذاته، وأما بحسب الذهن فالمتقدّم هي الماهيّة لأنّها مفهوم كلّيّ ذهنيّ يحصل بكنهها في الذهن، ولا يحصل من الوجود إلا مفهومه العامّ الاعتباريّ. فالماهيّة هي الأصل في القضايا الذهنيّة لا الخارجيّة، والتقدّم هنا تقدّم بالمعنى والماهيّة، لا بالوجود. فهذا التقدم خارج عن الأقسام الخمسة المعروفة.

(٧٨) فإن قلتَ: تجريد الماهيّة على الوجود عند التحليل أيضًا ضرب من الوجود لها في نفس الأمر، فكيف تُحفظ قاعدة الفرعيّة في اتّصافها بمطلق الوجود، مع أنّ هذا التجريد من أنحاء مطلق الوجود؟ قلنا هذا التجريد، وإن كان نحوًا من مطلق الوجود، فللعقل أن لا يلاحظ عند التجريد هذا التجريد، وأنّه نحو من الوجود، فتتّصف الماهيّة بالوجود المطلق

abstraction, [because] this is a mode of *wujūd*. As a result, quiddity would be qualified by [this] undetermined *wujūd* from which we had precisely abstracted [the quiddity]. This consideration consists of emptying quiddity of all acts of *wujūd*, even of this consideration and of this emptying, which is in reality a mode of *wujūd* without being an act. [This consideration] involves two points of view: there is the point of view according to which it is an abstraction and stripping, and there is the point of view according to which it is a mode of *wujūd*.

(79) According to the first point of view, quiddity is qualified by *wujūd*. According to the second point of view, it is mixed and is not qualified [by *wujūd*]. It is a stripping from one point of view and mixture from another. However, the position of each of these two points of view does not differ from that of the other. Otherwise, the difficulty would return, in the sense that the point of view according to which the quiddity is qualified by *wujūd* would imply its conjunction with *wujūd*; and thus, the principle of derivation would become null and void. That is because this abstraction [the quiddity] from the totality of *wujūd* is a mode of *wujūd*, not because it is something different from *wujūd*. It is *wujūd* and abstraction from *wujūd* in the same way that the *materia prima* possesses the potentiality of formal substances and others. This potentiality itself is realized in act for matter without its needing another potentiality for the actualization of this potentiality. The actualization [of this potentiality] is therefore the potentiality [of matter] with regard to multiple things, in the same way that the permanence of movement is its renewal and that the unity of number is [also] its multiplicity. Examine well the penetration of the light of *wujūd* and the permeation of its rule in the totality of meanings through the totality of mental considerations and actual realities, to such an extent that the abstraction of quiddity from *wujūd* presupposes the *wujūd* of this quiddity.[51]

الذي جرّدناها عنه. فهذه الملاحظة التي هي عبارة عن تخلية الماهيّة عن جميع الوجودات حتّى عن هذه الملاحظة وعن هذه التخلية — التي هي أيضًا نحو من الوجود في الواقع من غير تعمّل — لها اعتباران: اعتبار كونها تجريدًا وتعرية، واعتبار كونها نحوًا من الوجود.

(٧٩) فالماهيّة بالاعتبار الأوّل موصوفة بالوجود. وبالاعتبار الآخر مخلوطة غير موصوفة. فالتعرية باعتبار، والخلط باعتبار آخر. وليست حيثيّة أحد الاعتبارين غير حيثيّة الاعتبار الآخر، ليعود الإشكال جذعًا من أنّ الاعتبار الذي به تتّصف الماهيّة بالوجود. لا بدّ فيه أيضًا من مقارنته للوجود. فتنفسخ ضابطة الفرعيّة، وذلك لأنّ هذا التجريد عن كافة الوجود هو بعينه نحو من الوجود، لا أنّه شيء آخر غيره. فهو وجود وتجريد عن الوجود، كما أنّ للهيولي الأولى قوّة الجواهر الصوريّة وغيرها. ونفس هذه القوّة حاصلة لها لا بالفعل ولا حاجة لها إلى قوّة أخرى لفعليّة هذه القوّة. ففعليّتها قوّتها للأشياء الكثيرة، كما أنّ ثبات الحركة عين تجددها، ووحدة العدد عين كثرته. فانظر إلى سريان نور الوجود ونفوذ حكمه في جميع المعاني بجميع الاعتبارات والحيثيّات، حتّى أنّ تجريد الماهيّة عن الوجود أيضًا متفرّع على وجودها.

(80) Remark: It should be known that what we have mentioned has [as its goal] to complete the argument of the people in a way that it is in accordance with their [intellectual] taste and is adapted to their method concerning *wujūd* being a mental abstraction. However, for our part, we have no need of delving deeply into this matter, since we have established that *wujūd* is quiddity itself *in concreto* and that, moreover, *wujūd* is the affirmation of the thing itself and not the affirmation for it; therefore, the principle of derivation does not apply here. To apply qualification to the relationship that exists between quiddity and *wujūd* is to speak in a general and figurative sense, because the relation between the two [quiddity and *wujūd*] is of a unitive order. It is not like the relation between a subject and its accident, or between the subject qualified and the attribute that qualifies it. Rather, it is more like the qualification of a genus by its specific difference in the case of a simple species, when this is carried out by the mind with regard to them being a genus and specific difference and not with regard to them being intelligible matter and form.[52]

(٨٠) تنبيه. وليعلم أنّ ما ذكرنا تتميم لكلام القوم على ما يوافق مذاقهم و يلائم مسلكهم في اعتباريّة الوجود. وأمّا نحن، فلا نحتاج إلى هذا التعمّق، لما قرّرنا أنّ الوجود نفس الماهيّة عينًا، وأيضًا الوجود نفس ثبوت الشيء، لا ثبوت شيء له. فلا مجال للتفريع هنا. فكان إطلاق الاتّصاف على الارتباط الذي بين الماهية ووجودها، من باب التوسع والتجوز،لأن الارتباط بينهما اتّحاديّ لا كالارتباط بين المعروض وعارضه والموصوف وصفته، بل من قبيل اتّصاف الجنس بفصله في النوع البسيط عند تحليل العقل إيّاه إليهما، من حيث هما جنس وفصل، لا من حيث هما مادّة وصورة عقليّتين.

The Sixth Penetration

Concerning the particularization of individual existences and their ipseity—in a summary fashion

(81) Know this: You have already come to know that *wujūd* is a concrete, simple reality and that it is not a natural universal that, in the mind, would receive one of the five universals of logic, except from the point of view of the quiddity with which it is united when this quiddity is considered as such. Therefore, we say: The particularization of each individual *wujūd* consists of the following [three means]: [1] by its own reality, as in the case of the perfect Necessary Being—exalted be His Glory; or [2] by means of a degree of anteriority and posteriority, and of perfection and deficiency, as in the case of generated beings; or yet again, [3] by certain added elements, as in the case of the members of the world of creation.

(82) Some have said that the particularization of all existence consists in its relation with its substratum and with its cause, not that this relation is something added from the outside, because *wujūd* is an accident, and every accident subsists by its *wujūd* in its substratum. In the same way, the *wujūd* of every quiddity consists in the relation of this *wujūd* to this quiddity, not in the way that a thing is in space and time, because the existence of this thing in itself is other than its existence in space and time.[53] This argument is not without indulgence, because it is

المشعر السادس

في أنّ تخصيص أفراد الوجود وهويّاتها بماذا
على سبيل الإجمال

(٨١) اعلم أنّك قد علمت أنّ الوجود حقيقة عينيّة بسيطة، لا أنّه كلّي طبيعي يعرض لها في الذهن أحد الكلّيات الخمس المنطقيّة إلا من جهة الماهيّة المتّحدة بها إذا أُخذت من حيث هي هي. فإذن نقول: تخصيص كلّ فرد من الوجود إمّا بنفس حقيّقته، كالوجود التامّ الواجبي — جلّ مجده — و إمّا بمرتبته من التقدّم والتأخّر والكمال والنقص، كالمبدعات، أو بأمور لاحقة، كأفراد الكائنات.

(٨٢) وقيل تخصيص كلّ وجود بإضافته إلى موضوعه و إلى سببه، لا لأنّ الإضافة لحقته من خارج، فإنّ الوجود عرض، وكلّ عرض متقوّم بوجوده في موضوعه، وكذلك حال وجود كلّ ماهيّة بإضافته إلى تلك الماهيّة، لا كما يكون الشيء في المكان أو في الزمان. وهذا الكلام لا يخلو عن مساهلة، إذ قياس نسبة الوجود إلى الماهيّة بنسبة العرض إلى الموضوع فاسد، كما

false to establish an analogy between the relation of *wujūd* to quiddity on the one hand and accident to the substratum on the other. As was discussed before, quiddity does not subsist separately from *wujūd*, and *wujūd* is nothing other than the existence of a thing itself and is not the existence of something else for that thing, in the manner of an accident for a substratum or form for its matter. The *wujūd* of an accident in itself, while it is its *wujūd* for its substratum, is not, however, itself the *wujūd* of its substratum, contrary to the *wujūd* that is the very *wujūd* of this quiddity, insofar as it has a quiddity. There is a difference between the fact that a thing is in space and time and the fact that an accident is in its substratum. As it becomes clear from this argument, the existence of a thing in one of the two [meaning space and time] is different from its being in itself, while the existence of an accident is the same as being in itself. By the same token, there is a difference between the *wujūd* of the accident in the substratum and the *wujūd* of the substratum itself, because the *wujūd* in the first case [that of the accident] is other than the *wujūd* of the substratum, whereas in the second case, it is [this *wujūd*] itself.[54]

(83) Shaykh al-Raʾīs Ibn Sīnā has said in his *Taʿlīqāt* as follows: "The *wujūd* of accidents in themselves is their *wujūd* for their respective substrata, except for the accident [that is] *wujūd*. This latter differs from other accidents as a result of the fact that they have need of their substratum in order to exist, whereas *wujūd* does not need *wujūd* in order to exist. It is therefore not correct to say that *wujūd* in its substratum is *wujūd* in itself, if one means by that that *wujūd* has a *wujūd* other than itself, as whiteness has a *wujūd*. Rather, one can say that its *wujūd* in its substratum is the very *wujūd* of its substratum, whereas in the case of all other accidents, its *wujūd* in its substratum is simply the *wujūd* of this other [thing]."

(84) He has also said in the *Taʿlīqāt*: "The *wujūd* that is in the body is the very existentiality of the body itself, not as it is in the case of the whiteness of the body in its being white, because in this case it would not be sufficient to have only whiteness and the body."

مّر من أنّه لا قوام للماهيّة مجرّدة عن الوجود، وأنّ الوجود ليس إلا كون الشيء، لا كون شيء لشيء، كالعرض لموضوعه، أو كالصورة لمادّتها. ووجود العرض في نفسه، و إن كان عين وجوده لموضوعه، لكن ليس بعينه وجود موضوعه بخلاف الوجود، فإنّه نفس وجود الماهيّة فيما له ماهيّة. فكما أنّ الفرق حاصل بين كون الشيء في المكان وفي الزمان وبين كون العرض في الموضوع، كما ظهر من كلامه بأنّ كون الشيء في أحدهما غير كونه في نفسه، فكذا الفرق حاصل بين وجود العرض في الموضوع وبين وجود الموضوع، فإنّ الوجود في الأوّل غير وجود الموضوع وفي الثاني عينه.

(٨٣) قال الشيخ الرئيس في التعليقات «وجود الأعراض في أنفسها وجوداتها لموضوعاتها، سوى أنّ العرض الذي هو الوجود، لمّا كان مخالفاً لها لحاجتها إلى الموضوع حتّى يصير موجودًا، واستغنى الوجود عن الوجود حتّى يكون موجودًا، لم يصحّ أن يقال إنّ وجوده في موضوعه هو وجوده في نفسه، بمعنى أنّ للوجود وجودًا، كما يكون للبياض وجود، بل بمعنى أنّ وجوده في موضوعه نفس وجود موضوعه، وغيره من الأعراض وجوده في موضوعه وجود ذلك الغير.»

(٨٤) وقال أيضًا في التعليقات «فالوجود الذي في الجسم هو موجوديّة الجسم، لا كحال البياض والجسم في كونه أبيض، إذ لا يكفي فيه البياض والجسم.»

(85) I say: The majority of the later philosophers were not capable of understanding the purpose of such an explanation and those similar to it whereby they ascribed them to the conceptuality of *wujūd* [*wujūd* as a mental concept], [claiming that] *wujūd* is not a reality *in concreto*, and they caused the argument to deviate from its proper subject. As for myself, in the days gone by I was a vigorous defender of the thesis of the principiality of quiddities and the conceptuality of *wujūd*, until my Lord guided me and made me see its proof. Then it was unveiled to me with supreme evidence that [the case of the quiddities] was the reverse of what they conceived and decided [concerning this matter]. Glory be to God Who, through the light of veritable understanding, allowed me to leave the darkness of opinion, Who made the clouds of doubt in my heart dissipate through the rising of the Sun of the Truth, and Who established me on the "firm doctrine" in this life and in the Hereafter.[55] Existences are the principial realities, whereas quiddities are the "fixed essences" that have never smelled the perfume of real existence.[56] And [these] existences are none other than the rays and gleamings of the Light of Truth and the Eternal, exalted be His Sublimeness. For each of these existences, however, there are certain essential constitutive characteristics and intelligible meanings that one calls "quiddities."[57]

(86) *A clarification within which there is an investigation:* The particularization of *wujūd* through necessity [namely, the Necessary Being] consists in its sacred Reality being above all deficiency and shortcomings. Its particularization by Its degrees and Its levels of anteriority and posteriority, richness and indigence, intensity and weakness, and what pertains to It in its essential states and concrete realities is in accordance with Its simple Reality, which has no genus or specific difference. Nor does the

(٨٥) أقول: إنّ أكثر المتأخّرين لم يقدروا على تحصيل المراد من هذه العبارة وأمثالها، حيث حملوها على اعتباريّة الوجود وأنّه ليس أمرًا عينيًا، وحرّفوا الكلمة عن مواضعها. وإنني قد كنتُ في سالف الزمان شديد الذبّ عن تأصّل الماهيّات واعتباريّة الوجود، حتّى هداني ربي وأراني برهانه. فانكشف لي غاية الانكشاف أنّ الأمر فيه على عكس ما تصوّروه و قرّروه. فالحمد لله الذي أخرجني عن ظلمات الوهم بنور الفهم، وأزاح عن قلبي سحب تلك الشكوك بطلوع شمس الحقيقة وثبّتني على القول الثابت في الحياة الدنيا والآخرة. فالوجودات حقائق متأصّلة، والماهيّات هي الأعيان الثابتة التي ما شمّت رائحة الوجود أصلاً. وليست الوجودات إلا أشعّة وأضواء للنور الحقيقيّ والوجود القيّوميّ — جلّ كبرياؤه — إلا أنّ لكل منها نعوتًا ذاتيّة ومعانٍ عقليّة هي المسمّاة بالماهيّات.

(٨٦) توضيح فيه تنقيح. أمّا تخصيص الوجود بالواجبيّة، فبنفس حقيقته المقدّسة عن نقص وقصور. وأمّا تخصيصه بمراتبه ومنازله في التقدم والتأخّر، والغنى والحاجة، والشدّة والضعف، فبما فيه من شؤونه الذاتيّة وحيثيّاته العينيّة بحسب حقيقته البسيطة، التي لا جنس لها ولا فصل يعرض لها الكلّية، كما علم. وأمّا تخصيصه بموضوعاته — أعني الماهيّات

generality [of an abstract concept] occur to it, as has already been known. As for its particularization by its substratums—by which I mean the quiddities and essences qualified by it in the mind, as we have already explained—it is in regard to what is affirmed of each of the essential [properties] that issue from it on the level of knowledge and intellection. In confirmation of it, [particularization takes place with regard to] universal natures and essential meanings attributed to it by an attribution that is essential to it and that, in the language of the specialists of this science, is called quiddities. Among the Sufis, they are called the "fixed archetypes." And this is so while *wujūd* and quiddity, in everything that possesses *wujūd* and quiddity, are one and the same unique thing. And what is the object of knowledge is the existent itself. This is a strange secret. May God open[58] in thy heart the door for its understanding, if He wills.

(87) Ibn Sīnā says in his book *al-Mubāḥathāt:* "*Wujūd* in the essences of quiddities does not differ in [terms of] species. Rather, if there is a differentiation, it is through confirmation [that is, intensification] and weakness. Verily, the quiddities of things that pertain to *wujūd* are different from one another in terms of species. The human differs from the horse in terms of species because of his quiddity and not because of his act of existing." End of his word. Understood in the first way, particularization is produced in *wujūd* with regard to its essence and its ipseity; whereas, understood in the second way, it is produced in relationship to its essential and universal qualifications, which accompany it in every one of its degrees.

والأعيان المتّصفة به في العقل على الوجه الذي مرّ ذكره — فهو باعتبار ما يصدق عليه في كلّ مقام من ذاتيّاته التي تنبعث عنه في حدّ العلم والتعقّل، ويصدق عليه صدقًا ذاتيًا من الطبائع الكلّيّة والمعاني الذاتيّة، التي يقال لها في عرف أهل هذا الفنّ الماهيّات، وعند الصوفيّة الأعيان الثابتة، وأنّ كل الوجود والماهيّة فيما له وجود وماهيّة شيء واحد، والمعلوم عين الموجود. وهذا سرّ غريب فتح الله على قلبك فهمه إن شاء الله.

(٨٧) قال الشيخ الرئيس في المباحثات «إنّ الوجود في ذوات الماهيّات لا يختلف بالنوع، بل إن كان له اختلاف، فبالتأكّد والتضّعف. وإنّما تختلف ماهيّات الأشياء—التي تنال الوجود—بالنوع، وما فيها من الوجود فغير مختلف النوع. فإنّ الإنسان يخالف الفرس بالنوع لأجل ماهيّته، لا لأجل وجوده» انتهى كلامه. فالتخصيص في الوجود على الوجه الأوّل بحسب ذاته وهويّته وأمّا على الوجه الثاني، فباعتبار ما معه في كلّ مرتبة من النعوت الذاتيّة الكلّية.

(88) It is not farfetched to think that what is meant by the differentiation of existences in terms of species is what became famous according to the Peripatetics concerning this meaning. From one point of view, this is like the differentiation of the degrees of numbers; and from another point of view, it is their convergence in terms of species. In reality, it is correct to say that the degrees of numbers constitute a unified reality, since for each degree of numbers, there is nothing but an assemblage of units that are similar to one another. It is equally correct to say that they are differentiated [from one another] as far as their respective essential meanings are concerned, since from each degree [of numbers], the intellect can abstract qualities and essential properties that are not proven for others. And they have effects and differentiated characteristics that result from this degree with regard to its own conditions, which the intellect abstracts from each of its essential degrees as opposed to what it abstracts from each of the other degrees by virtue of their respective essences. They are, therefore, like particular existences in the sense that the subject to which these essential structures and universal qualities are attributed is essentially the respective essences of each of these numbers. Think deeply upon all of this because all of this comes from noble sciences.[59]

(٨٨) ولا يبعد أن يكون المراد بتخالف الوجودات نوعًا كما اشتهر من المشّائين هذا المعنى، وهو بعينه كتخالف مراتب الأعداد أنواعًا بوجهٍ، وتوافقها نوعًا بوجهٍ ما. فإنه يصّح القول بكونها متّحدة الحقيقة، إذ ليس في كلّ مرتبة من العدد سوى المجتمع من الوحدات التي هي أمور متشابهة. ويصح القول بكونها متخالفة المعاني الذاتيّة، إذ ينتزع العقل من كلّ مرتبة نعوتًا وأوصافًا ذاتيّة ليست ثابتة لغيرها. ولها آثار وخواصّ متخالفة تترتّب عليها بحسب أحكام نفسيّة ينتزع العقل من كلّ مرتبة لذاتها خلاف ما ينتزع من مرتبة أُخرى لذاتها. فهي بعينها كالوجودات الخاصّة في أنّ مصداق تلك الأحكام والنعوت الكلّية ذواتها بذواتها. فأتقن ذلك، فإنّه من العلوم الشرفية .

The Seventh Penetration

Concerning the subject that what is by essence the object of instauration and what emanates from the cause is wujūd *without quiddity*

And in it there are witnesses.

The first witness

(89) We say: That which is by essence the object of instauration is not what is called the quiddity, as was the path of those who followed the school of the Stoics (*riwāqiyyūn*),[60] such as the "Master who was killed" [Suhrawardī] and those who followed him, among whom are included ᶜAllāmah Dawānī and those who imitated him faithfully. Nor is it the quiddity becoming existent, as is well known among the Peripatetics. Furthermore, it is not the concept of existent *qua* existent, as has been professed by al-Sayyid al-Mudaqqiq [Ṣadr al-Dīn Dashtakī Shīrāzī]. Rather, what emanates in its essence [from the cause] and what

المشعر السابع

في أنّ الأمر المجعول بالذات من الجاعل
والفائض من العلّة هو الوجود دون الماهيّة

وعليه شواهد

الشاهد الأول

(٨٩) إنّا نقول: ليس المجعول بالذات هو المسمّى بالماهيّة، كما ذهب أتباع الرواقيّين كالشيخ المقتول ومن تبعه، ومنهم العلامة الدوّاني ومن يحذو حذوه؛ ولا ضرورية الماهيّة موجودة، كما اشتهر من المشّائين؛ ولا مفهوم الوجود بما هو موجود، كما يراه السيّد المدقّق، بل الصادر بالذات والمجعول بنفسه في كلّ ما له جاعل، هو نحو وجوده العينيّ جعلاً بسيطًا

is essentially the object of instauration in all that has an instaurer is the mode of its concrete *wujūd* through a simple act of instauration free of all multiplicity—[the latter view] requiring something that is instaured and something for which it is instaured. In fact, if quiddity with regard to its essence had need of an instaurer, it would follow that it would be subsisting by [the instaurer] in the very definition of itself and its meaning, because the consideration of the instaurer would be included in the very consistency of the essence [of the quiddity]—so much so that one would not be able to conceive it independent of its instaurer. And such is not the case.

(90) In fact, we can imagine a multiplicity of quiddities with their definitions without knowing if they have been actualized or not, let alone the actualization of their instaurer, because quiddities do not refer to things other [than themselves]. And among existing quiddities, there are those that we can conceptualize and consider with total disregard of other things since, considered in this way, quiddities are nothing but themselves.[61] Therefore, if quiddities were in themselves the objects of instauration, constituted by a cause and in need of the latter for their constitution, then it would not be possible to consider them separately from all other things. It would be no more possible to consider quiddities as such than it would be possible to consider the meaning of a thing independent of its parts and constitutive elements. Therefore, the effect exercised by the instaurer and what results from it is not quiddity, but something other than it. The object of instauration is none other than the *wujūd* of the object through a simple instauration, and its quiddity, only through the accident.[62]

(91) You might object: "This having been said, it follows that the *wujūd* of the instaurer is one of the constitutive elements of the thing being instaured and is not extrinsic to it, in the same way that one can deduce this consequence from the hypothesis of accepting the instauration of the quiddity and making the quiddity the object of the act of instauration." I would respond: Yes, it is so, and there is no harm in this, because the *wujūd* of the caused is constituted by its *wujūd* in the way that deficiency is constituted by perfection, weakness by strength, and contingency by necessity.

مقدّساً عن كثرة تستدعي مجعولاً ومجعولاً إليه، إذ لو كانت الماهيّة بحسب جوهرها مفتقرة إلى الجاعل، لزم كونها متقوّمة به في حدّ نفسها ومعناها، بأن يكون الجاعل معتبرًا في قوام ذاتها بحيث لا يمكن تصّورها بدونه. وليس كذلك.

(٩٠) فإننا قد نتصوّر كثيرًا من الماهيّات بحدودها، ولم نعلم أنّها هل هي حاصلة بعدُ أم لا، فضلاً عن حصول جاعلها، إذ لا دلالة لها على غيرها. ومن الماهيّات الموجودة ما نتصوّرها ونأخذها من حيث هي هي مع قطع النظر عما سواها، إذ هي بهذا الاعتبار ليست إلا نفسها. فلو كانت هي في حدّ نفسها مجعولة متقوّمة بالعلّة مفتقرة إليها افتقارًا قواميًّا، لم يكن بحيث يمكن أخذها مجرّدة عما سواها، ولا كونها مأخوذة من حيث هي هي، كما لا يمكن ملاحظة معنى الشيء إلا مع أجزائه ومقوّماته. فإذن أثر الجاعل وما يترتب عليه، ليس هو هي، بل غيرها. فإذن المجعول ليس إلا وجود الشيء جعلاً بسيطًا دون ماهيّته إلا بالعرض.

(٩١) فإن قلتَ: فعلى هذا يلزم أن يكون الجاعل مقوّماً للوجود المجعول غير خارج عنه، مثل ما يلزم من جعل الماهيّة ومجعوليّتها، —قلتُ: نعم لا محذور فيه. فإنّ وجود المعلول متقوّم بوجود علّته تَـقَـوُّم النقص بالتمام، والضعف بالقوّة والإمكان بالوجوب.

(92) It is not for you to object that we can imagine the *wujūd* of the caused while neglecting the *wujūd* of the cause that is necessary for it and that, therefore, the *wujūd* of the cause is not constituted by the *wujūd* of the caused; because we would respond: It is not possible to have the actualization of knowledge about the particularity of a mode of *wujūd* except by essential witnessing, and this cannot be realized except by witnessing its cause that emanates [this particular being]. That is why it has been said: "The knowledge of the caused does not come about except by the knowledge of its cause."[63] Contemplate this point.

The second witness

(93) If the quiddity were itself the object of instauration, the concept of the instaured would be predicated of the quiddity through "primary essential predication," not through "common technical predication." It would follow that the effect produced by the instaurer would be the concept of the thing instaured in exclusion of all other concepts, each concept differing from the other, since there is no unity among concepts with regard to quiddity. Now, primary essential predication is not conceivable except between a concept and itself, or between itself and its definition—for example, when we say, "Man is man" or "Man is a rational animal." But when we say, "The rational animal is a being who laughs," this predication is not possible through primary essential predication but [comes about] through common technical predication. The mode of this latter [predication] is unification in existence, not unification in concept.[64]

The third witness

(94) No quiddity rejects the multiplicity of particularization of existences. Now, as individuation is exactly the same as *wujūd*[65] (as is professed by the verifiers),[66] or is concurrent with it (as is the opinion of others), particularization cannot be one of the necessary components of the quiddity any more than can *wujūd*, as has already been demonstrated. If quiddity as an object of instauration were to be actualized in

(٩٢) وليس لك أن تقول: نحن نتصوّر وجود المعلول مع الغفلة عن وجود علّته الموجبة له، فلا يكون متقوّمًا به، — لأننا نقول: لا يمكن حصول العلم بخصوصيّة نحو من الوجود إلا بمشاهدة عينيّته وهى لا تتحقّق إلا من جهة مشاهدة علّته الفيّاضة. ولهذا قالوا: العلم بذي السبب لا يحصل إلا بالعلم بسببه، تأمّل فيه.

الشاهد الثاني

(٩٣) أنّ الماهيّة لو كانت في حدّ نفسها مجعولة، لكان مفهوم المجعول محمولاً عليها بالحمل الأوّليّ الذاتيّ، لا بالحمل الشائع الصناعي فقط. فيلزم أن يكون أثر الجاعل مفهوم المجعول دون غيره من المفهومات، إذ كلّ مفهوم مغاير لمفهوم آخر، إذ لا اتّحاد بين المفهومات من حيث المعنى والماهيّة، ولا يتصوّر الحمل الذاتيّ إلا بين مفهوم ونفسه، أو بينه وبين حده، كقولنا «الإنسان إنسان» أو «حيوان ناطق». وأمّا قولنا «الناطق ضاحك» فغير جائز بالحمل الذاتيّ، بل بالحمل الصناعيّ الذي مناطه الاتحاد في الوجود، لا الاتّحاد في المفهوم.

الشاهد الثالث

(٩٤) أنّ كلّ ماهيّة فهي لا تأبى عن كثرة التشخّصات والوجودات والتشخّص لمّا كان عين الوجود — كما قرّره المحقّقون — أو مساوقًا له — كما يظنّه الآخرون، — فلا يمكن أن يكون من لوازم الماهيّة كالوجود على ما برهن عليه. فلو كانت الماهيّة المجعولة متعدّدة

a multiple manner *in concreto*, in the same way that a single species is multiplied in its individuals, then the instauration of the quiddity could be multiple. Then the multiplication of instauration would require either the multiplication of the quiddity itself or the multiplicity of its actualizations, modalities, and existences. In this case, *wujūd* would be multiplied by itself, and the quiddity would be multiplied consecutively. The first alternative is impossible because a thing in its pure state is neither differentiable nor multipliable. How, then, can the quiddity itself be repeated and its instauration multiplied insofar as it is what it is? Such a thing would be impossible for a person who has intellect to conceive it, let alone approve of it. There remains the second alternative—that is, that what emanates essentially, which is primarily the object of instauration in a multiple manner, is the modes of actualizations (I mean the essential individualized existences), and that it is by their multiplication that one finds the one single quiddity multiplied.

The fourth witness

(95) If the existing quiddity were a species limited to a single individual—as, for example, the sun—and if it were this individual existent with the possibility of admitting multiplicity and participation among plural individuals, and [furthermore, if we assume that] it was before the instaurer, then what is essentially the object of instauration would be *wujūd* rather than the quiddity. This is what we wanted to establish. If it were before the quiddity, since the parity of a quiddity's relationship to its assumed individuals requires a preponderance without a preponderant, then the quiddity would be existent and particularized before *wujūd* and particularization. It would therefore be necessary for something to be anterior to itself, which is impossible. And furthermore, applying the same reasoning to the modality of *wujūd* and individualization of this thing [anterior to itself], one would end up with *petitio principi* or *regressio ad infinitum*.

الحصول في الأعيان، كالنوع الواحد المتكثّر أفراده، فلا محالة أن يكون جعلها متعددًا. فتعدد الجعل إمّا أن يقتضي أن يكون بحسب تعدّد نفس الماهيّة، أو تعدّد حصولاتها وأنحاء وجوداتها؛ فيكون الوجود متعددًا بالذات، والماهيّة متعدّدة بالتبع. والشق الأوّل مستحيل لأنّ صرف الشيء لا يتميّز ولا يتعدّد. فكيف تتكرّر نفس الماهيّة ويتعدّد جعلها من حيث هي هي؟ وهذا شيء لا مجال لذي عقل أن يتصوّره، فضلاً عن أن يجوّزه. فبقي الشقّ الثاني، وهو أن يكون الصادر بالذات والمجعول أولاً على نعت الكثرة، هي أنحاء الحصولات، أعني الوجودات المتشخّصة بذواتها، ويتكثّر بتكثّرها الماهيّة الواحدة.

الشاهد الرابع

(٩٥) أنّ الماهيّة الموجودة هذه إن كانت نوعًا منحصرًا في شخص كالشمس مثلاً، فكونها هذا الموجود الشخصيّ مع احتمالها بحسب نفسها التعدّد والاشتراك بين كثيرين، إن كان من قبل الجاعل، فيكون المجعول بالحقيقة هو الوجود دون الماهيّة، وهو المطلوب. وإن كان من قبل الماهيّة، فمع لزوم الترجيح من غير مرجّح لتساوي نسبة الماهية إلى أشخاصها المفروضة، يلزم أن تكون قبل الوجود والتشخّص موجودة متشخّصة. فيلزم تقدّم الشيء على نفسه، وهو ممتنع. ومع ذلك ننقل الكلام إلى كيفيّة وجوده وتشخّصه. فيلزم الدور أو التسلسل.

The fifth witness

(96) If the fact that there is an instaurer and the fact that there is an instaured object were to take place on the plane of the quiddities, and if *wujūd* were [nothing but] a rational consideration, it would follow that the object of instauration would be one of the concomitants of the instaurer. Now, the concomitants of quiddity are conceptual notions.[67] This, in turn, requires that all the substances and all the accidents of the universe be conceptual notions except the first instaured. [This would be true] for those who profess that the Necessary Being, glorified be His name, is the act of being of *wujūd* itself. If those who profess that the Necessary Being is *wujūd* itself were to know the reality of *wujūd* and understand that this reality is the very Divine Essence itself, transcending all quiddities, then they would of necessity understand that the act of each existent must correspond to its nature, even if it is imperfect in comparison to it and its degree deficient in comparison to it.[68] Whatever has a simple nature also has a simple act. And this is how it acts. Therefore, God's act in all things is the emanation of the good and the breathing of the spirit of *wujūd* and of life.[69]

(97) *A discourse [inspired by] the [Divine] Throne: Wujūd* has three degrees: (1) *wujūd* that is not related to anything other than itself and that is not limited by any particular limit ([this type of *wujūd*] deserves to be the principle of all things); (2) *wujūd* that is related to something else, such as intelligences, the souls of the heavens, the basic natures [heat, cold, dryness, and humidity], celestial bodies, and material substances; and (3) extended *wujūd*, whose comprehension and extension englobes the temples of individual concrete things and quiddities in a manner that is not like that of universal natures and intelligible quiddities, but, rather, in a manner that is understood by the gnostics and that they call the "Compassionate Breath," a name derived from His saying, transcendent is He: "And My Mercy embraces all things" ("Aʿrāf," Q. 7:156).[70] This *wujūd* is in reality the first emanated among contingent beings from the First Cause and is called "the Truth by which creation is created."[71] And this *wujūd* is the principle of the existence of the universe, its life and its

الشاهد الخامس

(٩٦) لو كانت الجاعليّة والمجعوليّة بين الماهيّات، وكان الوجود أمرًا اعتباريًا عقليًا، يلزم أن يكون المجعول من لوازم ماهيّة الجاعل. ولوازم الماهيّات أمور اعتباريّة، فيلزم أن يكون جواهر العالم وأعراضه كلّها أمورًا اعتباريّة، إلا المجعول الأوّل عند من اعترف بأنّ الواجب — جلّ اسمه — عين الموجوديّة، على أنّ القائلين بأنّ الواجب عين الوجود، لو علموا حقيقة الوجود، وأنّها عين ذاته تعالى المنزّهة عن الماهيّة، لعلموا أنّ كلّ موجود يجب أن يكون فعله مثل طبيعته، وإن كان ناقصاً عنه قاصراً درجته عن درجته، فما كانت طبيعته بسيطة، ففعله بسيط. وكذا فعل فعله. ففعل الله في كلّ شيء إفاضة الخير ونفخ روح الوجود والحياة.

(٩٧) قول عرشيّ. إنّ للوجود مراتب ثلاثًا. الأولى: الوجود الذي لا يتعلّق بغيره ولا يتقيّد بقيد مخصوص، وهو الحريّ بأن يكون مبدأ الكلّ. والثانية: الوجود المتعلّق بغيره، كالعقول والنفوس والطبائع والأجرام والموادّ. والثالثة: الوجود المنبسط الذي شموله وانبساطه على هياكل الأعيان والماهيّات ليس كشمول الطبائع الكلّيّة والماهيّات العقليّة بل على وجه يعرفه العارفون، ويسمّونه بالنَفَس الرحماني اقتباسًا من قوله تعالى: «وَرَحْمَتِي وَسِعَتْ كُلَّ شَيْءٍ» وهو الصادر الأوّل في الممكنات عن العلّة الأُولى بالحقيقة، ويسمّونه بالحقّ المخلوق به، وهو أصل وجود العالم وحياته ونوره الساري في جميع ما في السموات

light, and penetrates into all that there is in the heavens and the earths. It exists in all things according to that thing in such a way that in the intellect, it is intellect; in the soul, it is soul; in nature, it is nature; in the body, it is body; in substance, it is substance; and in accident, it is accident. Its relation to the Divine Being—exalted be He—is analogous to the relation of sensible light, and the rays shining upon bodies in the heavens and the earth, to the sun. And it is different from the affirmative, relational *wujūd* that is similar to other universal and rational concepts that are not attached to either the instauration of the Instaurer or to an effect. These latter ones do have a certain kind of *wujūd* in the manner of the principal intelligibles; but their *wujūd* is their very actuality in the mind in the same way that one sees non-thingness, non-possibility, and non-instauration in the concept of nonexistence. But in our view, there is no difference between these concepts and the others in the sense that they are only narratives and titles of certain things, except that some of them are titles for existent realities, whereas others are titles for something essentially false.

The sixth witness

(98) If the fact that there is an instaurer and the fact that there is an instaured were to be between the quiddities, it would follow that the quiddity of each contingent being would belong to the category of relation and become actualized under its genus. Since the consequent is false, the antecedent is equally false. As for the proof of the consequent, it is in what has been indicated before—that is to say, that there is an essential relationship and a conceptual relation between that which is essentially the object of instauration and that which is essentially the instaurer.

(99) It is not proper to say that this [objection] can be raised in regard to the two schools [mentioned above], because if the object of instauration is the very *wujūd* of the caused and not some qualification that has come to be added to it, then, if [*wujūd*] were to be linked in itself to something other than itself, its intellection would require the thinking of something else—namely, its agent. And whatever cannot be conceived without conceiving something else belongs to the category of relation. To this we would respond: The category of relation, [like] the

والأرضين. وهو في كل شيء بحسبه، حتى إنه يكون في العقل عقلاً، وفي النفس نفسًا، وفي الطبع طبعًا وفي الجسم جسمًا، وفي الجوهر جوهرًا، وفي العرض عرضًا. ونسبته إليه تعالى كنسبة النور المحسوس والضوء المنبثّ على أجرام السموات والأرض إلى الشمس. وهو غير الوجود الإثباتيّ الرابطيّ، الذي كسائر المفهومات الكليّة والمفهومات العقليّة لا يتعلّق بها جعل الجاعل ولا تأثير، ولها أيضًا كالمعقولات المتأصّلة وجود، لكن وجودها نفس حصولها في الذهن. وكذلك الحكم في مفهوم العدم واللاشيء واللاممكن واللامجعول، بل لا فرق عندنا بين هذه المفهومات وغيرها في كونها ليست إلا حكايات وعنوانات لأمور، إلا أنّ بعضها عنوان لحقيقة موجودة، وبعضها عنوان لأمر باطل بالذات.

الشاهد السادس

(٩٨) أنّه لو تحقّقت الجاعليّة بين الماهيّات، لزم أن تكون ماهيّة كلّ ممكن من مقولة المضاف وواقعة تحت جنسه. واللازم باطل بالضرورة، فكذا الملزوم. أمّا بيان الملازمة، فلِما سبقت الإشارة إليه من لزوم التعلّق الذاتيّ والارتباط المعنويّ بين ما هو المجعول بالذات وما هو الجاعل بالذات.

(٩٩) لا يقال هذا مشترك الورود على المذهبين، لأنّ المجعول إذا كان نفس وجود المعلول لا صفة زائدة عليه، فكان في ذاته مرتبطًا بغيره، فيلزم من تعقّله تعقّل غيره أعني فاعله. وكل مّا لا يمكن تعقّله إلا مع تعقّل غيره، فهو من مقولة المضاف، — لأنّنا نقول: مقولة المضاف — وكذا غيره من المقولات التسع — إنّما هي من أقسام الماهيّات دون الوجودات.

nine other categories, belongs to various kinds of quiddities, not existences. The higher genera are what one calls categories. All that has a definition in a species possesses genus and specific difference and must fall under one of the ten known categories. But as far as *wujūd* is concerned, it has been established that it has neither genus nor specific difference; it is neither a universal nor a particular, particularized by a particularity that would be added to its essence. That is why *wujūd* does not fall under any of the ten categories, except from the aspect of quiddity in the case of something that possesses a quiddity. And from this [discussion], it has become verified that the Creator—majestic is His remembrance—although He is the Principle of all things, and the relation of all things returns to Him, does not belong to the category of relation; for He is beyond something being of the same genus as He is, or resembling Him, or being analogous to Him or homologous with Him. He is beyond all that.[72]

The seventh witness

(100) According to their school, it would be necessary that the meaning of an essential reality—that of the substance, for example—would be equivocal, differentiated according to anteriority. For us as well as for them, the consequent is false, and so is the antecedent. The reason is that certain individual substances are causes for certain others—such as, for example, the causality of separate substances, some with regard to others; the causality of the [same] separate substances with regard to bodies; and the causality of matter and form for the body composed of them. The cause is in itself anterior to the caused; as a matter of fact, this sort of anteriority and posteriority has no other meaning than the [relation between] causality and the fact of being caused. Therefore, if

فالأجناس العالية هي المسمّاة بالمقولات، وكلّ ما له حدّ نوعي، فله جنس وفصل؛ وهو لا محالة يجب أن تكون واقعة تحت إحدى المقولات العشر المشهورة. وأمّا الوجود، فقد ثبت أنّه لا جنس له ولا فصل له، وليس هو بكلّيّ ولا جزئيّ متخصص بخصوصيّة زائدة على ذاته. فإذن لا يقع الوجود تحت شيء من المقولات بالذات، إلا من جهة الماهيّة فيما له ماهيّة. ومن هنا تحقّق أنّ الباريءَ — جلّ ذكره — وإن كان مبدأ كلّ شيء وإليه نسبة كلّ أمر، وليس من مقولة المضاف، تعالى عن أن يكون له مجانس أو مماثل أو مشابه أو مناسب، علوّا كبيرًا.

الشاهد السابع

(١٠٠) أنّه يلزم على مذهبهم أن يكون معنى الذاتيّ كالجوهر مشكّكاً متفاوتًا بالأقدميّة، والتالي باطل عندنا وعندهم جميعًا، فكذا الملزوم، لأنّ بعض أفراد الجوهر علّة لبعض آخر، كما في علّيّة الجواهر المفارقة بعضها لبعض، وعلّيّة الجواهر المفارقة للأجسام، وعلّيّة المادّة والصورة للجسم المركّب منهما. والعلّة في ذاتها أقدم من المعلول، بل لا معنى لهذا النحو من التقدّم والتأخّر إلا العلّيّة والمعلوليّة. فإذا كانت العلّة ماهيّة، وكان المعلول ماهيّة، كانت

the cause were a quiddity and the caused a quiddity, the quiddity of the cause would be anterior to the quiddity of the caused as such, and the latter would be in itself posterior to the quiddity of the cause. If they were two substances, the substantiality of one *qua* substantiality would be anterior to the substantiality of the other. This would necessitate equivocality in the meaning of the essential. This is false, according to the most accomplished philosophers. They maintain that the quiddity of a substance is neither anterior nor prior to the quiddity of another substance, either as to its substantification or to its substantiality—that is to say, as to the fact that the generic concept of substance is predicated of it. Rather, one can have anteriority over the other either in its act of existence (such as the anteriority of intellect over soul) or temporally (such as the anteriority of father to son).

The eighth witness

(101) According to the way of the philosophers, it has been established that the question of "what explains" [a thing] is different from the question of "what is the truth of" [that thing].[73] Now, the difference does not come from the concept of the answer to the two questions, because according to the verifiers (*muḥaqqiqīn*), the answer is only the definition of a thing, except when necessity requires [such a usage]. The difference between these two questions comes from the fact that the taking into consideration of *wujūd* is implied in the second without the first. It follows that *wujūd* cannot be simply an abstraction [made] by the intellect, but that it must be a reality. And this is what we wanted to establish.

ماهيّة العلّة بما هي هي متقدّمة على ماهيّة المعلول، وهي في ذاتها متأخّرة عن ماهيّة علّتها. وإذا كانتا جوهرَين، كانت جوهريّة أحدَيهما — بما هي جوهريّة الأخرى كذلك، فيلزم التشكيك في معنى الذاتيّ. وهذا باطل عند محصّليّ الحكماء، فإنّهم قالوا: لا أوّليّة ولا أولويّة لماهيّة جوهر على ماهيّة جوهر آخر في تجوهره، ولا في كونه جوهرًا، أي محمولاً عليه معنى الجوهر الجنسيّ، بل يتقدّم عليه إمّا في وجوده، كتقدّم العقل على النفس، أو في زمانه، كتقدّم الأب على الابن.

الشاهد الثامن

(١٠١) أنّه قد تقرّر عندهم أنّ مطلب «ماء الشارحة» غير مطلب «ماء الحقيقية»، وليست الغيريّة في مفهوم الجواب عنهما، لأنّه الحدّ عند المحقّقين لا غيره، إلا عند الاضطرار. فهذه المغايرة بين المطلبين ليست إلا من جهة اعتبار الوجود في الثاني دون الأوّل. ولزم من ذلك ألا يكون الوجود مجرّد أمر هو انتزاعيّ عقليّ، بل يكون أمرًا حقيقيًّا؛ وهو المطلوب.

The Eighth Penetration

Concerning the modality of instauration and effusion, and the proof of the First Creator, and [the reality] that the Effusing Instaurer is one, there being no multiplicity in it and no partner unto it

And in this section there are several penetrations.

The first penetration

Concerning the relationship of the instaured and the originated to the Instaurer[74]

(102) The relationship of the instaured and the originated to the Instaurer is the relationship of deficiency to perfection, of weakness to strength. And since you have learned that reality *in concreto* and the existent in truth is nothing other than existences without the quiddities, it has been proven that *wujūd* is a simple reality, that it has no genus and no specific difference constituting it, [that it has] no species and no specific difference dividing it, and that it has no particularization. Rather, its particularization is by its own essence, which is simple.

المشعر الثامن

في كيفيّة الجعل والإفاضة و إثبات البارئ الأوّل
وأنّ الجاعل الفياض واحد لا تعدّد فيه ولا شريك له

وفيه مشاعر

المشعر الأوّل

في نسبة المجعول المبدع إلى الجاعل

(١٠٢) إنّ نسبة المجعول المبدع إلى الجاعل نسبة النقص إلى التمام، والضعف إلى القوّة. لما علمت أنّ الواقع في العين والموجود بالحقيقة ليست إلا الوجودات دون الماهيّات، وثبت أنّ الوجود حقيقة بسيطة لا جنس لها، ولا فصل مقوّم لها، ولا نوع لها، ولا فصل مقسّم لها، ولا تشخّص لها، بل تشخّصها بنفس ذاتها البسيطة، وأنّ التفاوت بالذات بين

There is essentially no difference between its individual members and their identities except through degrees of intensity and weakness. As for differences in accidental matters, that comes about [only] in corporeal realities. There is no doubt that the instaurer is more perfect in its *wujūd* and more complete in its actualization than the instaured. The instaured is like a profusion and effusion from its instaurer. And the [production of] the effect in reality consists only in the modalization of the instaurer in its modalities and in the stations of its actions.

The second penetration

Concerning the Source of all existence, His qualities, and His effects

(103) That is what has been referred to as faith in God, His words, His signs, His books, and His messengers; and there are several paths in it.[75]

The first path

Concerning His wujūd*—transcendent is He—and His unity*

[In it there are several penetrations.]

The first penetration

Concerning the demonstration of the Necessary—sublime is His invocation—and that the chain of beings that are instaured of necessity ends in the Necessary Being

(104) *An illuminative demonstration,*[76] and that consists in our saying that the existent is either the reality of *wujūd* or something else. What we mean by "the reality of *wujūd*" is that which is not mixed with anything other than pure *wujūd*, having neither limit, nor end, nor deficiency, nor generality, nor particularity; and it is called the Necessary Being. And we say: If the reality of *wujūd* were not existent [by itself], then nothing would have existed; the consequent being evidently false, the subsequent is likewise false. As for the demonstration of the consequent, it is as follows: That which is other than the reality of *wujūd* is either a quiddity

آحادها وهويّاتها ليس إلا بالأشدّ والأضعف، والاختلاف بالأمور العارضة إنّما يتحقق في الجسمانيّات، ولا شكّ أنّ الجاعل أكمل وجودًا وأتمّ تحصّلاً من مجعوله، فالمجعول كأنه رشح وفيض من جاعله، وأنّ التأثير في الحقيقة ليس إلا بتطوّر الجاعل في أطواره ومنازل أفعاله.

المشعر الثاني

في مبدأ الموجودات وصفاته وآثاره

(١٠٣) وهو المشار إليه بالإيمان بالله وكلماته وآياته وكتبه ورسله وفيه مناهج.

المنهج الأول

في وجوده تعالى ووحدته

وفيه مشاعر

المشعر الأوّل

في إثبات الواجب — جل ذكره — وفي أنّ سلسلة الوجودات المجعولة يجب أن تنتهي إلى واجب الوجود

(١٠٤) برهان مشرقيّ، وهو أنّنا نقول: الموجود إمّا حقيقة الوجود أو غيرها. ونعني بحقيقة الوجود ما لا يشوبه شيء غير صرف الوجود من حدّ أو نهاية أو نقص أو عموم أو خصوص، وهو المسّمى بواجب الوجود. فنقول: لو لم يكن حقيقة الوجود موجودة، لم يكن شيء من الأشياء موجودًا. واللازم بديهيّ البطلان، فكذا الملزوم. أما بيان الملازمة، فلأنّ ما عدا حقيقة الوجود إمّا ماهيّة من الماهيّات أو وجود خاص مشوب بعدم أو نقص،

among quiddities or a particular *wujūd* mixed with nonexistence or deficiency. Now, all quiddity other than *wujūd* is existent through *wujūd*, not through itself. How else could it be since, if it is taken in itself absolutely or as abstracted from *wujūd*, then, far from its essence existing by itself, it is not even existent? [The reason is that] the affirmation of something for something is secondary to its own affirmation, and it is through *wujūd* that it is existent.

Now, if this *wujūd* [by which it exists] were to be other than the reality of *wujūd*, it would [be so] because there would be in it a compound of *wujūd qua wujūd* and some other particularity. [But] all particularity other than *wujūd* is nonexistence or nonexistent. Furthermore, all that is compound is posterior to that which is simple, [upon which it relies for its existence] and of which it has need. Nonexistence does not enter into the fact that something possesses the act of existence and its actualization, even if it does enter into its definition and meaning. The affirmation of any concept pertaining to a thing and its predication of it, whether it be a quiddity or another quality, affirmative or negative, is secondary to its *wujūd*. It would then be necessary to return our discussion to this *wujūd*. One would then have a *regressio ad infinitum* or a *circulus vitiosus*, or one would end with a pure *wujūd* with which nothing else is mixed. Therefore, it is evident that for all things the principle and source of the act of existing is the pure reality of *wujūd*, which is not mixed with anything other than *wujūd*.[77]

وكل ماهيّة غير الوجود فهي بالوجود موجودة، لا بنفسها. كيف ولو أخذت بنفسها مطلقة أو مجرّدةً عن الوجود، لم تكن بنفسها نفسها فضلاً عن أن تكون موجودة، لأنّ ثبوت شيء لشيء فرع على ثبوته في نفسه، فهي بالوجود موجودة. وذلك الوجود إن كان غير حقيقة الوجود، ففيه تركيب من الوجود بما هو وجود ومن خصوصيّة أخرى. وكلّ خصوصيّة غير الوجود فهي عدم أو عدميّ؛ وكلّ مركّب متأخّر عن بسيطه مفتقر إليه؛ والعدم لا دخل له في موجوديّة الشيء وتحصّله، و إن دخل في حده ومعناه. وثبوت أي مفهوم كان لشيء وحمله عليه، سواء كان ماهيّة أو صفةً أخرى، ثبوتيّة أو سلبيّة، فهو فرع على وجوده. والكلام عائد إلى ذلك الوجود أيضًا، فيتسلسل، أو يدور، أو ينتهي إلى وجود بحت لا يشوبه شيء. فظهر أنّ أصل موجوديّة كلّ موجود، وهو محض حقيقة الوجود الذي لا يشوبه شيء غير الوجود.

The second penetration

Concerning that the Necessary Being is unlimited in intensity and power and that what is other than It is finite and limited[78]

(105) Since you have come to know that the Necessary Being—transcendent is He—is the sheer reality of *wujūd*, with which nothing other than *wujūd* is mixed, neither limit nor end afflicts this reality since, if it had a limit and an end, there would be a delimiting and particularizing that is not in the nature of *wujūd*. It would then need a cause, which delimits and particularizes it and thus would not be the sheer reality of *wujūd*. So it is confirmed that the Necessary Being has no end, that no deficiency afflicts it, that there is no possible potentiality in it, that it has no quiddity, and that no generality or particularity is mixed with it.[79] So it has no specific difference, no particularization other than its essence, and no form—just as it has no active agent and no ultimate goal, and just as it has no end. Rather, it is the form of its essence that gives form to all things because it is the perfection of its essence and the perfection of everything, because its essence is actual from every point of view. There is nothing that makes it known[80] and nothing that unveils it except itself, and [there is] no demonstration of it, for its essence witnesses its essence and the uniqueness of its essence. As He has said: "God bears witness that there is no God but He" ("Āl ᶜImrān," Q. 3:16). We will explain this to you.[81]

The third penetration

Concerning His oneness

(106) Since the Necessary Being—transcendent is He—is the termination of the chain of needs and relations, and since it is the finality of everything and the plenitude of every reality, its *wujūd* does not rest upon anything and is not related to anything, as has already been said. It is absolutely simple reality from every point of view, and its essence is the Necessary Being from every perspective, since it is the Necessary Being by itself and there is no aspect of contingency or impossibility in it. Otherwise, that would result in a composition that would require contingency, and that is impossible for it [as the Necessary Being]—transcendent is He.

المشعر الثاني
في أنّ واجب الوجود غير متناهي الشّدة والقوّة
وأنّ ما سواه متناهٍ محدود

(١٠٥) لمّا علمت أنّ الواجب تعالى محض حقيقة الوجود الذي لا يشوبه شيء غير الوجود، فهذه الحقيقة لا يعتريها حدّ ولا نهاية، إذ لو كان له حدّ ونهاية، كان له تحدّد وتخصّص بغير طبيعة الوجود. فيحتاج إلى سبب يحدّده ويخصّصه، فلم يكن محض حقيقة الوجود. فإذن ثبت أنّ واجب الوجود لا نهاية له، ولا نقص يعتريه، ولا قوّة إمكانيّة فيه، ولا ماهيّة له، ولا يشوبه عموم ولا خصوص. فلا فصل له، ولا تشخّص له بغير ذاته، ولا صورة له، كما لا فاعل له ولا غاية له، كما لا نهاية له، بل هو صوره ذاته ومصوّر كلّ شيءٍ، لأنّه كمال ذاته وكمال كلّ شيءٍ، لأنّ ذاته بالفعل من جميع الوجوه، فلا معرّف له ولا كاشف له إلا هو. ولا برهان عليه فشهد ذاته على ذاته وعلى وحدانيّة ذاته، كما قال « شَهِدَ اللّهُ أَنَّهُ لاَ إِلَـهَ إِلاَّ هُوَ ». وسنشرح لك هذا.

المشعر الثالث
في توحيده تعالى

(١٠٦) لمّا كان الواجب تعالى منتهى سلسلة الحاجات والتعلّقات، وهو غاية كلّ شيء وتمام كلّ حقيقة، فليس وجوده متوقّفًا على شيء ولا متعلّقًا بشيء كما مرّ. فيكون بسيط الحقيقة من كلّ جهة. فذاته واجب الوجود من جميع الجهات، كما أنه واجب الوجود بالذات وليست فيه جهة إمكانيّة ولا امتناعيّة، وإلا لزم التركيب المستدعي للإمكان، وهو ممتنع فيه تعالى.

(107) Since this has been established, we will say: If we were to suppose two necessary beings in existence, the one that was supposed to be the second will be an essence that would be disconnected from the other, since it would be impossible for the Necessary Being—transcendent is He—to have an essential relationship between beings; for in that case, one would have to admit that one [being] was the cause of the other or that both were caused, which would be opposed to [our initial] assumption. Furthermore, each of the two would possess a degree of perfection of *wujūd* that the other did not possess and that did not flow and emanate from the other. Thus, each of the two would lack a certain perfection of *wujūd* and would miss a certain degree of existence.[82] In this case, the Essence of the Necessary Being would no longer consist of the pure state of actuality and the necessity of *wujūd*.[83] Rather, it would be composed of two attributes: the *wujūd* of one thing and the absence of another, both issuing from the nature of *wujūd qua wujūd*. It would have a type of necessity for a [particular] modality of *wujūd* and the possibility or impossibility of another modality [for *wujūd*]. It would therefore no longer be the Necessary Being from all points of view [in all modes of existence]. However, it was established that what is Necessary Being by itself is of necessity Necessary Being from all points of view.[84] Therefore, this is a contradiction. So the Necessary Being by itself constitutes a superabundance of actuality and perfect actuality containing all the modes of existence, all modes of becoming, and all cases of perfection. It has no analogue, no similitude, nothing comparable, nothing opposite, and nothing like unto it in [its] *wujūd*. Rather, its essence, by the perfection of its excellence, necessitates that it be the support of all perfections and the source of all good; thus, it is perfect and superior to all plenary perfection.

(١٠٧) فإذا تقرّر هذا، فنقول: لو فرضنا في الوجود واجبين، فيكون ما فرض ثانيًا منفصل الذات عن الواجب تعالى، لاستحالة أن يكون بين الواجبين علاقة ذاتيّة، و إلا لزم معلوليّة أحدهما أو كليهما، وهو خلاف الفرض. فلكلّ منهما إذن مرتبة من الكمال الوجوديّ ليس للآخر، ولا مترشّحًا منه فائضًا من عنده. فيكون كلّ منهما عادمًا لكمال وجوديّ وفاقدًا لمرتبة وجوديّة. فلم تكن ذات الواجب محض حيثيّة الفعليّة ووجوب الوجود، بل مؤلّفًا من جهتين ومصداقًا لوجود شيءٍ وفقد شيءٍ آخر — كليهما من طبيعة الوجود بما هو وجود ومناطًا لوجوب نحو من الوجود، و إمكان نحو آخر منه، أو امتناعه. فلم يكن واجب الوجود من كلّ جهة، وقد ثبت أنّ ما هو واجب الوجود بالذات يجب أن يكون واجب الوجود من جميع الجهات، وهذا خلف. فواجب الوجود بالذات يجب أن يكون من فرط الفعليّة، وكمال التحصّل، جامعًا لجميع النشآت الوجودية والأطوار الكونيّة والشؤون الكماليّة. فلا مكافئ له في الوجود ولا مماثل ولا ندّ ولا ضدّ ولا شبه، بل ذاته من كمال الفضيلة يجب أن تكون مستند جميع الكمالات و ينبوع كلّ الخيرات. فيكون تامًّا وفوق التمام.

The fourth penetration

That it is the origin and the end of all things

(108) The principles expounded until now have shown and firmly established [the fact] that the Necessary Being is one by itself, with no pluralization, and that it is perfect and above plenary perfection. Now we say that it emanates upon all that is other than itself, without this emanation producing an association [with it]; for what is other than it is, in reality, contingent quiddities and deficient essences—existences that depend upon something other than themselves. Now, all that whose *wujūd* depends upon another is in need of that other and finds its full completion with it, and this other is its origin and its end.[85]

So, all contingent beings, with their differentiations and grades in perfection and deficiency are, in their essences, in need of it [the Necessary Being] and derive their sufficiency in being from it. Considered in themselves, they are contingent beings made necessary by the First, the Necessary Being—transcendent is He. Indeed, they are, in themselves, illusory and perishing and are made real by the Real, the One, the Unique: "All things are perishing save His Face" ("al-Qaṣaṣ," Q. 28:88).[86] The relation between it and that which is other than it is analogous to the relation between the rays of the sun—supposing that it subsisted by itself—with the bodies that are illuminated by it and are dark in themselves. When you witness the rising of the sun in a place and the illumination of that place by its light, then another light resulting from this light, you will judge that this second light is also from the sun and will trace its origin back to the sun; likewise for the third light and the fourth light, until one ends with the weakest light perceptible to the senses. The same is true for the *wujūd* of contingent beings in which there is differentiation in their proximity and distance from the One, the Real; for everything proceeds from God.

المشعر الرابع
في أنّه المبدأ والغاية في جميع الأشياء

(١٠٨) الأصول الماضية دلّت وقامت على أنّ واجب الوجود واحد بالذات لا تعدّد له، وأنّه تامّ وفوق التمام. فالآن نقول إنّه فياض على كلّ ما سواه بلا شركة في الإفاضة، لأنّ ما سواه ممكنة الماهيّات، ناقصة الذوات، متعلقة الوجودات بغيرها؛ وكلّ ما يتعلق وجوده بغيره، فهو مفتقر إليه، مستتمّ به؛ وذلك الغير مبدؤه وغايته. فالممكنات كلّها على تفاوتها وترتّبها في الكمال والنقص، فاقرة الذوات إليه مستغنية به. فهي في حدود أنفسها ممكنة، واجبة بالأوّل الواجب تعالى بل باطلة هالكة بأنفسها، حقة بالحقّ الواحد الأحد «كُلُّ شَيْءٍ هَالِكٌ إِلاّ وَجْهَهُ». ونسبته إلى ما سواه كنسبة ضوء الشمس —لو كان قائمًا بذاته— إلى الأجسام المستضيئة منه، المظلمة بحسب ذواتها. وأنت إذا شاهدت إشراق الشمس على موضع وإنارته بنورها، ثمّ حصل نور آخر من ذلك النور، حكمتَ أنّ النور الثاني من الشمس وأسندته إليها وهكذا الثالث والرابع، إلى أن ينتهي إلى أضعاف الأنوار الحسّية. فعلى هذا المنوال وجودات الممكنات المتفاوتة في القرب والبعد من الواحد الحقّ، والكلّ من عند الله.

The fifth penetration

That the Necessary Being is the plenary perfection of everything

(109) You have come to know that *wujūd* is a single, simple reality. Its individuations are not differentiated by essential things, such as genus, specific difference, and the like. Rather, they are differentiated from each other by perfection or deficiency, self-sufficiency or poverty. Now, deficiency and poverty are not things that are postulated by the reality of *wujūd* itself. If this were so, there would be no Necessary Being. The consequent is false, as was established; the antecedent must therefore be false also. It is therefore evident that the reality of *wujūd* is, in itself, complete and perfect, infinite in power and intensity. Deficiency, shortcomings, contingency, and the like come only from what is secondary and caused. Inevitably, the caused is not equal to the cause, and the emanated is not equal to the source of emanation. It is thereby evident that the Necessary Being is the plenary perfection of all things; it is the *wujūd* of all existences and the light of all lights.[87]

The sixth penetration

That the Necessary Being is the point to which all affairs return

(110) Know that the Necessary Being is a simple reality. And all that is a simple reality is, by its oneness, the totality of things. "It [one's record] leaves nothing, neither small nor big, but has counted them" ("al-Kahf," Q. 18:49) and embraced them, except what falls under the category of nonexistences and deficiencies. Suppose that a simple thing is, for example, A and that you have said that A is not B. Now our point of view is A. If that rapport under which this thing is A were to be identical with the rapport that this thing is non-B, in the sense that this thing itself would be the subject of this negation, then affirmation and negation would be the same. [By the same token,] whoever thinks of man, for example, would also think, *ipso facto*, that he is not a horse, in the sense that his thinking of man would be the same as thinking that he is not a horse. But [since] the consequent is false, the antecedent is also false.

المشعر الخامس
في أنّ واجب الوجود تمام كلّ شيء

(١٠٩) قد علمت أنّ الوجود حقيقة واحدة بسيطة، لا تتفاوت أعدادها بأمور ذاتيّة من جنس وفصل ونحوهما، بل بكمال ونقص وغنى وفقر. وليس النقص والفقر ممّا يقتضيه نفس حقيقة الوجود، وإلا لم يوجد واجب الوجود. والتالي باطل كما ثبت، فالمقدم مثله. فظهر أنّ حقيقته في ذاتها تامة كاملة، غير متناهي القوّة والشدّة. وإنّما ينشأ النقص والقصور والإمكان ونحوه من الثانويّة والمعلوليّة، ضرورة أنّ المعلول لا يساوي علّته والفائض لا يكافئ المفيض. فظهر أنّ واجب الوجود تمام الأشياء، ووجود الوجودات، ونور الأنوار.

المشعر السادس
في أنّ واجب الوجود مرجع كلّ الأُمور

(١١٠) اعلم أنّ الواجب بسيط الحقيقة فهو بوحدته كلّ الأُمور، لا يغادر صغيرة ولا كبيرة إلا أحصاها وأحاط بها، إلا ما هو من باب الأعدام والنقائص. فإنّك إذا فرضت شيئًا بسيطًا هو ج مثلاً، وقلت ج ليس ب، فحيثيّة أنّه ج، إن كانت بعينها حيثيّة أنّه ليس ب، حتّى تكون ذاته بذاته مصدقًا لهذا السلب، فيكون الإيجاب والسلب شيئًا واحدًا. ولزم أن يكون كلّ من عقل الإنسان مثلاً، عقل أنّه ليس بفرس، بأن يكون نفس عقله الإنسان نفس عقله ليس بفرس. لكن اللازم باطل، فالملزوم كذلك. فظهر وتحقّق أنّ موضوع

Therefore, it is apparent and verified that proposition A is different from proposition non-B, even with regard to the mind. It is therefore understood that every existent in which one denies a certain form of *wujūd* is not an existent whose reality is simple. Rather, its essence is composed of two aspects: the aspect by which it is such-and-such, and the aspect by which it is not such-and-such. Reversing the opposite, [we obtain this proposition]: All that has a simple reality is all things. Safeguard this [principle], if you are of its people.[88]

The seventh penetration

That the Necessary Being intellects its own essence and, by its essence, intellects all things

(111) As for the fact that the Necessary Being intellects its own essence, that is because its essence is simple [and is] disengaged from mixture with all deficiency, contingency, and nonexistence. Now, the essence of all that which is such is present to itself without any veil. Knowledge is nothing other than the presence of *wujūd* without any veil. Every perception is produced by a mode of disengaging from matter and its veils, because matter is the source of nonexistence and absence. Therefore, each part of a body is, in effect, absent from each of the other parts; and the whole of the body is absent from each part; and the whole is absent from the whole. That is why the more a form is removed from matter, the more complete its presence is to itself. The lowest stage is the presence of a sensible form to itself; above it are the imaginal forms, according to their different degrees; above them still, there are the intelligible forms. The highest of the intelligibles is the existent whose *wujūd* is the most intense, and that is the Necessary Being. Its essence is the subject that intellects itself and the object of its own intellection, by the most exalted intellect. Its essence is the source of all emanation and all beneficence. Through its own essence, it intellects the totality of things in an intellection that contains absolutely no multiplicity.[89]

(112) Furthermore, all forms of perception, be they intelligible or sensible, are one in their *wujūd* with the *wujūd* of the subject that perceives it, according to a proof that was emanated upon us from God. And that is that, in every form of perception—let it be the form of intellection—its *wujūd* in itself, its state as object of intellection, and its *wujūd* as the

الجيميّة مغائر لموضوع أنّه ليس ب، ولو بحسب الذهن. فاعلم أنّ كلّ موجود سلب عنه أمر وجوديّ، فهو ليس بسيط الحقيقة، بل ذاته مركّبة من جهتين: جهة بها هو كذا، وجهة هو بها ليس كذا. فبعكس النقيض: كل بسيط الحقيقة هو كلّ الأشياء. فاحتفظ بهذا، إن كنت من أهله.

المشعر السابع
في أنّه تعالى يعقل ذاته و يعقل الأشـــياء كلّها من ذاته

(١١١) أمّا أنّه يعقل ذاته، فلأنه بسيط الذات مجرّد عن شوب كلّ نقص و إمكان وعدم، وكلّ ما هو كذلك، فذاته حاضرة لذاته بلا حجاب. والعلم ليس إلا حضور الوجود بلا غشاوة. وكلّ إدراك فحصوله يضرب من التجريد عن المادّة وغواشيها، لأنّ المادّة منبع العدم والغيبة، إذ كلّ جزء من الجسم فإنّه يغيب عن غيره من الأجزاء، ويغيب عنه الكلّ. فكلّ صورة هي أشد براءة من المادة، فهي أصحّ حضورًا لذاتها: أدناها المحسوسة على ذاتها؛ ثمّ المتخيّلة على مراتبها؛ ثمّ المعقولة، وأعلى المعقولات أقوى الموجودات، وهو واجب الوجود. فذاته عاقل ذاته ومعقول ذاته بأجل عقل، وذاته مبدأ كلّ فيض وجود: فبذاته يعقل جميع الأشياء عقلاً لا كثرة فيه أصلاً.

(١١٢) ثمّ إن كلّ صورة إدراكيّة—سواء كانت معقولة أو محسوسة—فهي متّحدة الوجود مع وجود مدركها ببرهان فائض علينا من عند الله. وهو أنّ كلّ صورة إدراكيّة،

subject that intellects are one thing, without differentiation. [This is so] in the sense that it is not possible to suppose that an intellective form possesses another mode of *wujūd* that is not the object of intellection for the subject that intellects. Otherwise, the intelligible form would not be an intelligible form.[90]

(113) This having been established, we say: It is not possible that this form has a *wujūd* that is distinct from the *wujūd* of the subject that intellects it, in the sense of itself having a *wujūd* and the subject that intellects it having another *wujūd*. This would establish between them a relation of the state of being the object of intellection and [that of being] the subject that intellects, as in the case of the father and the son, or the king and the city, and other things in the state of relationality upon which the relation is imposed as an accident after they already exist. Otherwise, the *wujūd* of this form of intellection would not be the object of intellection itself. But that was the hypothesis; therefore, it is contradictory.

From this, it follows of necessity that the intellective form by itself, when considered in isolation from all that is other than it, is the object of intellection. Moreover, it is equally the subject that intellects, since it would be inconceivable that the state of being intellected would be actualized in the absence of a subject that intellects it, as is the case with relational objects. From the moment that we suppose the intellected form to be separate from all that is other than itself, it must be the object of intellection for itself and to itself. Consequently, what one began by presupposing is that there is here an essence that intellects things that are intelligible to it. Furthermore, it follows of necessity from our demonstration that the objects of intellection are one with that which intellects them. Now, this is none other than what we had presupposed. From what has been mentioned, it is apparent and clear that the *wujūd* of every subject that intellects must be united with the object that it intellects. And this is what we wanted to establish.

(114) This demonstration is applicable to all the other perceptions—the estimative, the imaginal, and the sensible in the sense that the sensible substance in us becomes united with the form that is sensible to it in itself—besides what lies outside representation, as, for example, in the case of the sky, the earth, and all material realities whose *wujūd* is not [merely] perceptible.[91] Reflect deeply; the best of actions is your vision of it, for it is a matter to which access is difficult. God is the Master of virtue and the virtuous.

ولتكن عقليّة، فوجودها في نفسها ومعقوليّتها ووجودها لعاقلها شيء واحد بلا تغاير، بمعنى أنّه لا يمكن أن يفرض لصورة عقليّة نحوٌ آخر من الوجود لم يكن هي بحسبه معقولة لذلك العاقل؛ وإلا لم يكن هي هي.

(١١٣) فإذا تقرّر هذا، لا يمكن أن تكون تلك الصورة متباينة الوجود عن وجود عاقلها، حتّى يكون لها وجود ولعاقلها وجود آخر، عرضت لهما إضافة المعقوليّة والعاقليّة، كما للأب والابن والملك والمدينة وسائر الأُمور المضافة التي عرضت لها الإضافة بعد وجود الذات. وإلا لم يكن وجودها بعينه معقوليّتها، وقد فرضناها كذلك؛ هذا خلف. فإذن لزم من ذلك أنّ الصورة العقليّة في حدّ نفسها، مع فرض تفرّدها عمّا عداها، هي معقولة، فتكون عاقلة أيضًا إذ المعقوليّة لا يتصوّر حصولها بدون العاقليّة، كما هو شأن المتضائفين؛ وحيث فرضناها مجرّدة عمّا عداها فتكون معقولة لذاتها. ثمّ الموضوع أوّلاً أنّ هاهنا ذاتًا تعقل الأشياء المعقولة لها، ولزم من البرهان أنّ معقولاتها متّحدة مع من يعقلها، وليس إلا الذي فرضناه. فظهر وتبيّن ممّا ذكر، أنّ كلّ عاقل يجب أن يكون متّحد الوجود مع معقولة فهو المطلوب.

(١١٤) وهذا البرهان جاز في سائر الإدراكات الوهميّة والخياليّة والحسّيّة، حتّى أنّ الجوهر الحسّاس منّا يتّحد مع الصورة المحسوسة له بالذات، دون ما خرج عن التصوّر كالسماء والأرض وغيرهما من المادّيّات، التي ليس وجودها وجودًا إدراكيًا فتدبّر وأحسن إعمال رؤيتك فيه، فإنّه صعب المنال. والله وليّ الفضل والأفضال.

The eighth penetration

Concerning that wujūd *in reality is the One Reality—transcendent is He—and all that is other than it, if it be considered in itself, is perishing except His august face*[92]

(115) You have come to know that the quiddities have no principial reality in existence, that the perfect Instaurer is instaurer by its very *wujūd*, that the instaured is none other than a mode of *wujūd*, and that it [the perfect Instaurer] is instaured by itself and not by some qualification added to it. Otherwise, it would be instaured through this quality; but the instaured is instaured by itself in the sense that its essence and its being instaured are a single thing without differentiation of rapport, in the same way that the instaurer is Instaurer by its essence, in the sense already mentioned. Therefore, it has been proven, and what we have mentioned has been well established—that is, that the cause is the cause by itself and that the caused is the caused by itself, according to what has already been mentioned. This assertion follows the fact that the act of being instaurer and the act of being instaured occur between existences and not between quiddities, because the latter are mental things abstracted in diverse ways from existences.

(116) It has been established and verified that what bears the name of the instaured does not constitute in reality an ipseity that is separated from the ipseity of its existentiating cause. It is impossible for the intellect to indicate, through a presential indication, a caused object whose ipseity is separate from the ipseity of its existentiator, in the sense that there would be two independent ipseities in this intellective allusion, one of them being the emanating ipseity and the other being the emanated ipseity. Certainly, it is possible for one to conceive the quiddity of the caused as something other than the cause, and you have already learned that what constitutes the caused in reality is not the quiddity of the caused but its *wujūd*. It has therefore become evident that the *wujūd* of

المشعر الثامن
في أنّ الوجود بالحقيقة هو الواحد الحقّ تعالى
وكلّ ما سواه بما هو مأخوذ بنفسه
هالك دون وجهه الكريم

(١١٥) لمّا علمتَ أنّ الماهيّات لا تأصّل لها في الكون، وأنّ الجاعل التام بنفس وجوده جاعل، وأنّ المجعول ليس إلا نحوًا من الوجود، وأنّه بنفسه مجعول لا بصفة زائدة، وإلا لكان المجعول بتلك الصفة، فالمجعول مجعول بالذات، بمعنى أنّ ذاته وكونه مجعولاً شيء واحد من غير تغاير حيثيّة، كما أنّ الجاعل جاعل بالذات بالمعنى المذكور. فإذن ثبت وتقرّر ما ذكرناه من كون العلّة علّة بذاتها والمعلول معلولاً بذاته بالمعنى المذكور، بعد ما تقرّر أنّ الجاعليّة والمجعوليّة أنّما يكونان بين الوجودات، لا بين الماهيّات، لأنّها أُمور ذهنيّة تنتزع بنحو من أنحاء الوجودات.

(١١٦) فثبت وتحقّق أنّ المسمّى بالمجعول ليس بالحقيقة هويّة مباينة لهويّة علّته الموجدة إيّاه، ولا يمكن للعقل أن يشير إشارة حضوريّة إلى معلول منفصل الهويّة عن هويّة موجده، حتّى يكون عنده هويّتان مستقلتان في الإشارة العقليّة، أحداهما مفيضة والأخرى مستفيضة. نعم، له أن يتصوّر ماهيّة المعلول شيئًا غير العلّة، وقد علمتَ أنّ المعلول بالحقيقة ليس ماهيّة المعلول، بل وجوده. فظهر أنّ وجود المعلول في حد نفسه ناقص الهويّة، مرتبط

the caused constitutes in itself a deficient ipseity, related in its essence to its existentiator and dependent upon it for its existence. Therefore, all *wujūd* other than the One Reality—transcendent is He—is a flash among the flashes of His essence and a face among His faces. Furthermore, all existences have a single origin, which is the Reality that bestows reality upon all realities, that which bestows the quality of being things upon all things, and that which bestows essence upon all essences. It is the Reality; everything else is its states. It is Light; everything else is its effusions. It is the Origin; what is other than it is its manifestations and theophanies. "And He is the First and the Last, the Outward and the Inward" ("*al-Ḥadīd*," Q. 57:3). Among the prayers handed down by tradition, there is the following: "O He, O He who is He, O He other than whom there is no He, O He of whom no one knows where He is except He."[93]

(117) Remark: Be careful not to lose your footing in hearing these phrases and in imagining that the relationship of contingent beings to Him—transcendent is He—is by incarnation, unification, or something like that! Far be it from that! For this would imply a duality in the Origin of *wujūd*. When the Sun of the Truth rises and its penetrating Light spreads in all regions of contingent beings, expanding upon the "temples" (*hayākil*) of quiddities, it becomes evident and manifest that all to which the name *wujūd* is given is nothing but a state among the states of the One, the Self-Subsistent, and a flash among the flashes of the Light of lights. Thus, what we have posed in the beginning, according to the exalted consideration—namely, that there is a cause and a caused in *wujūd*—finally leads us, through sapiential journeying and intellectual piety (*al-nasak al-ʿaqlī*), to the result that what is named the cause is the origin and that the caused is a state among its states and a modality among its modalities. Causality and emanation thus lead back to the modalization of the First Principle in its modalities, and to its theophany in its different manifestations. Remain firm in this station, where so often feet have slipped. How many, having fallen from the ship of the intellect, have drowned in the abyss of the sea; and God is the guardian of virtue and bounties.

الذات بموجده، تعلّقيّ الكون به. فكلّ وجود سوى الواحد الحق تعالى لمعة من لمعات ذاته، ووجه من وجوهه. وأنّ لجميع الموجودات أصلاً واحدًا محقّق الحقائق ومشّيئ الأشياء، ومذوّت الذوات. فهو الحقيقة، والباقي شؤونه. وهو النور، والباقي سطوعه. وهو الأصل، وما عداه ظهوراته وتجلّياته. وهو الأوّل والآخر، والظاهر، والباطن. وفي الأدعية المأثورة «يا هو، يا من هو، يا من ليس هو إلا هو، يا من لا يعلم أين هو إلا هو!»

(١١٧) تنبيه: إيّاك أن تزلّ قدمك من استماع هذه العبارات، وتتوّهم أنّ نسبة الممكنات إليه تعالى بالحلول والاتّحاد ونحوهما ! هيهات أنّ هذا يقتضي الإثنينيّة في أصل الوجود! وعندما طلعت شمس الحقيقة وسطع نورها النافذ في أقطار الممكنات المنبسط على هياكل الماهيّات، ظهر وانكشف أنّ كلّ ما يقع عليه اسم الوجود، ليس إلا شأنًا من شؤون الواحد القيّوم، ولمعة من لمعات نور الأنوار. فما وضعناه أولاً بحسب النظر الجليل من أنّ في الوجود علّة ومعلولاً، أدّى بنا أخيرًا من جهة السلوك العلميّ والنسك العقليّ، إلى أنّ المسمّى بالعلّة هو الأصل، والمعلول شأنٌ من شؤونه، وطور من أطواره. ورجعت العلّية والإفاضة إلى تطوّر المبدأ الأوّل بأطواره وتجلّيه بأنْحاء ظهوراته. فاستقم في هذا المقام الذي قد زلّت فيه الأقدام. وكم من سفينة عقل غرقت في لجج هذا القمقام والله وليّ الفضل والإنْعام.

The second path

Fragments concerning the states of His attributes—transcendent is He

In it there are several penetrations.

The first penetration

Concerning that His attributes—transcendent is He—are the same as His essence

(118) His attributes (transcendent is He) are the same as His essence (transcendent is He). It is not according to what is professed by the Ashᶜarites, who are the followers of Abū al-Ḥasan al-Ashᶜarī, in affirming the [plurality of] attributes in *wujūd*. This would imply the plurality of eternal principles (*al-qudamāʾ*)—and He transcends that in sublime transcendence. And it is not according to what is professed by the Muᶜtazilites and their later followers, who are experts in dialectic and conceptual analysis—people who, while negating the concepts of the attributes and affirming their effects, nevertheless substitute the essence for their source. Furthermore, it is not according to what is done concerning the principle of *wujūd* by some of them, such as the author of *Glosses upon al-tajrīd* [Jalāl al-Dīn Dawānī]. Rather, the matter is as it is understood by "those who are firm in knowledge" ("Āl ᶜImrān," Q. 3:7). That is to say, His *wujūd*—transcendent is He—which is His very reality, is itself the attributes of perfection and the locus in which are manifest His attributes of beauty and majesty. The attributes, despite their plurality and multiplicity, exist by a single *wujūd*, without there being any necessity for multiplicity, passivity, receptivity, and activity. So, just as, for us, the *wujūd* of the contingent exists by essence and the *wujūd* of the quiddity exists by this very *wujūd* accidentally, because this *wujūd* is the subject of which the quiddity is the attribute, so, too, it is true concerning the fact that the attributes of God exist through the *wujūd* of His sacrosanct essence, with the difference that the Necessary Being does not possess a quiddity.[94]

المنهج الثاني
في نُبذ من أحوال صفاته تعالى

وفيه مشاعر

المشعر الأوّل
(في أنّ صفاته تعالى عين ذاته)

(١١٨) إنّ صفاته تعالى عين ذاته تعالى، لا كما يقول الأشاعرة أصحاب أبي الحسن الأشعريّ من إثبات تعدّدها في الوجود، ليلزم تعدّد القدماء—تعالى عن ذلك علوًّا كبيرًا—ولا كما يقوله المعتزلة وتبعهم الآخرون من أهل البحث والتدقيق، من نفي مفهوماتها رأسًا و إثبات آثارها، وجعل الذات نائبة منابها، كما في أصل الوجود عند بعضهم كصاحب حواشي التجريد؛ بل على نحو يعلمه الراسخون في العلم من أنّ وجوده تعالى الذي هو عين حقيقته، هو بعينه مصداق صفاته الكماليّة، ومظهر نعوته الجماليّة والجلاليّة. فهي على كثرتها وتعدّدها موجودة بوجود واحد من غير لزوم كثرة وانفعال وقبول وفعل. فكما أنّ وجود الممكن عندنا موجود بالذات، والماهيّة موجودة بعين هذا الوجود بالعرض لكونه مصداقًا لها. فكذلك الحكم في موجوديّة صفاته تعالى بوجود ذاته المقدّس، إلا أنّ الواجب لا ماهيّة له.

The second penetration

Concerning the modality of His knowledge—transcendent is He—of all things, according to an illuminative principle

(119) This principle is the following: Knowledge possesses a reality in the same way that *wujūd* possesses a reality. Just as the reality of *wujūd* is a single reality and, with its oneness, attaches itself to all things, it is necessary that *wujūd* repel nonexistence from all things, being the *wujūd* of all things and their plenary perfection. Now, the plenary perfection of a thing is more primary for a thing than the thing itself, because the thing exists through possibility in itself, while in its plenary perfection and in that which makes it necessary, it exists through necessity; and necessity is more [clearly] confirmed than possibility. Likewise, it is necessary that His knowledge—transcendent is He—be the reality of knowledge.[95] Now, the reality of knowledge is a single reality and, with its oneness, the knowledge of everything: "It [one's record] leaves nothing, neither small nor big, but has enumerated them" ("al-Kahf," Q. 18:49)—since, if there were to be left aside a single thing from among things and that knowledge were not a knowledge of it, it would not be the pure reality of knowledge, but knowledge in one respect and ignorance in another respect. The pure reality of a thing does not mix with something other than itself; otherwise, it would not completely leave the state of potentiality for actuality.

It has been explained before that God's knowledge—praised be He—comes back to His *wujūd*. Now, just as His *wujūd* does not mix with nonexistence and deficiency, so, too, His knowledge, which is His presence to Himself, cannot be mixed with the absence of anything. How could this be, since He is the Reality that bestows reality upon all realities and that which bestows thing-ness upon all things? For His essence is more real concerning things than the things themselves.[96] Thus, the presence of His essence—transcendent is He—is the presence of all things. What are with God are the principal realities, which make descent into the station of apparitions and shadows.[97]

المشعر الثاني
في كيفيّة علمه تعالى بكّل شيء
على قاعدة مشرقيّة

(١١٩) هي أنّ للعلم حقيقة كما أنّ للوجود حقيقة. وكما أنّ حقيقة الوجود حقيقة واحدة، ومع وحدتها يتعلّق بكلّ شيء، ويجب أن يكون وجودًا يطرد العدم عن كل شيء وهو وجود كل شيء وتمامه وتمام الشيء أولى به من نفسه، لأنّ الشيء يكون مع نفسه بالإمكان ومع تمامه وموجبه بالوجوب، والوجوب آكد من الإمكان، فكذا علمه تعالى يجب أن يكون حقيقة العلم، وحقيقة العلم حقيقة واحدة، ومع وحدتها علم بكلّ شيء «لا يُغَادِرُ صَغِيرَةً وَلا كَبِيرَةً إِلاَّ أَحْصَاهَا»، إذ لو بقي شيء من الأشياء ولم يكن ذلك العلم علمًا به، لم يكن صرف حقيقة العلم، بل علمًا بوجهه وجهلاً بوجه آخر. وصرف حقيقة الشيء لا يمتزج بغيره، وإلا فلم يخرج جميعه من القوّة إلى الفعل. وقد مّر أنّ علمه سبحانه راجع إلى وجوده، فكما أنّ وجوده لا يشوب بعدم ونقص، فكذلك علمه الذي هو حضور ذاته، لا يشوب بغيبة شيء من الأشياء. كيف وهو محقّق الحقائق ومشيّئ الأشياء؟ فذاته أحق بالأشياء من الأشياء بأنفسها. فحضور ذاته تعالى حضور كلّ شيء. فما عند الله هي الحقائق المتأصّلة التي تنزل هذه الأشياء منزلة الأشباح والأظلال.

The third penetration

Concerning the allusion to His other attributes of perfection

(120) The aforementioned principle concerning the generality of the connection of God's knowledge of things applies to His other attributes. Therefore, His power with its oneness is of necessity the power over all things, because His power is the reality of power.[98] If it were not connected to all things, then [His] power would cause one thing to exist rather than another. Thus, His power would not be the pure reality of power. The same reasoning holds true for His will, His life, His hearing, His seeing, and His other attributes of perfection. All things are so many degrees of His power, His will, His love, His life, and so on. If someone finds it difficult to conceive that His knowledge, for example, in spite of its oneness, is knowledge of all things and, likewise, that His power, with its oneness, is connected to all things, that is because he conjectures that His oneness—transcendent is He—and the oneness of His essential attributes is numerical oneness and that He—transcendent is He—is one numerically. The truth of the matter is, however, otherwise; for this oneness is another sort of oneness and is not numerical—nor [is it] of species, nor of genus, nor of conjunction, [nor of any other kind]. No one knows this [oneness] except "those who are firm in knowledge" ("Āl ᶜImrān," Q. 3:7).[99]

The fourth penetration

Concerning the allusion to His word—transcendent is He—and His book[100]

(121) His word—transcendent is He—is not as the Ashᶜarites have professed, who make the word an attribute residing in the soul, comprised of ideas subsisting by the Divine Essence. This is not so, because it is impossible that the Divine Being—transcendent is He—should be a substratum for something other than Himself. Nor does the word of God consist of the creation of sounds and letters with a referent; otherwise, all words would be the word of God. Similarly, His command and His speech precede all existents, as He has also said: "Verily, His command is that if He wills a thing, He says to it, 'Be!' and it is" ("Yā-Sīn," Q. 36:82). Rather, the word of God consists of the production of the "perfect words" and the descent of "the firmly established verses which are the archetype of the Mother Book, and others which are metaphorical"

المشعر الثالث
في الإشارة إلى سائر صفاته الكماليّة

(١٢٠) القاعدة المذكورة في عموم تعلّق علمه تعالى بالأشياء مطرّدة في سائر صفاته. فقدرته مع وحدتها يجب أن يكون قدرة على كل شيء لأنّ قدرته حقيقة القدرة. فلو لم تكن متعلّقة بجميع الأشياء، لكانت قادرة على إيجاد شيء دون شيء آخر؛ فلم تكن قدرته صرف حقيقة القدرة. وكذا الكلام في إرادته وحياته وسمعه وبصره وسائر صفاته الكماليّة. فجميع الأشياء من مراتب قدرته و إرادته ومحبّته وحياته وغير ذلك. ومن استصعب عليه أنّ علمه مثلاً مع وحدته علم بكلّ شيء وكذا قدرته مع وحدتها متعلّقة بكلّ شيء، فذلك لظنّه أنّ وحدته تعالى ووحدة صفاته الذاتية وحدة عدديّة، وأنّه تعالى واحد بالعدد. وليس الأمر كذلك، بل هذه ضرب آخر من الوحدة غير العددّية والنوعيّة والجنسيّة والاتصاليّة وغيرها. لا يعرفها إلا «الرَّاسِخُونَ فِي الْعِلْمِ».

المشعر الرابع
في الإشـــارة إلى كلامه تعالى وكتابه

(١٢١) كلامه تعالى ليس كما قالته الأشاعرة من أنّه صفة نفسيّة هي معانٍ قائمة بذاته، لاستحالة كونه تعالى محلاً لغيره. وليس أيضًا عبارة عن خلق أصوات وحروف دالّة و إلا لكان كلّ كلام كلام الله. وأيضًا أمره وقوله سابق على كلّ كائن، كما قال أيضًا «انما اَمْرُهُ اِذَا ارادَ شيئاً اَن يقولَ لهُ كُنْ فيكون» بل هو عبارة عن إنشاء كلمات تامّات و إنزال «آيَاتٌ

("Āl ᶜImrān," Q. 3:7) in the dress of words and expressions. Furthermore, He has said: "His word did He project unto Mary, and a spirit from Him" ("al-Nisāᵓ," Q. 4:171). And [it is said] in the ḥadīth: "I take refuge in all the perfect words of God from the evil of what He has created."[101]

(122) The word that descends from the Divine [Proximity] is word from one aspect and book from another aspect. The word, since it belongs to the world of the Divine Command, is other than the book, since it belongs to the world of creation.[102] The speaking subject is the one through whom the word subsists, in the same manner that the existent subsists through its existentiator. The writer [of the book] is He who makes the word exist—that is to say, [as] the book. The word and the book possess different stations and stages. Now, every speaker is also a writer, in a certain respect; and every writer is also a speaker, in a certain respect. The example of it is witnessed in the fact that when man speaks a word, the word emanates from his soul upon the tablet of his breast, and the different organs serving to form letters produce the forms and figures of these letters [as he] pronounc[es] them. His soul, therefore, is that which makes the word exist.[103] He is a writer inasmuch as that, with the pen of his power, he reproduces the letters on the tablet of his heart in the stations of his voice and the channels of his breath; while his physical person is that through which the word subsists, and thus he becomes a speaker. Place this in comparison with what is mentioned above.

The word is recitation (*qurᵓān*)[104] from one point of view and discernment (*furqān*) from another point of view. The word, because it belongs to the world of the [Divine] Command, has for its abode the breasts (hearts; *ṣudūr*), and no one perceives it except "those who possess heart-knowledge."[105] "Rather, it is evident signs in the hearts of those who are given knowledge" ("al-ᶜAnkabūt," Q. 29:49), "and no one intellects it except those who know" ("al-ᶜAnkabūt," Q. 29:43). As for the book, because it belongs to the world of creation, it has for its abode the tablets of power [or destiny], which everyone perceives; as His word asserts—transcendent is He: "We have written for him upon the tablets an exhortation of everything" ("al-Aᶜrāf," Q. 7:145). As for the word, "No one touches it except the pure" ("al-Wāqiᶜah," Q. 56:79). Rather, it is the Noble Qurᵓan that possesses an exalted grade in the Guarded Tablet: "No one touches it except the pure; it is a descent of revelation from the Lord of the worlds" ("al-Wāqiᶜah," Q. 56:79–80). It is this descent [of revelation] that is the book.

مُحْكَمَاتٌ هُنَّ أُمُّ الْكِتَابِ وَأُخَرُ مُتَشَابِهَاتٌ» في كسوة ألفاظ وعبارات. قال «وَكَلِمَتُهُ أَلْقَاهَا إِلَى مَرْيَمَ وَرُوحٌ مِنْهُ»، وفي الحديث «أعوذ بكلمات الله التامّات كلّها من شرّ ما خلق».

(١٢٢) والكلام النازل من عند الله هو كلام وكتاب من وجهين. والكلام لكونه من عالم الأمر غير الكتاب، لكونه من عالم الخلق. والمتكلّم من قام به الكلام قيام الموجود بالموجد. والكاتب من أوجد الكلام، يعني الكتاب. ولكلّ منهما منازل ومراتب. فكلّ متكلّم كاتب بوجه، وكل كاتب متكلّم بوجه. ومثاله في الشاهد أنّ الإنسان إذا تكلّم بكلام، فقد صدر عن نفسه في لوح صدره ومخارج حروفه صور وأشكال حرفيّة. فنفسه من أوجد الكلام، فيكون كاتبًا بقلم قدرته في ألواح صدره ومنازل صوته ومجارى نفَسه — بفتح الفاء — وشخصه الجسمانيّ ممّن قام به الكلام، فيكون متكلّمًا. فاجعل ذلك مقياسا لما فوقه. والكلام قرآن وفرقان باعتبارين. والكلام لكونه من عالم الأمر منزله الصدور، ولا يدركه إلا أولو الألباب، «بَلْ هُوَ آيَاتٌ بَيِّنَاتٌ فِي صُدُورِ الَّذِينَ أُوتُوا الْعِلْمَ» وما يعقلها إلا العالمون. والكتاب لكونه من عالم الخلق منزله الألواح القدريّة، يدركه كلّ واحد لقوله تعالى «وَكَتَبْنَا لَهُ فِي الْأَلْوَاحِ مِنْ كُلِّ شَيْءٍ مَوْعِظَةً» والكلام لا يمسّه إلا المطهّرون بل هو « قُرْآنٌ كَرِيمٌ» وله مرتبة عظيمة في لوح محفوظ «لاَ يَمَسُّهُ إِلاَّ الْمُطَهَّرُونَ تَنزِيلٌ مِّن رَّبِّ العَالَمِينَ» فتنزيله هو الكتاب.

The third path

Concerning the allusion to formative creation (ṣunᶜ) *and creation without intermediary* (ibdāᶜ)

In it there are several penetrations.

[The] first penetration

Concerning the activity of the agent

(123) The activity of every agent is either by nature, by coercion, by domination, by intention, by agreement, by providence, or by theophany.[106] What is other than the first three is, of course, voluntary. The third [that is, domination] can have either aspect. In the view of the atheists and the naturalists, the Creator of the universe acts according to nature. According to the Muᶜtazilites, He acts according to intention, as well as [in response to] something that invites Him; and according to the majority of the theologians, [He acts] without something that invites Him. For the Ishrāqīs, He acts according to agreement. He acts by providence, according to the majority of the philosophers, and by theophany, according to the Sufis. "To everything there is a direction toward which it orients itself; so vie in good works" ("al-Baqarah," Q. 2:148).

The second penetration

Concerning His activity—transcendent is He

(124) His activity—transcendent is He—consists of command and creation. His command is with God [Himself], and His creation is a temporal origination. And [it is in the ḥadīth] that the Prophet of God—may God's blessings be upon him and his family—said: "The first thing that God created was the Intellect," according to another narration, "the Pen," and according to yet another narration, "My Light." The meaning of all of these is the same.[107]

المنهج الثالث
في الإشارة إلى الصنع والإبداع

وفيه مشاعر

المشعر الأوّل
(في فاعليّة الفاعل)

(١٢٣) إنّ فاعليّة كل فاعل إمّا بالطبع، أو بالقسر، أو بالتسخير، أو بالقصد، أو بالرضا، أو بالعناية، أو بالتجلّي. وما سوى الثلاث، الأوّل، إراديّ البتّة؛ والثالث يحتمل الوجهين. وصانع العالم فاعل بالطبع عند الدهريّة والطباعيّة؛ وبالقصد مع الداعي عند المعتزلة؛ وبغير الداعي عند أكثر المتكلّمين؛ وبالرضا عند الإشراقيّين؛ وبالعناية عند جمهور الحكماء؛ وبالتجلّي عند الصوفيّة. ولكلٍّ وجهة هو مولّيها، فاستبقوا الخيرات.

المشعر الثاني
في فعله تعالى

(١٢٤) فعله تعالى أمر وخلق. وأمره مع الله، وخلقه حادث زماني وفي الحديث أنّه قال رسول الله—صلّى الله عليه وآله—«أوّل ما خلق الله العقل». وفي رواية «القلم». وفي رواية «نوري» والمعنى في الكلّ واحد.

(125) In the book *Baṣā'ir al-darajāt* (The Degrees of Vision), one of our people among the Imāmiyyah—may God be content with them—said: "Yaᶜqūb ibn Yazīd narrated to us from Muḥammad ibn Abī ᶜUmayr from Hishām ibn Salīm, who said: 'I heard Abū ᶜAbd Allāh [Imam Jaᶜfar al-Ṣādiq]—may peace be upon him—say: "They will ask you concerning the Spirit. Say: 'The Spirit is from the command of my Lord!'" [17:87]. He said: 'It is a creation more sublime than Gabriel and Michael. It is not with any of those in the past, except with Muḥammad (may God's blessings be upon him and upon his family), and he is with the Imams (may peace be upon them), directing them.'"[108]

(126) Muḥammad ibn ᶜAlī ibn Bābūyah al-Qummī [d. 381/991]—may God sanctify his spirit—has said in his *Kitāb al-iᶜtiqādāt* (The Book of Creeds): "Our belief concerning souls is that they are spirits by which subsist the life of souls and that they are the first creation, since the Prophet—may God's blessings and peace be upon him—has said: 'The first things that God created [without intermediary] were the sanctified and pure souls; then He made them state His unity. After that, He created the rest of His creation.' Therefore, our belief in this matter is that they were created for subsistence and not at all for annihilation; as has been said by him—may God's blessings and peace be upon him: 'You were not created for annihilation; rather, you were created for subsistence, and verily, you are transferred from one abode to another.' In this world, the spirits are strangers and imprisoned in bodies. What we profess concerning them is that when they separate from bodies, they subsist, some to be showered upon with blessings, others to suffer chastisement, until they are returned by Him—exalted and majestic is He—to their bodies."

(127) Jesus, the son of Mary—peace be upon him—said to the apostles: "I say unto you the truth that nothing ascends to heaven except what has descended from it."[109]

(128) He—majestic is His praise—has said: "And had We wanted We would have uplifted him by means of them [the signs of God]; but he attached himself to the earth and followed his passion" ("al-Āᶜrāf," Q. 7:176).

(129) He [Ibn Bābūyah] also said—may his secret be sanctified—in *Kitāb al-tawḥīd* (The Book of Unity), transmitting by a continuous chain from Abū ᶜAbd Allāh [Jaᶜfar al-Ṣādiq]—may peace be upon him: "Truly, the spirit of the believer is connected to the Spirit of God in a way that is stronger than the connection of the rays of the sun to the sun."

(١٢٥) وفي «كتاب بصائر الدرجات» لبعض أصحابنا الإماميّة — رضي الله عنهم قال «حدّثنا يعقوب بن يزيد عن محمَد بن أبي عمير عن هشام بن سالم، قال: سمعت أبا عبد الله (الإمام جعفر الصادق) — عليه السلام — يقول: يسألونك عن الروح، قل الروح من أمر ربّي. قال: خلق أعظم من جبرئيل وميكائيل لم يكن مع أحد ممّن مضى غير محمّد — صلّى الله عليه وآله — وهو مع الأئمّة — عليهم السلام — يسدّدهم» انتهى.

(١٢٦) وقال محمّد بن عليّ «بن بابويه القمّيّ — قدّس الله روحه — في كتاب الاعتقادات « اعتقادنا في النفوس أنّها هي الأرواح التي تقوم بها حياة النفوس، وأنّها الخلق الأوّل لقول النبيّ صلعم : إنّ أوّل ما أبدع الله تعالى هي النفوس المقدّسة المطهّرة، فأنطقها بتوحيده؛ ثمّ خلق بعد ذلك سائر خلقه. واعتقادنا فيها أنّها خلقت للبقاء. ولم تخلق للفناء لقوله صلعم: ما خلقتم للفناء بل خلقتم للبقاء، وإنّما تنقلون من دار إلى دار. وأنّ الأرواح في الدنيا غريبة وفي الأبدان مسجونة. واعتقادنا فيها أنّها إذا فارقت الأبدان، فهي باقية، منها منّعمة ومنها معذّبة، إلى أن يردّها — عزّ وجلّ — إلى أبدانها.»

(١٢٧) وقال عيسى بن مريم — عليه السلام — للحواريّين «أقول لكم الحقّ إنّه لا يصعد إلى السماء إلا ما نزل منها.»

(١٢٨) وقال — جلّ ثناؤه — «وَلَوْ شِئْنَا لَرَفَعْنَاهُ بِهَا وَلَكِنَّهُ أَخْلَدَ إِلَى الْأَرْضِ وَاتَّبَعَ هَوَاهُ».

(١٢٩) وقال أيضًا قدّس سرّه — في كتاب التوحيد ناقلاً بسنده المتّصل عن أبي عبد الله — عليه السلام — «إنّ روح المؤمن لأشد اتصالاً بروح الله من اتّصال شعاع الشمس بها».

(130) Furthermore, al-Shaykh al-Mufīd [d. 413/1022]—may peace be upon him—has recounted in *Kitāb al-maqālāt* (The Book of Treatises), one of the precious books of wisdom by one of our Imamate scholars professing unity—may God be content with them—based on a chain from Layth ibn Abī Salīm, from Ibn ᶜAbbās—may God be content with him—who said: "I heard the Messenger of God—may God's blessings and peace be upon him—when he made the nocturnal journey to the seventh heaven and then descended to the earth, say to ᶜAlī ibn Abī Ṭālib—may God's blessings be upon him: 'O ᶜAlī, verily, God—transcendent is He—was God and there was nothing with Him. Then He created me and created you, two spirits from the light of His majesty, and we were standing before the throne of the Lord of the worlds, praising God, thanking Him and uttering the testimony to His oneness. That was before the heavens and the earth were created. When He willed to create Adam—may peace be upon him—He created me and you from the clay of ᶜIlliyyīn,[110] and I was kneaded in this light, and we were plunged in all the streams and the streams of paradise. Then He created Adam—may peace be upon him—and consigned in his loin this clay and this light. When he created him and had his posterity brought forth from his back, He taught them speech and made them proclaim His lordship. So what God created first, and made perfect through justice and unity, was I and thou and the prophets, according to their stations and their proximity to God—exalted and majestic is He.'" All of this is in a long ḥadīth.

(131) It has become evident from these transmitted sayings, after the witness of intellectual demonstration, that the spirits possess an existence before the world of bodies. The sacrosanct intelligences and the universal spirits subsist, according to us, through the subsistence of God—transcendent is He—rather than God sustaining them, because they are evanescent in essence, lights concealed under the luminosity of the Light of Majesty, not casting a look upon their own essences and humble before God—transcendent is He.

(132) Saᶜd ibn Jubayr said: "God has not created a creation more sublime than the Spirit; if it wanted to devour the seven heavens and the two earths in a single bite, it would do that."

(١٣٠) ونقل الشيخ المفيد — رحمه الله — في كتاب المقالات من كتاب نوادر الحكمة لبعض علمائنا الإماميّة أصحاب التوحيد — رضي الله عنهم — مستندًا إلى ليث بن أبي سليم عن ابن عباس — رضي الله عنه — قال «سمعتُ رسول الله صلعم لمّا أسْري به إلى السماء السابعة، ثّم أهبط إلى الأرض، يقول لعليّ بن أبي طالب — صلوات الله عليه — يا عليّ ! إنّ الله تعالى كان الله ولا شيء معه. فخلقني وخلقك روحين من نور جلاله. فكنّا أمام عرش ربّ العالمين، نسبّح الله ونحمّده ونهلّله. وذلك قبل أن يخلق السماوات والأرض. فلمّا أراد أن يخلق آدم عم، خلقني و إيّاك من طينة عليّين، وعجّنت بذلك النور وغمّسنا في جميع الأنّهار وأنّهار الجنة. ثمّ خلق آدم عم واستودع صلبه تلك الطينة والنور. فلمّا خلفه واستخرج ذرّيته من ظهره، فاستنطقهم وقرّرهم بربوبيّته. فأوّل ما خلق الله وأتّمّ له بالعدل والتوحيد، أنا وأنت والنبيّون على قدر منازلهم وقربهم من الله عزّ وجل»، في حديث طويل.

(١٣١) فقد ظهر من هذه النقول بعد شهادة البرهان للعقول، أنّ للأرواح كينونة سابقة على عالم الأجسام. والعقول القادسة والأرواح الكلّيّة عندنا باقية ببقاء الله تعالى فضلاً عن إبقائه، لأنّها مستهلكة الذات، مطويّة الأنوار تحت سطوع نور الجلال لا يرمون النظر إلى ذواتهم، خاضعين لله تعالى.

(١٣٢) قال سعد بن جبير «لم يخلق الله خلقًا أعظم من الروح، ولو شاء أن يبلع السماوات السبع والأرضيين في لقمة، لفعل.»

(133) Some have said that "the Spirit never proceeds from 'Be!' because if it were to proceed from 'Be!,' it would have to submit itself to something before it." From what, then, would it proceed? He said: "From between His beauty and His majesty." I say: The meaning of this word is that the Spirit is precisely His command (transcendent is He) in the same way that His word "Be!" is precisely His command (transcendent is He) by which all things are existentiated. Other existents are created by and come from His command. And His command does not come from His command; otherwise, it would necessitate a vicious circle and an infinite regression. Rather, the world of His command—praised be He—issues from His essence, like the issuing of the rays of the sun from the sun and of humidity from the sea.

(134) Ibn Bābūyah has also said in his *Kitāb al-iʿtiqādāt* (The Book of Creeds): "Our belief concerning the prophets, the messengers, and the imams—may peace be upon them—is that there are with them five spirits: the Sacred Spirit, the spirit of faith, the spirit of power, the spirit of desire, and the spirit of growth. Among the believers, there are four spirits; and among the disbelievers and the animals, there are three spirits. As for His word—transcendent is He: 'They will ask you concerning the Spirit. Say: "The Spirit is from the command of my Lord!"' ("al-Isrāʾ," Q. 17:85), it means that the Spirit is a creation more sublime than Gabriel, Michael, and Sarafael. It was with the Messenger of God—may God's blessings and peace be upon him—and with the angels, and it belongs to the world of dominion." That is the end of his word.

(135) This saying is taken from the traditions of our inerrant Imams—may the blessings of God be upon them all. By the Sacred Spirit is meant the first Spirit that is with God, without returning upon itself. It is what the philosophers call "the Active Intellect." By the spirit of faith is meant the acquired intellect that has become intellect in act after having been intellect in potentiality. By the spirit of power is meant the human rational soul, which is the hylic potential intellect. By the spirit of desire is meant the hylic soul, whose condition contains concupiscence and irascibility. And by the spirit of growth is meant the natural spirit, which is the origin of physical growth and nourishment. These five spirits become actualized one after another in man gradually. When man is in the womb, he possesses only the vegetal soul. Then, after his birth, there grows the animal soul, by which I mean the imaginal faculty. Then there occurs within him, in the period of physical growth and

(١٣٣) وقال بعضهم «الروح لم يخرج من» كُن» لأنّه لو خرج من «كُن» كان عليه الذلّ قبل. فمن أيّ شيءٍ خرج؟ قال: من بين جماله وجلاله» انتهى. أقول: معنى كلامه أنّ الروح هو أمره تعالى، وقوله «كُن» هو نفس أمره تعالى، الذي به تتكوّن الأشياء. فسائر الموجودات خُلقت وكانت من أمره، وأمره لا يكون من أمره؛ وإلا، لزم الدور أو التسلسل، بل عالم أمره سبحانه ينشأ من ذاته نشوء الضوء من الشمس والنداوة من البحر.

(١٣٤) وقال ابن بابويه أيضًا في كتاب الاعتقادات «اعتقادنا في الأنبياء والرسل والأئمّة — عليهم السلام — أنّ فيهم خمسة أرواح: روح القدس، وروح الإيمان ، وروح القوّة، وروح الشهوة، وروح المدرّج. وفي المؤمنين أربعة أرواح. وفي الكافرين والبهائم ثلاثة أرواح. وأمّا قوله تعالى «وَيَسْأَلُونَكَ عَنِ الرُّوحِ قُلِ الرُّوحُ مِنْ أَمْرِ رَبِّي» فإنّه خلق أعظم من جبرائيل وميكائيل وإسرافيل، وكان مع رسول الله صلعم، ومع الملائكة، وهو من الملكوت»، انتهى كلامه.

(١٣٥) وقد أخذ هذا الكلام من أحاديث أئمّتنا المعصومين — صلوات الله عليهم أجمعين — والمراد منه «روح القدس» الروح الأوّل الذي هو مع الله من غير مراجعة إلى ذاته، وهو المسمّى عند الحكماء بـ»العقل الفعّال». ومن روح الإيمان، والعقل المستفاد الذي صار عقلاً بالفعل بعدما كان عقلاً بالقوّة. ومن روح القوّة، النفس الناطقة الإنسانيّة وهي علق هيولانيّ بالقوّة. ومن روح الشهوة، النفس الحيوانيّة التي شأنها الشهوة والغضب. ومن روح المدرّج الروح الطبيعيّ الذي هو مبدأ التنمية والتغذية. وهذه الأرواح الخمسة متعاقبة الحصول في الإنسان على التدريج. فالإنسان ما دام في الرحم، ليس له إلا النفس النباتيّة. ثم ينشأ له بعد الولادة النفس الحيوانيّة، أعني القوّة الخياليّة. ثم يحدث له في أوان

the intensification of forms [in him], the rational soul, and that is the practical intellect. As for the intellect in act, it does not occur except in a small number of human beings; these are the knowers and those who have true faith in God, His angels, His books, His messengers, and the Day of Judgment. As for the Sacred Spirit, it is particular to the saints of God. Furthermore, these five spirits are lights differing in the strength and weakness of their luminosity, all of them existing by a single *wujūd* but possessing different degrees that are actualized gradually in those in whom they are found.

(136) That which comes to our aid in this matter is what was mentioned by the author of the *Iᶜtiqādāt*, by the path of the tradition transmitted from Kumayl ibn Ziyād, who said: "I asked our master Amīr al-Muʾminīn ᶜAlī—may a thousand benedictions and peace be upon him—and I said: 'O Amīr al-Muʾminīn, I would like you to make me know my soul.' ᶜAlī—peace be upon him—said: 'O Kumayl, which soul would you like me to make known to you?' I said: 'O my master, is there not but a single soul?' He said: 'O Kumayl, there are, in fact, four: the vegetative soul, which causes growth; the animal, which has sensibility; the rational, which is sacred; and the universal, which is divine. Each of these souls has five powers and two properties. The vegetative soul, which causes growth, has five powers—the attractive, the retentive, the digestive, the repulsive, and the reproductive—and it has two properties: one is growth, and one is diminution. It issues from the liver. The animal soul, which is sensible, has five powers—hearing, sight, smell, taste, and touch—and it has two properties: concupiscence and irascibility. It issues from the heart. The rational soul, which is sacred, has five powers: thinking, remembering, knowledge, patience, and nobility. It does not issue from any organ; it is that which, among all things, most resembles the angelic souls; and it has two properties: purity and wisdom. The universal [soul], which is divine, has five powers—subsistence in annihilation, well-being in hardship, glory in debasement, richness in poverty, and patience in tribulation—and it possesses two properties: contentment and surrender. It is this soul whose origin is from God and which returns to Him.'" God—transcendent is He—has said: "And I breathed into him from My Spirit" ("al-Ḥijr," Q. 15:29). And He has said: "O soul pacified, return unto thy Lord, satisfied and satisfying" ("al-Fajr," Q. 89:27–28). And the intellect is the medium of everything.

البلوغ الحيوانيّ والاشتداد الصوريّ النفس الناطقة، وهو العقل العلميّ. وأما العقل بالفعل، فلا يحدث إلا في قليل من أفراد البشر، وهم العرفاء والمؤمنون حقًا بالله وملائكته وكُتبه ورسُله واليوم الآخر. وأمّا روح القدس، فهو المخصوص بأولياء الله. وهذه الأرواح الخمسة أنّوار متفاوتة في شدّة النوريّة وضعفها، كلّها موجودة بوجود واحد ذي مراتب متدرّجة الحصول فيمن وجدت له.

(١٣٦) والذي يعضد ما ذكره صاحب الاعتقادات من طريق الرواية، ما نقل عن كميل بن زياد أنّه قال «سألتُ مولانا أمير المؤمنين عليّا — عليه ألف التحية والسلام — فقلت يا أمير المؤمنين! أريد أن تعرفني نفسي قال عم: يا كميل ! وأيّ النفس تريد أن أعرّفك؟ قلت: يا مولاي، وهل هي إلا نفس واحدة؟ قال يا كميل إنّما هي أربعة: الناميّة النباتيّة، والحسّيّة الحيوانيّة، والناطقة القدسيّة، والكلّيّة الإلهيّة. ولكل واحدة من هذه خمس قوى وخاصّيّتان فالنامية النباتيّة لها خمس قوى: جاذبة، وماسكة، وهاضمة، ودافعة، ومولّدة. ولها خاصّيّتان: الزيادة والنقصان، وانبعاثها من الكبد. والحسّيّة الحيوانيّة لها خمس قوى: سمع، وبصر، وشمّ، وذوق، ولمس. ولها خاصّيّتان: الشهوة والغضب وانبعاثها من القلب. والناطقة القدسية لها خمس قوى: فكر، وذكر، وعلم، وحلم، ونباهة. وليس لها انبعاث، وهي أشبه الأشياء بالنفوس الملكيّة. ولها خاصّيّتان: النزاهة والحكمة. والكلّيّة الإلهيّة لها خمس قوى: بقاء في فناء، ونعيم في شقاء، وعزّ في ذّل، وغنى في فقر، وصبر في بلاء. ولها خاصّيّتان: الرضا والتسليم. وهذه التي مبدؤها من الله و إليه تعود. قال الله تعالى «وَنَفَخْتُ فِيهِ مِنْ رُوحِي» وقال «يَا أَيَّتُهَا النَّفْسُ الْمُطْمَئِنَّةُ ارْجِعِي إِلَى رَبِّكِ رَاضِيَةً مَرْضِيَّةً» والعقل وسط الكلّ.

The third penetration

Concerning the temporal origination of the world

(137) The world, with all that is in it, is generated temporally because the existence of everything in it is preceded by its nonexistence in time, in the sense that there is no ipseity among individual ipseities whose nonexistence had not preceded its existence in time. Briefly, there is nothing among corporeal things and material corporealities—be it celestial or elemental, be it a soul or a body—except that its identity is renewed and its existence and individuality are not permanent.[111] This has come to us as a luminous demonstration from God, as a result of meditating upon the signs of God—transcendent is He—and His glorious Book, such as His saying—praised be He: "Are they in doubt about a new creation?" ("Qāf," Q. 50:15); His saying: "From changing your forms and creating you again in forms that ye know not" ("al-Wāqiᶜah," Q. 56:61); His saying—transcendent is He: "Thou seest the mountains and thinkest them to be firmly fixed; but they shall pass away as clouds pass away" ("al-Naml," Q. 27:88); His saying—transcendent is He: "If He so will, He can remove you and put [in your place] a new creation" ("Ibrāhīm," Q. 14:19; "al-Fāṭir," Q. 35:16); His saying: "And the heavens will be rolled up in His right Hand" ("al-Zumar," Q. 39:67); His saying—transcendent is He: "It is We who shall inherit the earth and all beings therein; to Us will they all be returned" ("Maryam," Q. 19:40); His saying—transcendent is He: "All things other than Him perish, and there abideth the face of thy Lord, the Possessor of Majesty and Bounty" ("al-Raḥmān," Q. 55:26–27); and His saying—transcendent is He: "There is not one thing in the heavens and the earth but [that it] must come as a servant to the Most-Merciful" ("Maryam," Q. 19:93). And everyone comes unto Him individually.[112]

المشعر الثالث
في حدوث العالم

(١٣٧) العالم بجميع ما فيه حادث زمانيّ. إذ كلّ ما فيه مسبوق الوجود بعدم زمانيّ. بمعنى أنْ لا هويّة من الهويّات الشخصيّة إلا وقد سبق عدمها وجودها. ووجودها عدمها سبقًا زمانيًّا. وبالجملة لا شيء من الأجسام والجسمانيّات الماديّة فلكيّا كان أو عنصريًّا، نفسًا كان أو بدنًا، إلا وهو متجدّد الهويّة غير ثابت الوجود والشخصيّة، مع برهان لاح لنا من عند الله لأجل التدبّر في آيات الله تعالى وكتابه العزيز، مثل قوله سبحانه «بَلْ هُمْ فِي لَبْسٍ مِنْ خَلْقٍ جَدِيدٍ» وقوله «عَلَى أَنْ نُبَدِّلَ أَمْثَالَكُمْ وَنُنْشِئَكُمْ فِي مَا لا تَعْلَمُونَ» وقوله تعالى «وَتَرَى الْجِبَالَ تَحْسَبُهَا جَامِدَةً وَهِيَ تَمُرُّ مَرَّ السَّحَابِ» وقوله تعالى «إِنْ يَشَأْ يُذْهِبْكُمْ وَيَأْتِ بِخَلْقٍ جَدِيدٍ» وقوله «والسَّماواتُ مَطْوِيَّاتٌ بِيَمِينِهِ» وقوله تعالى «إِنَّا نَحْنُ نَرِثُ الأَرْضَ وَمَنْ عَلَيْهَا وَإِلَيْنَا تُرْجَعُوْنَ»، وقوله تعالى « كُلُّ مَنْ عَلَيْهَا فانٍ وَيَبْقَى وَجْهُ رَبِّكَ ذُو الْجَلالِ وَالإِكْرَامِ» وقوله تعالى «إِنْ كُلُّ مَن فِي السَّمَاوَاتِ وَالأَرْضِ إِلاَّ آتِي الرَّحْمَنِ عَبْدًا» وكلّ أتوه فردًا.

(138) The origin of the demonstration to which we have sometimes referred comes from the side of the incessant renewal of nature, which is a substantial form penetrating the body. It is the proximal principle for its essential movement and rest, and it is the source of its effects.[113] No body exists that is not constituted in its essence of this substantial form, which penetrates all of its parts. And the body is permanently in a state of change, flow, renewal, rupture, cessation, and destruction. Therefore, there is no permanence to nature; and there is no cause for its temporal origination and incessant renewal, because what is essential is not caused by any cause other than the cause of its essence. When the Instaurer instaured it [nature], It instaured its essence in incessant renewal. As for its incessant renewal, it does not occur through a new instauration by the Instaurer or creation by an agent. And it is through it [nature] that what is temporal and what is eternal are connected, because the *wujūd* [of nature] is precisely this *wujūd*, which is gradual; its subsistence is its very generation, and its stability is its very change. Therefore, the Creator, who possesses the quality of permanence and stability, originated, without intermediary, this being whose essence and ipseity are in incessant renewal.[114]

(139) The fact that the philosophers have proposed motion as an intermediary between the temporally originated and the eternal is not suitable for this [argument]. In fact, motion is an intellectual and relational entity, consisting of the passing of a thing from potentiality to actuality, but not that by which it passes from potentiality to actuality. It is from a *wujūd* in becoming and an origination that is realized gradually. Time is the quantity of this passage and renewal. As for motion, it is the gradual passage of this substance from potentiality to actuality, and time is the measure of it. But neither [movement nor time] is appropriate to be the intermediary in the link between the temporally originated and the eternal. The same is true for accidents because they depend upon their substratum for stability and renewal. Therefore, there only remains what we have mentioned.[115] In order to prove this argument, we have expanded the discussion in our other writings, to which there is nothing more to add.[116]

(١٣٨) ومبدأ هذا البرهان المشار إليه تارة من جهة تجّدد الطبيعة، وهي صورة جوهريّة سارية في الجسم، هي المبدأ القريب بحركته الذاتيّة وسكونه ومنشأ آثاره. وما من جسم إلا ويتقوّم ذاته من هذا الجوهر الصوريّ الساري في جميع أجزائه، وهو أبدًا في التحوّل والسيلان والتجدّد والانصرام والزوال والانهدام. فلا بقاء لها، ولا سبب لحدوثها وتجدّدها، لأنّ الذاتيّ غير معلّل بعلّة سوى علّة الذات. والجاعل إذا جعلها، جعل ذاتها المتجدّدة. وأمّا تجدّدها، فليس بجعل جاعل وصنع فاعل. و بها يرتبط الحادث بالقديم، لأنّ وجودها بعينه هذا الوجود التدريجيّ وبقاءها عين حدوثها، وثباتها عين تغيّرها. فالصانع بوصف ثباته وبقائه أبدع هذا الكائن المتجدّد الذات والهويّة.

(١٣٩) والذي جعل الحكماء واسطة لارتباط الحادث بالقديم، وهي الحركة، غير صالح لذلك. فإنّ الحركة أمر عقليّ إضافيّ عبارة عن خروج الشيء من القوّة إلى الفعل لا ما به يخرج منها إليه، وهو من الوجود الحدوثيّ والحدوث التدريجيّ، والزمان كميّة ذلك الخروج والتجدّد. فالحركة خروج هذا الجوهر من القوّة إلى الفعل تدريجيًا، والزمان مقداره. وشيء منهما لا يصلح أن يكون واسطة في ارتباط الحادث بالقديم، وكذا الأعراض، لأنّها تابعة في الثبات والتجدّد لمحالّها. فلم يبق إلا ما ذكرناه. وقد بسطنا القول المشبع لإثبات هذا المرام في سائر صحفنا بما لا مزيد عليه.

(140) Sometimes it comes from the aspect of the proof of the final ends for elemental natures. They require, from the point of view of the process of perfection of their essence and substantial motions, that *wujūd* bring upon them a radical mutation that causes this becoming to cease; that growth and generation be terminated, that everything on the earth and heaven fall into a state of swoon, that this present abode be destroyed, and that the matter be transferred to the One, the Victorious.

(141) The prince of believers and the Imam of those who truly profess the doctrine of Divine Unity—may peace be upon him—has said in the sermons of the *Nahj al-balāghah* (The Path of Eloquence), in referring to the evanescence of the world and its cessation in view of affirming the end and the return to the beginning:

> All things are humbled before Him, and all things subsist by Him. He is the richness of all the poor, the glory of all the lonely, the power of all the weak, and the shelter of all the pitiable. Whosoever speaketh, He heareth his speech; and whosoever keepeth silent, He knoweth his secret. Whosoever liveth, his livelihood depends upon Him; and whosoever dieth, to Him is his return.

Then the sermons of the Imam—may peace be upon him—lead to his words concerning the states of man and the gradual penetration of death into him:

> Death doth not cease to penetrate into his body until his tongue behaveth like his ear [ceasing to function], and he lieth among his people without speaking with his tongue or hearing with his ear. He rotateth his glance on their faces, seeing the movement of their tongues but unable to hear their speech. Then death increaseth its sway upon him, and his sight is taken away, as his hearing was taken away before. Then the spirit departeth from his body, and he becometh a carcass among his people. They depart from his side and distance themselves from his proximity. He cannot join the mourner crying near him nor answer the person who calleth him. He is then carried to a [narrow] burial place in the earth and is surrendered in it to his deeds. They cease visiting him . . . until [what is written in] the Book reacheth its fixed term, affairs attain their destined limits, the end of creation joineth its beginning, and there cometh from the

(١٤٠) وتارة من جهة إثبات الغايات للطبائع، وأنّها تستدعي من جهة استكمالاتها الذاتيّة وحركاتها الجوهريّة، أنْ يتبدّل عليها هذا الوجود، ويزول عنها هذا الكون، وينقطع الحرث والنسل، وينهدم هذا البناء، ويصعق من في الأرض والسماء، وتخرب هذه الدار، وينتقل هذا الأمر إلى الواحد القهّار.

(١٤١) قال أمير المؤمنين وإمام الموحّدين — عليه السلام — في خطب نهج البلاغة مشيرًا إلى دثور العالم وزواله من جهة إثبات الغاية والرجوع إلى البداية:

> كلّ شيء خاضع له وكلّ شيء قائم به، غنى كلّ فقير، وعزّ كلّ ذليل، وقوّة كل ضعيف، ومفزع كلّ ملهوف. من تكلّم سمع نطقه، ومن سكت علم سره، ومن عاش فعليه رزقه، ومن مات فإليه منقلبه.

ثمّ ساق الكلام إلى قوله — عليه السلام — في أحوال الإنسان وولوج الموت فيه على التدريج:

> فلم يزل الموت يبالغ في جسده، حتّى خالط سمعه، فصار بين أهله لا ينطق بلسانه، ولا يسمع بسمعه. يردّد طرفه في وجوههم؛ يرى حركات ألسنتهم، ولا يسمع رجع كلامهم. ثمّ ازداد الموت التياطًا به. فقبض بصره، كما قبض سمعه. وخرجت الروح من جسده. فصار جيفة بين أهله، قد أوحشوا من جانبه، وتباعدوا من قربه. لا يسعد باكيًا، ولا يجيب داعيًا. ثم حملوه إلى محطّ في الأرض. وأسلموه فيها إلى عمله. وانقطعوا عن زورته، حتّى إذا

command of Allah whatever He willeth concerning the renewal of His creation. He will then cause the sky to fall into convulsion and will split it, and [He will] cause the earth to quake and will shake it. He will uproot its mountains and scatter them. They will crush each other out of awe of His majesty and fear of His dominion.

He will then take out everyone who is in it [the earth] and renew them after they have become decrepit and assemble them after they have become scattered. He will then set them apart in order to question them according to His will concerning their hidden actions and secret acts, and [He] will divide them into two groups; He will reward one group and punish the other. As for those who were obedient, He will reward them with proximity to Him and will preserve them forever in His abode, a place from which those who have settled therein are not removed. Their state undergoeth no change, fear overcometh them not, sickness befalleth them not, danger affecteth them not, and there are no journeys to cause them the pain of moving from place to place. As for those who have committed sin, they are made to descend to the worst of places, with their hands tied to their necks, their forelocks to their feet, clothed in shirts of tar and short garments of fire.

بلغ الكتاب أجله، والأمر مقاديره، وألحق آخر الخلق بأوّله. وجاء من أمر الله ما يريده من تجديد خلقه. أمار السماء وقطرها، وأرجّ الأرض وأرجفها وقلع الجبال ونفسها.

ودكّ بعضها بعضًا من هيبة جلاله وبخوف سطوته، وأخرج من فيها. فجدّدهم بعد إخلاقهم، وجمعهم بعد تفريقهم. ثم ميّزهم لما يريده من مساءلتهم عن خفايا الأعمال وخبايا الأفعال، وجعلهم فريقين: أنعم على هؤلاء، و انتقم من هؤلاء. فأما أهل الطاعة، فأثابهم بجواره، وخلّدهم في داره، حيث لا يظعن النزال، ولا يتغيّر الحال، ولا تهولهم الأفزاع، ولا تنالهم الأسقام، ولا يعرض لهم الأخطار ولا تشخصهم الأسفار. فأمّا أهل المعصية، فأنزلهم شرّ دار، وغلّ الأيدي إلى الأعناق، وقرن النواصي بالأقدام، وألبسهم سرابيل القطران ومقطّعات النيران.

[The] Seal of the Treatise

(142) Know that the paths to God—transcendent is He—are multiple because He possesses countless virtues and aspects "and each one hath a goal to which he turneth" ("al-Baqarah," Q. 2:148). However, certain of them are more luminous and of superior virtue, are more rigorous, and possess firmer demonstrations. The most trustworthy path and the one of the greatest virtue leading to Him, His qualities, and His actions is the one in which the middle term in the demonstration is none other than He. In this case, the path leading to the desired object comes from the desired object because He is the proof of all things. And this was the path of all the prophets and the people of sincerity, may the peace of God be upon them all. "Say: This is my way: I call on God with clear vision—I and whosoever followeth me" ("Yūsuf," Q. 12:108). "This is in the earliest books of revelation, the book of Abraham and Moses" ("Aᶜlā," Q. 87:18–19). And these are those who seek the witness of God—transcendent is He—through Himself. "God Himself is witness that there is no God save He" ("Āl ᶜImrān," Q. 3: 18). Then they seek to bear witness through the Divine Essence to His divine attributes and, one after another through His attributes, to His acts and effects.

(143) Others take recourse to the knowledge of His essence—transcendent is He—and of His attributes by the intermediary of something other than He. Thus, the majority of the philosophers take recourse to contingency, the philosophers of nature to the movement of the body [of the universe], the theologians to the creation of the world in time, and so on. And these [foregoing proofs] are also reasons and witnesses. However, this path [of which we have spoken] is the most firm and of the greatest virtue. In fact, it is to these different paths that the divine

خاتمة الرسالة

(١٤٢) اعلم أنّ الطرق إلى الله تعالى كثيرة، لأنّه ذو فضائل وجهات غير عديدة «وَلِكُلٍّ وِجْهَةٌ هُوَ مُوَلِّيهَا» لكن بعضها أنور وأشرف وأحكم وأشدّ البراهين. وأوثقها وأشرفها إليه و إلى صفاته وأفعاله، هو الذي لا يكون الوسط في البرهان غيره. فيكون الطريق إلى البغية من البغية، لأنّه البرهان على كلّ شيء. وهذه سبيل جميع الأنبياء والصدّيقين — سلام الله عليهم أجمعين — «قُلْ هَذِهِ سَبِيلِي أَدْعُو إِلَى اللَّهِ عَلَى بَصِيرَةٍ أَنَا وَمَنِ اتَّبَعَنِي» «إِنَّ هَذَا لَفِي الصُّحُفِ الْأُولَى صُحُفِ إِبْرَاهِيمَ وَمُوسَى» فهؤلاء هم الذين يستشهدون به تعالى عليه «شَهِدَ اللَّهُ أَنَّهُ لا اله إِلا هُوَ» ثمّ يستشهدون بذاته تعالى على صفاته، وبصفاته على أفعاله وآثاره واحدًا بعد واحد.

(١٤٣) وغير هؤلاء يتوسّلون في السلوك إلى معرفته تعالى وصفاته بواسطة أمر آخر غيره، كجمهور الفلاسفة بالإمكان، والطبيعيّين بالحركة للجسم، والمتكلّمين بالحدوث للخلق أو غير ذلك. وهي أيضًا دلائل وشواهد، لكنّ هذا المنهاج أحكم وأشرف. وقد أُشير

book alludes when He—transcendent is He—says: "We shall show them our signs on the horizons and within their souls until it will become manifest unto them that it is the truth" ("Fuṣṣilat," Q. 41:53). And it is to this path that allusion is made in His word: "Doth not thy Lord suffice, since He is witness over all things?" ("Fussilat," Q. 41:53).

(144) The lordly sages (*rabbāniyyūn*) look first of all at the reality of *wujūd*. Then they realize it and come to know that it is the principle of all things and that it is, according to the truth, the Necessary Being. As for contingency, indigence, and the state of being caused, these are conditions adjoined to *wujūd* not because of the reality of *wujūd*, but because of the deficiencies and nonexistence, which are extrinsic to the source of its reality. Then, by looking at what requires necessity and contingency, richness and indigence, they reach the unity of His attributes and, through the understanding of His attributes, [attain] to the how-ness of His states and effects.

(145) In what we have given before in our demonstrations, there is something, in which the light of the Divine Truth shone from the horizon of explanation and the sun of the truth arose from the rising place of gnosis, [proving] that *wujūd*, as we have already said, is a simple reality, possessing neither genus nor specific difference, neither definition nor that by which it can be known, nor a demonstration [that] can be given for it. The difference between its individuals and numbers does not exist, except through perfection and deficiency, anteriority and posteriority, richness and indigence, or [else] in accidental matter, as it is among individuals of a single quiddity. The summit of its perfection is pure *wujūd*, of which there is nothing more perfect; and it is the necessary, simple reality, requiring complete perfection and the most exalted majesty and infinitude of intensity. Therefore, every degree [of *wujūd*] below this degree in intensity is not pure *wujūd*. Rather, it is combined with imperfections and deficiencies.

(146) The deficiency of *wujūd* does not come from the reality of *wujūd*, nor from matters inherent to it, because these deficiencies are nonexistent; and nonexistence is precisely the negation of the principle of *wujūd*, or the negation of its perfection. That is why the First [Being]—transcendent is He—excludes it [non-being] completely, and this matter is evident. Imperfections are not adjoined to the source of *wujūd* but, rather, to the occurrence of *wujūd* on a second level and on all the levels that come after it. Imperfections and negativities occur to the second levels because of their position as second levels and because of

في الكتاب الإلهيّ إلى تلك الطرق بقوله تعالى «سَنُرِيهِمْ آيَاتِنَا فِي الآفَاقِ وَفِي أَنفُسِهِمْ حَتَّى يَتَبَيَّنَ لَهُمْ أَنَّهُ الْحَقُّ» وإلى هذه الطريقة أشار بقوله «أَوَلَمْ يَكْفِ بِرَبِّكَ أَنَّهُ عَلَى كُلِّ شَيْءٍ شَهِيدٌ».

(١٤٤) فالربّانيّون ينظرون إلى حقيقة الوجود أولاً، ويحقّقونها ويعلمون أنّها أصل كلّ شيءٍ وأنّها واجب الوجود بحسب الحقيقة. وأمّا الإمكان والحاجة والمعلوليّة، فإنّما تلحق الوجود لا لأجل حقيقته، بل لأجل نقائض وأعدام خارجة عن أصل حقيقته. ثمّ بالنظر فيما يلزم الوجوب والإمكان، والغنى والحاجة، يصلون إلى توحيد صفاته، ومن صفاته إلى كيفيّة أحواله وآثاره.

(١٤٥) وقد مرّ فيما أسلفنا من البرهان ما بزغ به نور الحقّ من أفق البيان، وطلعت شمس الحقيقة من مطلع العرفان، من أنّ الوجود — كما مرّ — حقيقة بسيطة، لا جنس ولا فصل لها، ولا حدّ لها ولا معّرف لها، ولا برهان عليه، وليس الاختلاف بين آحادها وأعدادها إلا بالكمال والنقص، والتقدّم والتأخّر، والغنى والحاجة، أو بأُمور عارضة كما في أفراد ماهيّة واحدة. وغاية كمالها هي صرف الوجود الذي لا أتمّ منه، وهي حقيقة الواجبيّة البسيطة المقتضية للكمال الأتمّ، والجلال الأرفع، وعدم التناهي في الشدة، إذ كل مرتبة دون تلك المرتبة في الشدّة، ليست هي صرف الوجود، بل مع قصور ونقص.

(١٤٦) وقصور الوجود ليس من حقيقة الوجود، ولا من لوازمه، لأنّة عدم. والعدم سلب أصل الوجود أو سلب كماله، والأوّل تعالى لا يجامعه، وهو ظاهر. فالقصور لاحق لا لأصل الوجود، بل لوقوعه في مرتبة ثانية وما بعدها. فالقصورات والأعدام إنّما طرأت للثواني من حيث ثانويّتها وتأخّرها. فالأوّل على كماله الأتمّ الذي لانهاية له. والعدم

their anteriority. The First Being persists in the most complete perfection, which has no limit, whereas nonexistence and indigence for *wujūd* have their issuing forth in emanation and instauration. It goes without saying that the instaured is not equal to the Instaurer and that emanation is not equal to the Source of emanation in the degree of *wujūd*. Moreover, the ipseities belonging to the secondary levels are suspended hierarchically in relation to the First Being, so that their imperfections are compensated for by its plenitude and their indigence by its richness. The greater the retardation of an existent in relation to the First Being, the greater its deficiencies and negativity.

(147) The first realities that emanate from Him—transcendent is He—are of necessity the most majestic and glorious beings after Him. And this is the creative *wujūd*, which does not possess the quality of contingency except to a certain extent that is veiled by the first Necessary Being. And it is the world of the Divine Command. In it are contained only the sacred spirits that are differentiated from each other by their degree of proximity to the unique Divine Essence, because those sacred spirits are like divine rays. The expression "sacred spirit" signifies their ensemble because they are like a single person. And the sacred spirit is not of this world and does not fall under the saying "Be," because the sacred spirit is precisely the creative command and the Word. And after it [the sacred spirit], there are the levels of the souls in their hierarchy.

(148) After that come natures and forms, according to their own levels. And then [come] the simple bodies, one after the other, to the *materia ultima*, whose condition is pure receptivity and capability. And it is the limit of lowness and darkness. Then *wujūd* is elevated from this matter by the process of becoming more subtle and more perfect. In this way, it returns toward that from which it descended and regresses to that from which it began by a process of excitation of materials, movement of bodies, and creation of celestial heat within the elements, resulting from excitation through the revolution of heavenly luminaries. All of this causes the formation of plants after minerals, pushing compounds to the degree of the acceptance of life and the ardent desire of souls to attain to the degree of the acquired intellect, returning to God, the most munificent.

والافتقار إنّما ينشئان عن الإفاضة والجعل ضرورة أنّ المجعول لا يساوي الجاعل، والفيض لا يساوي الفيّاض في مرتبة الوجود. فهويّات الثواني متعلّقة على ترتيبها بالأوّل، فتنجبر قصوراتها بتمامه وافتقارها بغنائه. وكلّ ما هو أكثر تأخّرًا عنه، فهو أكثر قصورًا وعدمًا.

(١٤٧) فأوّل الصوادر عنه تعالى يجب أن يكون أجلّ الموجودات بعده، وهو الوجود الإبداعيّ الذي لا مكان له إلا ما صار محتجبًا بالوجوب الأوّل، وهو عالم الأمر الإلهيّ. ولا يسع فيه إلا الأرواح القادسة على تفاوتها في القرب من الذات الأحديّة، لأنّها بمنزلة الأضواء الإلهيّة. والعبارة عن جملتها روح القدس، لأنّها كشخص واحد. وهي ليست من العالم، ولا واقعة تحت قول «كن»، لأنّها نفس الأمر والقول. وبعدها مرتبة النفوس على درجاتها.

(١٤٨) ثمّ الطبائع والصور على مراتبها، ثم بسائط الأجسام واحدًا بعد واحد إلى المادّة الأخيرة، التي شأنها القبول والاستعداد، وهي النهاية في الخسّة والظلمة، ثمّ بترقّي الوجود منها بالتلطيف والتكميل راجعًا إلى ما نزل منه، عائدًا إلى ما بدأ منه بتهيّج الموادّ، وتحريك الأجساد، وإحداث الحرارة المهيّجَة السماويّة في الاسطقسات من تداوير النيّرات الموجبة لنشوء النبات بعد الجماد وسياقة المركّبات إلى درجة قبول الحياة وتشويق النفوس إلى أن تبلغ إلى درجة العقل المستفاد الراجعة إلى الله الجواد.

(149) Observe, then, the wisdom of the unique Originator of being, how He originated things and brought beings into existence from degree to degree of excellence. He first generated the sacred lights and active intellects. He cast His theophanies upon them and projected His image upon them. Through them He manifested His actions, and by their intermediary He created the noble bodies, pure and luminous, possessing living souls in constant movement in order to come closer to God and His worship. These celestial bodies He carries in a ship "possessing broad planks and caulked with palm fiber" ("al-Qamar," Q. 54:13), flowing in the ocean of decree and destiny. "In the name of God be its course and its mooring" ("Hūd," Q. 11:41), "and unto thy Lord belongeth the term thereof" ("al-Nāziᶜāt," Q. 79:44).

(150) He made the celestial souls different in motions and gave [them] rays of light that would help in the growth of [sublunary] creatures. Then He created the *hylé* of the elements, which are the lowest of contingent beings and which are the final term in the economy of the divine command. The divine command operates first in descending from heaven to earth. He then operates the ascent toward Himself by bringing into being the minerals from the equilibrium of the elements and the pillars of the corporeal world. Then the plants are created from the purest substance of the elements, and then animals, and finally the human [person]. When the human [state] is perfected through knowledge and perfection, [the person] attains the degree of the Active Intellect. And here terminates the [divine] economy of the good and the munificent, and the final point of the cycle of *wujūd* rejoins the initial point.

This book has been completed with the aid of the
Loving Sovereign, who is the dispenser
of the good and of munificence.

(١٤٩) فانظر إلى حكمة المبدع البديع: كيف أبدع الأشياء وأنشأ الأكوان من الأشرف فالأشرف. فأبدع أوّلاً أنوارًا قدسيّة وعقولاً فعّالة، تجلّى بها وألقى فيها مثاله. فأظهر منها أفعاله، واخترع بتوسطها أجسامًا كريمة صافية نيّرة، ذوات نفوس حيوانيّة، دائمة الحركات تقرّبًا إلى الله وعبوديّة له. وحملها في سفينة «ذَاتِ أَلْوَاحٍ وَدُسُرٍ» جارية في بحر القضاء والقدر «بِسْمِ اللَّهِ مَجْرَاهَا وَمُرْسَاهَا» «إِلَى رَبِّكَ مُنتَهَاهَا»

(١٥٠) وجعلها مختلفة في الحركات. ونسب أضواء النيرات المعدّة لنشوء الكائنات. ثّم خلق هيولى العناصر التي هي أخسّ الممكنات، وهى نهاية تدبير الأمر، فإنّه يدبّر الأمر من السماء إلى الأرض. ثمّ يعرج إليه بتكوين الجماد من تعديل العناصر والأركان. ثّم النبات من صفوتها. ثمّ الحيوان. ثمّ الإنسان. وإذا استكمل بالعلم والكمال، بلغ إلى درجة العقل الفعّال. فيه وقف تدبير الخير والجود، واتّصل بأوّله آخر دائرة الوجود.

تمّ بعون الملك الودود الذي هو

مفيض الخير والوجود.

Notes

1. The word *ᶜirfān*, translated here as "gnosis," is derived from the verb *ᶜa-r-f*, meaning "to know," "to understand," and "to cognize." *ᶜIrfān* refers to a state of deeper understanding and cognition, an epistemic and spiritual ability achieved through such methods as contemplation, reflection, inner purification, and moral refinement. In the later Islamic tradition, the word came to signify a specific method of attaining knowledge, and the expression *ᶜilm al-maᶜrifah* began to be used for metaphysical and theoretical *taṣawwuf*. We have chosen to render it in English as "gnosis" to revive this old meaning of the word. While *gnosis* in English conjures up the Gnostic tradition in early Christianity—a school considered heretical by some—our usage of the word obviously has nothing to do with that particular school of thought in the Christian tradition. But just as the Gnostic Christians' quest was realized knowledge and inner purification, the followers of *ᶜirfān* also expressed a desire to go beyond merely demonstrative arguments in logic and philosophy. Kāshānī, for instance, defined *al-āarif*, the one who knows through *ᶜirfān* and *maᶜrifah*, as someone who "witnesses God Himself, His qualities, names and acts." Accordingly, "*maᶜrifah* is the state that comes about from witnessing Him." Kāshānī, *Iṣṭilāḥāt al-ṣūfiyyah*, 124. For the uses of *ᶜirfān* and *maᶜrifah* in Ibn Sīnā, see A. M. Goichon, *Lexique de la langue philosophique d'Ibn Sīnā (Avicenne)*, 221. In a similar way, al-Ghazālī used *ᶜirfān* and *maᶜrifah* as knowledge based on experience and witnessing (*mushāhadah*); see Jabre, *Essai sur le lexique de Ghazali*, 174–78.

2. *Manāsik*, plural of *mansik*, refers to specific acts and rituals conducted during the pilgrimage (*manasik al-hajj*).

3. Cf. the following statement Ṣadrā made in regards to Suhrawardī's claim that *wujūd* is only a mental concept: "If someone is ignorant about the question of existence, he is of necessity ignorant about all of the principles and foundations of knowledge, for it is through existence that everything is known, and it is the beginning of all description (*taṣawwur*) and more known than anything that provides description. When someone ignores it, he ignores everything besides it. As we have mentioned before, the true knowledge of existence comes about only through unveiling (*kashf*) and witnessing (*mushāhadah*). It has thus been said that 'he who has no unveiling has no knowledge.' It is strange that this great master [i.e., Suhrawardī], after establishing a number of arguments in the *Talwīḥāt* that existence is a mental concept (*iᶜtibārī*) possessing no form and reality in the

external world, explained towards the end of this book that the human souls and what is above them are simple beings without quiddity. Is this not a clear contradiction on his part?" *Al-Shawāhid al-rubūbiyyah*, 14. The expression "He who has no unveiling has no knowledge" comes from Ibn al-ᶜArabī, *Futūḥāt*, 1.218.19, translated in Chittick, *The Sufi Path of Knowledge*, 170.

4. This is based on one of the key principles of Ṣadrā's epistemology: "True demonstration (*al-burhān al-ḥaqīqī*) does not contradict witnessing based on unveiling (*al-shuhūd al-kashfī*)." See Ṣadrā, *Asfār*, 1.2 (315).

5. Ṣadrā's commentator Mullā Muḥammad Lāhījī added: "*Wujūd* itself is presence, manifestation, essential. It is not caused by anything else; rather it is through [*wujūd*] that everything else is manifest and present. It is the principle in manifestation and presence." Lāhījī, *Sharḥ risālat al-mashāᶜir*, 12. Lāhījī's commentary makes it clear that "presence" and "manifestation" refer to the way in which *wujūd* is particularized in the world of creation.

6. For a more detailed discussion of the impossibility of giving a formal-logical definition of *wujūd*, see Ṣadrā, *Asfār*, 1.1 (25).

7. Ṣadrā insisted that no matter how perfect our conceptualizations are, the reality of *wujūd* as it is remains outside the ken of the human mind because the mind operates through concepts and universals. For Ṣadrā, concepts, while indispensable for organizing human thought, have the possibility to distort reality. That is why the true philosopher must constantly check his concepts and arguments against the reality of things. Cf. the following paragraph in *Asfār*, 1.1 (37–38): "Every concrete being represented in the mind with its reality ought to maintain its quiddity, despite the change in its modality of existence. The reality of existence is such that it is in the extramental world (*fī al-aᶜyān*). Everything whose reality is such that it is in the extramental world cannot be found in the mind [as it is]; otherwise, this would lead to the alteration (*inqilāb*) of something from its own reality [into something else]. Therefore, the reality of existence cannot be found in any mind. What is represented of existence in the soul, whereby it takes on universality and generality, is not the reality of existence, but one of the aspects of its constitution and one of its names."

8. As Ṣadrā explained later in paragraph 22, "external" (*fī al-ᶜayn*), which we also rendered as *in concreto*, means a particular state of existence, not a place "out there." Ṣadrā has said: "The meaning of something existing in the external world is that it has an existence from which particular effects result and specific states (*aḥkām*) emanate. Its being in the mind is not like this." *Aṣālat jaᶜl al-wujūd*, 191.

9. *Maṣdarī* can also be translated as "unconditional" because it refers to a state of existence "conditioned by nothing" (*bi-sharṭ lā*). See n. 40 below.

10. Cf. the following: "Beings (*wujūdāt*) are actual identities particularized by themselves. They are not qualified by genus, species, universality, and particularity in the sense that they belong to a species or genus or in the sense that they become particular through something added to them from outside. Rather, they are differentiated by themselves, not through differentia (*faṣl*) or accident (*ᶜaraḍ*). In this sense, they have no genus, differentia, or definition." Ṣadrā, *Asfār*, 1.1 (53).

11. Ṣadrā confirmed that God cannot have a quiddity (*māhiyyah*) because a quiddity is, by definition, something shared by a multitude of subjects. In the case of God, He can be the only member of a class to which He belongs; otherwise, divine unity is jeopardized. It is important to note that while Ṣadrā introduced "meanings and quiddities" to account for differentiation and particularization among things, he posited *wujūd* as the only principle of both identity and difference.

12. The word *shumūl* does not have an exact equivalent in English. It refers to something that applies to many things, comprises many members, and includes or encapsulates multiplicities. But as Ṣadrā explained, *wujūd*'s encapsulation or comprising of all things is different from generic concepts being applied to more than one member: "Existence's encapsulation of things is not like the universal's encapsulation of particulars, but through expansion (*inbisāṭ*) and flow (*sarayān*) in the temples of essences in such a way that no full description of it can be given." *Al-Maẓāhir al-ilāhiyyah*, 26–27.

13. Ṣadrā equated the natural universal with quiddity (*māhiyyah*) in *Asfār*, 3.1, 472.

14. It is clear from the paragraph that *shumūl al-wujūd* is a creative act by which God creates and fashions things in the way they are. Lāhījī explained this with the notion of "relative truth" (*al-ḥaqq al-iḍāfī*): "the reality by which things are created . . . that is to say, the relative truth which is created by the true [absolute] truth (*al-ḥaqq al-ḥaqīqī*) without an instrument or by the truth through which things are created." *Sharḥ risālat al-mashāʿir*, 23.

15. Cf. the following: "Existence in everything is the principal reality in existentiation, and it is the principle of its particularity, the source of its quiddity, and the measure of its essence. Existence belongs to the category of things that allow intensification and diminution in terms of perfection and imperfection, and it has essential qualities and modes in every degree of intensification and diminution as different from what it had before." Ṣadrā, *Ittiḥād al-ʿāqil*, 22.

16. The language of "effects (*āthār*) and conditions (*aḥkām*)" confirms the creative act of *wujūd* through which things come to be what they are. It is not the case that *wujūd* exerts an effect on things that are already fully established. Rather, it is *wujūd* that makes and shapes them by throwing its "effects and conditions" on them. Lāhījī quoted the following statement from ʿAbd al-Razzāq Qāshānī: "*Wujūd* is the *wujūd* of something, not something that exists." *Sharḥ risālat al-mashāʿir*, 32.

17. A further discussion of these concepts appears in paragraph 42.

18. Essential primary predication refers to predication where the predicate is an essential part of the definition of the subject. In this kind of predication, subject and predicate are one and the same, both in concept and in reality. Existential propositions such as "man is man" are of this kind. Although existential propositions are tautological and yield no new knowledge about the predicate, they play an important role in logic. Having said that, essential primary predications are also applied to such propositions as "man is a rational animal," whereby "rational animal" is essential for the definition of "man." The second kind of predication, called "common predication" (*ḥaml shāiʿī ṣināʿī*) or simply "secondary predication"

(*ḥaml thānī*), refers to predication where the predicate is not an essential property of the subject. The proposition "man is a writer" is of this kind in that being a writer is a quality shared by some human beings but not an essential part of the definition of man. Cf. *Asfār*, 1.3 (324–25, 351).

19. As Ṣadrā explained in the next paragraph, all things exist through a composition of *wujūd* and *māhiyyah*, the only exception being *wujūd* itself. Ṣadrā's concern was to show that *wujūd* exists by itself and does not need any other agent—such as a quiddity, substance, or cause—to make it exist, either in a generic or a specific way. This is the primacy of *wujūd* over quiddity (*aṣālat al-wujūd*), a principal teaching that Ṣadrā developed and defended in his works. This is also a criticism of Suhrawardī, who argued that *wujūd* does need the quiddity in order to exist. For Ṣadrā's criticism, see *Asfār*, 1.1 (41, 66).

20. Ṣadrā asserted the self-determination of *wujūd* as follows: "It becomes determined by itself, without the addition of anything else, with all of the existential determinations and external realizations. It is better to say that external realities are generated from the degrees of its essence and modes of its determinations and states. It is the principle of the cosmos, the sphere of life, the Throne of the Merciful, the 'real through whom creation takes place' in the tradition of the Sufis, and the Truth of all truths. In its very unity, it becomes many with the multiplicity of existents united with quiddities. Thus, it becomes eternal with eternal, temporally originated with temporally originated, intelligible with intelligible, and sensible with sensible. In this regard, people think that it is a universal, but it is not. Expressions used to explain its expansion on the quiddities and its comprehensiveness of existents are deficient signs, [and it cannot be expressed] except through symbol and similitude." *Asfār*, 1.2 (328).

21. Dāwūd al-Qayṣarī, a prominent figure of the school of Ibn al-ᶜArabī and one of the sources of Ṣadrā's metaphysics, added the following: "Existence, insofar as it is being, is predicated of all relational beings (*al-wujūdāt al-muḍāfah*) because we say that: [this particular] being exists. And whatever is predicated of things has to have a relationship of unity and difference towards them. In the case of existence [as predicated of things], that which unites [that is, the principle of unity] is nothing but existence, and that which differentiates [that is, the principle of difference] is again existence itself." *Muqaddamāt*, 36.

22. In Ṣadrā's vocabulary, this is known as the "principle of derivation" (*al-qaʾidah al-farᶜiyyah*). It states that if one affirms a quality or a property of something, this presupposes the affirmation of the actual reality of that thing in the first place. In order to predicate whiteness of the "white wall," the wall must exist before the predicate white. Ṣadrā's main point is that *wujūd*, in its all-embracing reality, precedes all predicates, qualities, and properties. Every predicative statement regarding existing bodies presupposes the preexisting reality of *wujūd*.

23. As Lāhījī put it: "The realization of *wujūd* happens [through the modality of being] in the external world, and the quiddity is united with it in the external world in the sense that the quiddity corroborates it and occurs to it [as a quality]." *Sharḥ risālat al-mashāᶜir*, 54.

24. Ṣadrā wanted to make sure that the relationship between *wujūd* and quiddity is not understood to be a relationship between two independent and self-

subsisting entities. Rather, *wujūd* is the source, principle, and cause of all attributions. That is why he brought up the example of the Necessary Being: things are dependent upon the Necessary Being in an absolute sense. For Ṣadrā, contingent beings vis-à-vis the Necessary Being are "pure relations" (*rawābiṭ maḥḍah*) and thus possess no substantiality on their own. Cf. *Asfār*, 1.3 (37).

25. As indicated in the previous paragraphs and made clear by the quote from Bahmanyār, Ibn Sīnā's famous student, the concrete reality of existence is twofold: First, it exists in a generic or absolute way, without qualification by anything. *Wujūd qua wujūd* exists in such a way as to let other things exist as particular beings. In this sense, *wujūd* also exists as a particular being, such as Zayd, the sky, and so forth. This second aspect of *wujūd* does not contradict its first aspect, because when we say, "Zayd exists," we refer both to the fact that such a person as Zayd exists and to the fact that Zayd exists as a concrete being. Furthermore, being *qua* tree or being *qua* table exists through predication in that the qualities of being tree or table are predicated of being to make it a specific object. But the First Being, or what Plotinus has called Non-Being, remains above any predication and qualification. It is this non-predicative Being that is the source and principle of all beings. For this aspect of Non-Being in Plotinus, see Kenney, *Mystical Monotheism*, 136–37. This specific question of ontology is part of a larger issue in metaphysics. The Muslim philosophers had to develop a metaphysics of impersonal divine principle on the one hand and a theology of personal God on the other. Theologically, God is absolute and beyond all qualification. But He is also creating, speaking, hearing, forgiving, and so on.

26. The word *jaʿl*, translated here as "instauration," and its derivatives *jāʿil* and *majʿūl* occupy a special place in Ṣadrā's philosophical vocabulary. Briefly stated, it signifies putting something into a specific state or condition in conformity with its essential properties. Ṣadrā divides it into two kinds: simple and composite. Simple instauration refers to the construction of something by itself—when we say, for instance, "man is man." In logic, this corresponds to essential primary predication (*al-ḥaml al-dhātī al-awwalī*). As for composite instauration, it refers to cases where the definition of a quiddity involves the convergence of both essential and accidental properties, such as when we say, "Man is a rational animal" and "Man is a writer." For Ṣadrā, what is instaured by itself (*al-majʿūl bi'l-dhāt*) is not essence, but *wujūd*, because *wujūd* does not need an external agent to make it a specific substance, whereas all essences need some cause external to them in order to exist in the external world. In this sense, essences are instaured, or produced "by accident" (*al-majʿūl bi'l-ʿaraḍ*). Cf. *Asfār*, 1.1 (65–66); *Aṣālat jaʿl al-wujūd*, 184–85; *Sharḥ risālat al-mashāʿir*, 2:805. See also Ṣadrā's extensive analysis in *Asfār*, 1.1 (396–423), concerning concept (*taṣawwur*) and judgment (*taṣdīq*) as cases of simple and composite instauration.

27. The word *ʿurūḍ*, derived from the root *ʿa-r-ḍ*, does not have an equivalent in English. Its verbal form denotes something "becoming an accident to" or "occurring to" something. Lāhījī defined it as "something being existent for something else." *Sharḥ risālat al-mashāʿir*, 65. Since "accidenting" does not make much sense, we have rendered it in several ways. In the translation, however, the link between something *being* an accident and something *becoming* an accident is lost.

28. According to Gutas, Ibn Sīnā uses *muḥaṣṣil* "to describe the most accomplished philosophers in the Aristotelian tradition, and in particular Alexander of Aphrodisias." *Avicenna and the Aristotelian Tradition*, 189. Ṣadrā seemed to follow Ibn Sīnā in this particular issue.

29. This premise is related to the famous debate as to whether existence is an accident or not. Ṣadrā rejected the idea of existence being an accident because accidents are, by definition, dependent upon those of which they are accidents. Concerning Ibn Sīnā's statement that "existence is an accident in things with quiddities to which existence is attached, as we see in the case of ten categories" (*Mubāḥathāt*, 154), Ṣadrā argued that what Ibn Sīnā meant here is a special kind of accident in the sense that contingent beings derive or borrow their existence from the Necessary Being. In other words, it is only in relation to the source of being that existence can be considered an accident. *Asfār*, 1.1 (48; see also 258).

30. In contrast to the Peripatetics, Ṣadrā took existence, rather than the Aristotelian fixed substances, as the primary agent of qualitative and quantitative change in his natural philosophy. For Ṣadrā, when an object becomes black, it does not simply assume blackness as an accident. While this is true as far as the black object is concerned, what really happens is that the *wujūd* of that object increases in blackness. This general principle applies to substances as well: when substances realize their potentials, they increase in existence, rather than simply taking on new properties as accidents. Peripatetics and Suhrawardī had a difficult time explaining quantitative change because their ontology had practically no room for gradation in existence. Ṣadrā noted this: "The problem of motion [in the sense of change] in the category of quantity . . . caused later thinkers many problems—so much so that the author of [*Ḥikmat*] *al-ishrāq* [Suhrawardī] and his followers denied it by saying that adding a definite quantity to another quantity necessitates its dissolution." *Asfār*, 1.3 (89–90). See also the discussion by F. Rahman, *The Philosophy of Mullā Ṣadrā*, 99–100.

31. *Ṣūrah ʿayniyyah*, a concrete or objective form in the extramental world. This usage of the word *ṣūrah* reveals its epistemic and ontological functions. In epistemology, form is that by which we know things. In ontology, form is that by which a thing is what it is. Ṣadrā says that "in our view, what is meant by the form is *wujūd*, not a generic concept." *Asfār*, 1 (332; see also 294, 307). In both cases, *ṣūrah* is contrasted to *māddah*—a tradition that goes back to Aristotelian hylomorphism. Like the previous Muslim philosophers, Ṣadrā accepts Peripatetic hylomorphism in broad outlines. But his metaphysics of being makes hylomorphism rather secondary.

32. In other words, *wujūd* is more than the total sum of existing beings (*mawjūdāt*) that issue forth from it. Cf. *Asfār*, 1.1 (54), where Ṣadrā provided a discussion of why *wujūd* is always more than its manifestations.

33. As Lāhījī commented, the difference between essential necessity and pre-eternal necessity concerns the creation and preservation of beings. When things exist *in concreto*, they exist through a kind of necessity that is conditional upon their source of existence. In relation to their source, they exist necessarily; but in relation to themselves, they exist only as pure relations or as mere shadows. This pertains to what Ṣadrā calls "essential necessity." "Pre-eternal necessity" refers to

God's act of creation that, when it happens, necessitates things into existence. Cf. *Sharḥ risālat al-mashāʿir*, 83.

34. In the *Asfār*, Ṣadrā provided the following answer to the same question: "The meaning of the Necessary Being is that it necessitates its own existence and reality by itself, without being in need of any active agent and performer, whereas the meaning of the realization of existence by itself is that when it is realized, it is either by itself, like the Necessary Being, or through an active agent whose realization is not in need of another existence by which it subsists. This realization takes place only after the effect of the agent with its existence and its qualification with existence." *Asfār*, 1.1 (40–41).

35. As Ṣadrā stated in the *Asfār* and other works, the distinction between *wujūd* and *māhiyyah* is a "rational operation of the mind" (*iʿtibār al-ʿaql*). It is not the case that things are composed of two separate qualities called existence and quiddity, which the mind puts together. It is the opposite: beings exist as single units, and the mind analyzes them into existence and quiddity. Ṣadrā put it as follows: "Beings (*wujūdāt*) are actual identities particularized by themselves. They are not qualified by genus, species, universality, and particularity in the sense that they belong to a species or genus or in the sense that they become particular through something added to them from outside. Rather, they are differentiated by themselves, not through differentia (*faṣl*) or accident (*ʿaraḍ*). In this sense, they have no genus, differentia, or definition." *Asfār*, 1.1 (53).

36. Like the word *muḥaṣṣilīn*, Ṣadrā uses the word *al-muḥaqqiqīn* to refer to some of the prominent philosophers with whom he associates himself. Literally, the word means "those who verify the truth." It plays a significant role in the school of Ibn al-ʿArabī.

37. Ṣadrā asserted that the relation between *wujūd* and quiddity is not causal but ontological. *Wujūd* does not simply precede quiddity and other states of existence in terms of temporal priority; it does so through a generative act.

38. For Ṣadrā, the kind of cognition proper to *wujūd* is different from knowing its different modalities, such as sensation, imagination, and abstraction. We can have an intuition of *wujūd* through "illuminative presence and real witnessing," but even this experience of *wujūd* is bound to remain subjective and mental. At any rate, knowledge by presence (*al-ʿilm al-ḥuḍūrī*) is the best possible way to perceive the reality of *wujūd*. Cf. *Asfār*, 3.1 (292ff).

39. Lāhījī commented: "The reality (*kunh*) of *wujūd* is not actualized [in the mind] because its reality is itself the external reality, the source of [existential] effects and the source of particularization and mental [qualities]. What is actualized in the mind is an aspect of universality and ambiguity. They [the two modes of being] are separate from one another and do not join, and the transformation of one into another is without addition and diminution. The *wujūd* of every existent is what dispels nonexistence, and it is external reality because the "external" and the "mind" are not receptacles and places. Rather, they are *wujūd*, which is called "external" when [existential] effects occur to it and is called "mental" when [these effects] do not occur to it." *Sharḥ risālat al-mashāʿir*, 104.

40. Referring to existence "conditioned by nothing" (*bi-sharṭ lā*) as opposed to "unconditioned by anything" (*lā bi-sharṭ shayʾ*). The difference between the two is

one of degree and modality and can be compared to the difference between "whiteness" and "white." While "whiteness" refers to an accident, "white" refers to an object that has whiteness as an accident. Cf. Āshtiyānī's note in Lāhījī's *Sharḥ risālat al-mashāʿir*, 138. Dāwūd al-Qayṣarī makes the following comment: "Know that existence insofar as it is existence—namely, existence *qua* existence (*min ḥaythu huwa*)—is different from external and mental existence. Each of these (modes) is a species of it. Therefore, existence insofar as it is existence—namely, existence not conditioned by anything (*lā bi-sharṭ shayʾ*)—is not limited by absoluteness and delimitation. [In this sense,] it is neither universal nor particular, neither general nor specific, and neither one with a [numerical] oneness added to its essence [*a posteriori* and from outside] nor many. On the contrary, it necessitates these things [meaning these qualities] in accordance with its degrees and stages, to which God refers as 'He is the One who raises the degrees and possesses the Throne.' And it becomes absolute, conditioned, universal, particular, general, specific, one, and many without there being any change in its essence and reality." *Muqaddamāt*, 29.

41. Ṣadrā's concern was to establish *wujūd* as the primary constituting agent in particular beings. When we say, "A tree exists," it is not the case that there are two things: *wujūd* on the one hand and the tree on the other. Rather, in the case of an existing tree, *wujūd* exists "as a tree," and the tree is a particular modality of *wujūd*. In contrast to Suhrawardī and his followers, this peculiar relationship between *wujūd* and its particularizations prevents any regression and vicious circle.

42. The relationship between existence and quiddity is not like the relationship between two independently existing entities: "*Wujūd* is the principal reality in existence, and the quiddity is derived from it." *Asfār*, 1.3, 373.

43. I.e., the "principle of derivation" (*al-qāʿidah al-farʿiyyah*), discussed in n. 22 above.

44. Ṣadrā relegated all existential attributes, properties, and qualifications to the self-subsistent and all-inclusive reality of *wujūd*. In its various modalities, *wujūd* is particularized by itself, not by something exterior to it. The diversification and particularization of *wujūd* stems from the internal structure of the *wujūd* itself. It is the mind that analyzes these modalities as quiddities and properties that qualify *wujūd*. In reality, they are nothing but the manifestation of the self-delimiting act of *wujūd*. Cf. *Asfār*, 1.1, 44–46. See also *al-Masāʾil al-qudsiyyah*, 207–8.

45. As Lāhījī pointed out, the principle of derivation does not apply to *wujūd* and *māhiyyah*, because the relationship between the two is not one of qualification (*ittiṣāl*), but unification (*ittiḥād*). "Applying qualification to *wujūd* and *māhiyyah* belongs to a wider category because qualification is between two [separate] things from the point of view of actualization, and it means [a kind of] occurring (*al-ʿurūḍ*). But qualification can be used in a sense more general than occurring and unification. What is meant by qualification here is unification from the point of view of realization. The principle of derivation requires two separate things in terms of realization; whereas *wujūd* and its relation [to quiddity] and *māhiyyah* fall outside this [consideration]." *Sharḥ risālat al-mashāʿir*, 117–18. The distinction between *ittiṣāl* and *ittiḥād* has a long history in Islamic philosophy and plays a key role in Ṣadrā's ontology and epistemology. Besides his other works,

Ṣadrā devoted a separate treatise to the question of unification called *Ittiḥād al-ᶜāqil wa'l-maᶜqūl* (Unification of the Intellector and the Intelligible). For Ṣadrā's discussion of the three types of unification, see *Ittiḥād*, 22–24. For the English translation of the treatise, see Kalin, *Knowledge in Later Islamic Philosophy*, 256–86.

46. This is a key element of Ṣadrā's ontology: *wujūd* exists both as *wujūd* and as concrete-specific entities. Things are real not because they are specific or have such-and-such qualities, but because they partake of the reality of *wujūd*. While Ṣadrā makes a clear distinction between *wujūd* and *mawjūd* (something that exists), he also states that what really exists in reality is nothing other than *wujūd*. The "thing that really exists" (*al-mawjūd al-ḥaqīqī*) is existence (*wujūd*): "The existent is existence and its modes (*aṭwār*), affairs (*shu'ūn*), and modalities (*anḥā'*)." *Asfār*, 1.2, 341.

47. This is the problem of mental existence to which Ṣadrā devoted considerable space in his works. For a clear analysis, see Rizvi, *Mulla Sadra and Metaphysics*, 77–101.

48. This is an indirect response to those who consider *wujūd* an accident just like any other quality or property. As mentioned before, *wujūd* appears to be an accident that comes to inhere in actually existing beings. This was the position taken by Ibn Sīnā. But even if we admit that *wujūd* is an accident, it is a special accident in the sense that things receive *wujūd* from the Source of *wujūd*—namely, the Necessary Being—as something by which they exist. Ṣadrā's concern was to distinguish the relationship between *wujūd* and *māhiyyah* from all other comparable relations. To use one of Ṣadrā's examples, the body as an actually existing quiddity can exist without the quality or accident of whiteness because a body can be white, black, or red. Accidents do not add anything to the existential constitution of actually existing beings. But this is not the case with *wujūd*, because it is the Source of existence and nothing can exist and have any property without it.

49. One of the principles of classical Islamic philosophy going back to the Greeks states that the mind can know only forms, not matter. In other words, the mind can know things as universals; it cannot perceive their sensate and material properties. Al-Fārābī was the first Muslim philosopher to state this principle with considerable clarity: "As for the occurrence of the form in the intellect, it happens when the form of a thing exists in the intellect as singular and unattached into matter . . . and as disengaged from all with which it is connected. In short, sensible objects are not known; sensibles are parables for what can be known." Al-Fārābī, *Jawābāt li-masā'il su'ila ᶜanhā*, 104. The mind not only turns actually existing beings into abstract, generic, and universal concepts, but it also prioritizes what is conceptual in them. Ṣadrā put it as follows: "Essence is united with existence *in concreto* in a kind of essential unity (*ittiḥād*). When the mind analyzes them into two things, it asserts the precedence of one over the other *in concreto*. Now, this [reality that precedes the other] is existence, because it is the principle of being the reality emanating from the [First] Principle (*al-mabda'*). As for the essence, it is united with and predicated of existence, not like an attached accident, but in its own reality [as essentially united with existence]. Insofar as the mind is concerned, the essence precedes the latter [namely, existence] because essence is the principle in mental judgments." *Asfār*, 1.1 (56).

50. The five types of anteriority (*taqaddum*) can be explained as follows: Anteriority by nature applies to cases such as the whole preceding the part. Anteriority by causality refers to causal priority, as in the case of the finger with which the ring moves. Anteriority by time implies temporal sequence, such as today preceding tomorrow. The other two types of anteriority have an axiological and normative dimension. Anteriority by rank or degree and anteriority by dignity (*afḍal*) refer to the place of things or states in a hierarchical order. A saint has a higher spiritual state and thus precedes others in rank. Cf. Corbin's note in *Le livre des pénétrations métaphysiques*, 149. It is clear that this system of anteriority and posteriority introduces a hierarchical order of things and extends from physical beings to spiritual beings. This hierarchy is generated and sustained by the gradational nature of existence (*tashkīk al-wujūd*), whereby *wujūd* manifests itself in different degrees and gradations of intensity and weakness. In the *Asfār*, Ṣadrā explained this being-centered hierarchy as follows: "As for its equivocal predication by primacy, priority, precedence, and intensity, this is so because, as we shall explain, existence requires itself in some beings, has precedence in some in terms of its nature, and is more perfect and stronger in some others. A being that has no cause has priority in existence compared to others and is, by definition, prior to all other beings. By the same token, the existence of each one of the active intellects has a priority over the existence of other intellects, and the existence of substance is prior to the existence of accident." *Asfār*, 1.1 (36). It should be noted that Ṣadrā took this paragraph almost verbatim from Ibn Sīnā's student Bahmanyār: "Know that existence is predicated of what is under it equivocally, not univocally. This means that an existence that has no cause precedes by nature an existence that has a cause. By the same token, the existence of substances precedes the existence of accidents. Similarly, some beings are stronger and some weaker. One cannot say that existence is a generic term predicated, for instance, on the existence of man, donkey, and stars univocally, like the colors yellow and red. As you shall learn, some things are prior to others, and the meaning of this is that the existence (*wujūd*) of those things is prior to the existence of other things; not that thing-ness (*al-jismiyyah*) itself is prior to thing-ness. Therefore, when we say that cause is prior to effect, it means that its existence is prior to the existence of the effect." Bahmanyār, *Kitāb al-taḥṣīl*, 281.

51. As the examples of *materia prima* and light imply, the penetration of *wujūd* into the world of particular beings is not based on a mechanical model. Rather, it encapsulates and fills the world of beings in the same way that the light of the sun shines upon dark objects. While this analogy gives an idea about the particular modalities of *wujūd*, it runs the risk of assuming self-existing beings before or without the prior agency of *wujūd*. But as Ṣadrā repeatedly states, *wujūd* does not come to things that already exist. It makes them exist as it forms and shapes them in myriad ways.

52. Such universal categories as species, genus, and specific difference, into which we divide things, do not exist in the extramental world. They are mental constructions that enable us to classify, analyze, and thus better understand things. What exists outside is a man who writes as a single and unified being, not

something composed of a person on the one hand and a writer on the other. Ṣadrā does not go into it here, but it is clear that this point had been raised by the Muᶜtazilites and some philosophers to explain the precise relationship between God and His names and qualities. The Ashᶜarites made a distinction between God and His names and qualities to save God from change, which implied imperfection for the Greeks and the Muslim philosophers who followed them. The divine essence had to stay above and beyond all names and qualities that account for God's actions in the world, such as creating, forming, hearing, speaking, forgiving, and punishing. But the Ashᶜarite theology never succeeded fully in explaining how God's names and qualities are different from but at the same time identical with God himself. The Muᶜtazilite answer was similar to what Ṣadrā described here concerning the relationship between *wujūd* and its particular instantiations. For them, God's names and qualities were not separate from His essence. Rather, God is both Himself and loving, creating, forgiving, and so on, all at the same time. In other words, when we say that God is a speaker (*mutakallim*), what we mean is that "God speaks," not that God has the quality of speech. For Ṣadrā's discussion of God's names and qualities, see *Asfār*, 3.1 (121), where Ṣadrā quoted al-Fārābī to affirm the identity of God's essence with His names and qualities.

53. As Ṣadrā (paragraph 94) further elaborates, *wujūd* and its individuations are one and the same thing in the sense that *wujūd* remains the generic source and particular modality of all things. Given the centrality of existence, it is a mistake to explain particular beings in terms of substance, cause, or substratum.

54. As this and the following two paragraphs make clear, accidents are second-order beings that are, in turn, derived from the first-order reality of *wujūd*.

55. Ṣadrā's short autobiography in *Asfār*, 1.1 (11), describes this dramatic change in terms of both an intellectual and a spiritual transformation.

56. Given the unrealness of quiddities in Ṣadrā's metaphysics, his employment of *māhiyyah* as "fixed essences" (*al-aᶜyān al-thābitah*) needs to be explained. Fixed essences refer to the universal patterns according to which entities receive the particular form of their existence. In this sense, they do not belong to the world of actually existing beings. They have an existence of their own only in relation to *wujūd* and its particularizations. Lāhījī explained this point as follows: "Existences are effects that come about by way of effusion (*fayḍ*) from the instaurer. The relation of effusion to the source of effusion is like the relation of a ray to the source of the ray itself. Existences are illuminative effusions from the *wujūd*, which is the true reality and is purely self-subsisting to the essences of contingent beings and fixed quiddities (*al-māhiyyāt al-thābitāt*). Relations between existences are themselves the realization of things; the quiddities have no realization in principle and by themselves. They have not smelled the perfume of existence primarily and by themselves; rather, the judgment of existence applies to them only in relation to what is attached to them [in the extramental world]. There are two ways of looking at contingent beings and particular things that exist in the world: [The first is] summary consideration, by which they are judged to exist and [by which] they do exist. [The second is] detailed consideration, because every contingent being is a composite pair and has two aspects: the aspect that looks toward its Lord, and

the aspect that looks toward itself. The aspect of the Lord is *wujūd* [and is] included in the exception [which states that] 'everything is perishing except its [His] Face.' The aspect of itself is the quiddity included in the things that perish by themselves and have not smelled the perfume of existence. . . . That is why it has been said that quiddities are nonexistent by themselves and existent [only] in judgment." *Sharḥ risālat al-mashāʿir*, 147.

57. Here Ṣadrā reverts back to the standard meaning of *māhiyyah*.

58. The rich connotations of *fatḥ*, rendered as "open(ing)," are lost in translation. As Lāhījī and Āshtiyānī point out, Ṣadrā's use of the word here is not casual; it alludes to understanding a subtle point as a special gift from God. "Close opening" (*fatḥ qarīb*), "clear opening" (*fatḥ mubīn*), and "absolute opening" (*fatḥ muṭlaq*) refer to different modes and degrees of spiritual illumination and unveiling "from the station of the heart and the disclosure of God's Attributes and Perfections." Cf. *Sharḥ risālat al-mashāʿir*, 149–50.

59. This paragraph is a response to the Peripatetic and Ishrāqī understanding of the particularization of *wujūd* through species. For the Peripatetics, the species refers to an actually existing and delimiting property by which things are distinguished from one another. While Ṣadrā agrees with this interpretation at one level, he rejects it at another level when he posits *wujūd* as the reality that accounts for both identity and difference in existence. "Noble sciences" translates *al-ʿulūm al-sharīfah*. *ʿUlūm* is the plural of *ʿilm*, meaning both "knowledge" and what we now call "science" and "discipline." It makes more sense to understand the term *ʿulūm* as the plural of knowledge and understanding rather than as any particular science. As Lāhījī pointed out in *Sharḥ risālat al-mashāʿir*, 153–54, the reference to "noble knowledge" indicates the subtlety of the point Ṣadrā was making in the paragraph.

60. For references to Suhrawardī as a Stoic, see *Asfār*, 3.1 (181); 1.3 (291). For the relation between Suhrawardī and "Stoicism" in Islamic philosophy, see Walbridge, *The Leaven of the Ancients*, 187–90.

61. Lāhījī makes an important observation about this point. Considered in themselves, all things are self-referential. In the larger scale of things, however, everything is related to everything else all the way to God, who, as the Cause of all causes, stands above causal links. Lāhījī noted that everything has two aspects: one in regard to itself and the other in regard to its Lord. In regard to their Lord, things exist as real beings but also as an emanation from God. In regard to themselves, they exist as "quiddities which have not smelled the smell of [real] existence." This dual nature of things penetrates the entire creation and explains the dialectical relationship between God and His creation. Cf. *Sharḥ risālat al-mashāʿir*, 161.

62. As discussed above, *jaʿl* designates a particular mode of existentiating whereby an already-existing being is made to exist in a certain way. Rahman renders *jaʿl* as "causation," but it is clear that what is involved here is more than simply something causing something else. Rather, *jaʿl* refers to a process of existentiating whereby something comes to exist in a way specific to the nature of that thing. Ṣadrā's main point is that it is *wujūd* and not quiddity that makes things into

concrete and specific beings. Therefore, *wujūd* remains fully active throughout the process of existing.

63. This Aristotelian argument (*Posterior Analytics* 71b 10) has been widely used and expanded upon in the Islamic philosophical tradition. Ṣadrā agreed that the full knowledge of something can be achieved only when its cause is known. In a hierarchical sort of way, this goes all the way to God as the ultimate Cause of all things: to fully know the world, one needs to know God. This can be taken to be a version of what medieval Christian philosophers would call "natural theology," whereby one moves from the knowledge of the world to the knowledge of God. But Ṣadrā also refined the argument by saying that "the knowledge of the building does not necessitate the knowledge of the builder but leads to the knowledge of the need of the building for its builder." *Asfār*, 1.3 (397). In other words, we have an idea about the generic knowledge of the cause but cannot know it in its full details on our own. In the language of theology, this refers to the need for revelation and prophets for a proper knowledge and worship of God.

64. Ṣadrā's concern was to emphasize the difference between the order of thought and the order of existence. From the point of view of the mind, everything is analyzed as belonging to the order of thought, where predication, judgment, qualification, derivation, "occurring," or "accidenting" (*ᶜurūḍ*) and other modalities of relation take precedence over *wujūd* and its modalities. For Ṣadrā, the Peripatetics and the Illuminationists had failed to understand the full implications of the difference between the concept (*mafhūm*) and the reality (*ḥaqīqah*) of beings. All other philosophical errors result from confounding the two orders of reality. For Ṣadrā's discussion of this point, see *Asfār*, 1.1 (37–49). For an analysis of this point in the school of Mullā Ṣadrā, see Izutsu, *The Concept and Reality of Existence*.

65. Ṣadrā insisted that *wujūd* remains the same in its essence even when it is particularized "a thousand times." A tree is a tree not because it has a quiddity called "tree-ness," which is secondary to its existential constitution, but because it is the form or essence in which *wujūd* has been particularized. Instead of saying that "a tree exists," it would be more proper to say that "*wujūd* exists as a tree." In the former, the emphasis is on the essence, whereas the latter underlies the priority of *wujūd*. As is clear from the preceding discussions, what is essential is to understand the way in which *wujūd* particularizes and manifests itself, not how quiddities come to be named.

66. The insertion of the word *muḥaqqiqūn* (the verifiers) shows Ṣadrā's attachment to the school of Ibn al-ᶜArabī. It seems that Ṣadrā inserted the word to draw attention to the subtlety of the point he is making concerning the relationship between *wujūd* and its modalities.

67. *Lawāzim*, which is the plural of *lāzim* and has been rendered here as "concomitant," refers to an essential aspect of things that is required by their own nature. The *lāzim* of something expresses both logical and ontological necessity. For instance, the fact that light makes things visible is a logical necessity of the definition and existence of light. When Ṣadrā says that "the concomitants of quiddity are conceptual notions," he refers to the mental-conceptual nature of the quiddities. Since the quiddities are eventually mental abstractions created by the mind, their

corresponding reality is notions and concepts, not actually existing properties. Therefore, instauration as a subset of existentiating can take place only at the level of existential effects and properties. Cf. the note by Āshtiyānī in *Sharḥ risālat al mashāʿir*, 169.

68. Ṣadrā devoted considerable space to the way in which *wujūd* generates the world of multiplicity and interacts with it. This is understandable, given his attempt to construct a dynamic cosmology underpinned by a gradational ontology. Unlike Aristotle, whose metaphysics was based on fixed substances and a static world order, Ṣadrā saw everything undergoing an existential journey. His famous concept to describe this is substantial motion (*al-ḥarakat al-jawhariyyah*), which upholds that all existing beings, including substances, undergo substantial change to reach their *telos* (*ghāyah*). In contrast to the Peripatetic tradition, Ṣadrā allowed change in substances because he defined them in terms of existence and its degrees of existentiating. For more on this, see Kalin, "Between Physics and Metaphysics," 65–93. Concerning the way in which *wujūd* "penetrates" into the world of creation through instauration, substantial motion, and other forms of existentiating, Ṣadrā used an elaborate vocabulary and borrowed several terms from Ibn al-ʿArabī—for instance, "flow of existence" (*sarayān al-wujūd*) in *Asfār*, 1.1 (67, 146, 381) and 1.2 (327), "expanding existence" (*al-wujūd al-munbasiṭ*) in *Asfār*, 1.2 (328, 331–33) and 3.2 (10–11), and "Breath of the Compassionate" (*nafas al-raḥmān*) in *Asfār*, 2.3 (5) and 1.1 (47, 164, 381), to describe the flow of existence into the various levels and planes of being. Ibn al-ʿArabī uses the richly suggestive term "Breath of the Compassionate" for the generation and sustenance of the universe with God's "Breath." See Chittick, *The Sufi Path of Knowledge*, 127–30, and idem., *The Self-Disclosure of God*, 69–70.

69. This is a key point in Ṣadrā's metaphysics and pertains to his conception of the universe as a living being. Ṣadrā's "cosmological vitalism" is thoroughly ontological and thus different from the Bergsonian élan vital. Rather, it is based on a particular understanding of existence as the creative Act of God. For Ṣadrā, "whatever is established in existence is capable of being intelligible even potentially." *Ittiḥād*, 71. Ṣadrā considered this to be self-evident because *wujūd* contains in itself all of the primary and secondary qualities, including life, intelligence, volition, and goodness. But "the majority of intelligent people are incapable of understanding the penetration of knowledge, power, and volition in all things, including stones and inanimate objects, just like the penetration of existence in them." *Asfār*, 3.1 (335–36). Just as *wujūd* manifests itself in a hierarchical order, the sharing of the "vital qualities" of existence is also hierarchical: "The abode of existence is one, and the whole universe is a big living being. Its dimensions are conjoined with one another, but not in the sense of the conjunction of measurement and the unification of surfaces and environs. Rather, what is meant is that each degree of existential perfection must be adjacent to a degree that befits it in (a similar) existential perfection." *Asfār*, 2.2 (342). He also said: "All existence, from its highest to the lowest and from its lowest to the highest, is [united] in a single relationship by which some parts of it are related to some others. All things are united in spite of their external diversity. Their unity is not like the conjunction of corporeal bodies whereby their goals are conjoined and their surfaces

linked. Rather, the whole universe is one single animate being (*ḥayawān wāḥid*), just like a single soul." *Asfār*, 2.2 (349–50). Attributing life and intelligence to inanimate objects has a long history among both the ancient Greeks and the Muslim thinkers. Aristotle opposed the idea in *De Anima* 404b and 433a and in *Metaphysics* 980b. For the history of this idea in Western philosophy, see Sorabji, *Animal Minds and Human Morals*, especially 12–16.

70. In the *Asfār*, Ṣadrā gave a different classification of *wujūd*. Quoting ʿAlāʾ al-Dawlah al-Simnānī, one of the prominent commentators of Ibn al-ʿArabī, Ṣadrā said that the proper subject matter of metaphysics is not actual substances and their properties, as Aristotle would say, but divine theophany (*tajallī*): "The True Being (*al-wujūd al-ḥaqq*) is God the Exalted, the absolute Existence (*al-wujūd al-muṭlaq*) is His Act (*fiʿl*), and the conditioned existence (*al-wujūd al-muqayyad*) is His Work (*athar*). And what we mean by the absolute existence is not existence as a generic abstract term but expanding existence." *Asfār*, 1.2 (330).

71. Cf. *Asfār*, 1.2 (328). For the use of this expression in Ibn al-ʿArabī, see Chittick, *The Sufi Path of Knowledge*, 133.

72. Genus is a category in which multiple beings participate. Since God is the only being of His kind, He does not share a set of qualities with other beings. That is why God has no genus, species, or differentiae. Lāhījī adds that "the Necessary Being is pure being and pure goodness outside all categories, including the category of relation." *Sharḥ risālat al-mashāʿir*, 181.

73. This is another way of stating the difference between the concept (*mafhūm*) and reality (*ḥaqīqah*) of something—a difference that Ṣadrā used profusely in his analyses of *wujūd*. As he stated in *Asfār*, 1.1 (37): "Existence as a concept is a generic term predicated of concrete existents univocally (*biʾl-tafāwut*), not equivocally (*biʾl-tawāṭi*)." But "the reality of existence *qua* existence is not limited by generality and delimitation, universality and particularity, and inclusiveness and specificity. It is neither one [numerically] by a oneness added to it, nor many. . . . In its essence, it is nothing but full realization, actuality, and manifestation. These meanings of contingency, concepts of universality, attributes of rational consideration, and terms of mental analysis are attached to it on account of its degrees and stations." *Asfār*, 1.1 (259). Lāhījī's comment is also illuminating: "Meaning without the consideration of *wujūd* is quiddity . . . and meaning and concept with the consideration of *wujūd* is reality." *Sharḥ risālat al-mashāʿir*, 187.

74. The Eighth Penetration (paragraphs 102–3) and the First Path (paragraphs 104–15) are devoted to the proofs for the existence of God. While establishing God as the source, cause, plenitude, and return point of all things, Ṣadrā also hinted at the utter contingency of the world to the point of calling it a shadow, pure relation, and even an "imaginary reality." This immediately raises questions about the reality of the world in which God manifests His names and qualities. Given God's overpowering being, is the world a mirage? Ṣadrā did not delve into this question here, but his commentator Lāhījī cautioned against declaring the world to be a mere image, a mirage, or a figment of imagination: "There is no doubt that the instaured beings in the universe are many; and the one that is emanated in reality is real, not as some have imagined, that what is in existence is a fancy/delusion (*wahm*) and a mirage. This *wahm* is by necessity a mistake. That the sage attributes imagination (*al-khayāl*) to those things in existence has an aspect to it. But by 'imagination,' he does not mean an imagined (*mawhūm*) thing

that has no referent in reality." *Sharḥ risālat al-mashāʿir*, 189–90. Mullā Fanārī added further clarification to this point when he said that "forms have no real existence because they are nonexistent relational forms, and the meaning of their existence comes from the fact that *wujūd* is related to them . . . [but] the claim about the fallacy of contingent beings is based on the fact that their reality would necessitate their nonexistence had the divine manifestation not turned to them." *Miṣbāḥ al-uns*, 247–48, quoted in *Sharḥ risālat al-mashāʿir*, 190 n. 1.

75. This is a passage from ontology to theology and corresponds to "general matters of metaphysics" (*al-umūr al-ʿāmmah*) and *uthūlūjiyā*, or "the science of the Lord" (*al-ʿilm al-rubūbī*). This does not involve a hierarchy between ontology and theology in the modern senses of these terms. In Ṣadrā, as in all traditional philosophy, metaphysics comprises both ontology and theology because the ultimate sources of all that is, from existence to quiddities, is eventually God Himself.

76. *Burhān mashriqī* can also be translated as "oriental proof"; but in both cases, the meaning is related to enlightenment and illumination: it is a kind of demonstration obtained through spiritual vision and intellectual illumination. Mullā Ismāʿīl al-Iṣfahānī called it "a demonstration that comes from the real orient, which is the source of all effusion, exalted is His Glory." *Sharḥ risālat al-mashāʿir*, 199. For the school of Mullā Ṣadrā, this type of argument is stronger and more convincing than "logical proof" (*burhān manṭiqī*).

77. In stating more clearly the distinction between God and His creation, Lāhījī disagreed slightly with Ṣadrā: "When we say that 'God is the source of all existents,' it is an allegorical expression in the sense that His act is the source of things, because nothing originates from Him [directly] and He acts by Himself—namely, through His own action. God is above His own action because He is the eternal (*al-azal*), whereas action is in the world of preferred contingency. Nothing has descended from eternity (*al-azal*) to contingency (*al-imkān*); likewise, nothing has ascended from contingency to eternity in one respect. The intelligibles are from His act of creation (*al-takwīn*) and establishing (*al-inshāʾ*)." *Sharḥ risālat al-mashāʿir*, 204.

78. In his important gloss on this paragraph, Lāhījī developed an argument for the ontological servitude of all creation to God. God is plenitude because He is pure being. But He is also above plenitude because even plenitude implies some sort of relation. All creatures depend on God and thus worship Him in their own way. Those who worship Him in a "general and absolute way" are those who profess His oneness, whereas those who worship Him in a "limited and conditioned way" are those who take partners unto Him. In this sense, the disbelievers (*al-kuffār*), Magians, materialists (*dahriyyah*), and naturalists (*ṭibāʿiyyah*) are not outside the category of ontological dependence and servitude. Jews and Christians worship God, but in an incomplete way because they mistake some of His names and qualities for His absoluteness. Lāhījī added that "among all the past nations, Christians are closest to God besides the Muḥammadiyyīn." The Christians worship God in the person of Jesus, Mary, and the Holy Spirit. This does not befit God's absolute oneness and moves Christians away from the "state of affirming the oneness of God (*al-muwaḥḥidīn*)." Yet they remain closer to the truth of the Divine because "whoever has witnessed God in man has a witnessing more perfect

than all those who have witnessed God in anything other than man." *Sharḥ risālat al-mashāʿir*, 207. This is a reference to the Islamic belief that while God has revealed His Names and Qualities in His creation, they are manifested most perfectly in the human state. Lāhījī's view of Christians as being closer to the truth of God is in tandem with the attitude of early Muslims to see them in a more favorable light than they see other communities. This is based on Q. 5:82–84, which states: "Thou wilt surely find that, of all people, they who say, 'Behold, we are Christians,' come closest to feeling affection for those who believe [in this divine writ]: this is so because there are priests and monks among them, and because these are not given to arrogance." The classical commentaries interpreted this verse as referring to Negus or Najāshī, the Christian king of Abyssinia, who had sheltered the Muslim delegation from the Makkans. See Ibn Kathīr, *Tafsīr*, 521. See also Ibn Qayyim al-Jawziyyah, *Zād al-Masīr fī ʿilm al-tafsīr*, 401. The Muʿtazilite theologian al-Jāḥiẓ (d. 868) mentioned Najāshī as one of the reasons Muslims consider Christians closer to them. See al-Jāḥiẓ, *al-Rad ʿalá al-naṣārā*, 260. Historically speaking, this positive attitude toward Christians has led to a clearly more favorable view of the Byzantine Empire than that of the Sassanids in early Islamic history. For more on this matter, see El Cheikh, *Byzantium Viewed by the Arabs*, 24–33. See also Shboul, "Byzantium and the Arabs," 235–60.

79. In the *Asfār*, 1.1 (54), Ṣadrā stated the same point as follows: "Existence, insofar as it is existence, has no agent from which it emanates, no matter into which it transforms, no subject in which it is found, no form by which it is clothed, no goal for which it is [established]. Rather, it itself is the agent of all agents, the form of all forms, and the goal of all goals."

80. Sabziwarī elaborated on the same point when he said: "Existence is the source of all explanations in which all descriptions come to an end. And it is the source of all sources and descriptions. When the Prophet, may peace and blessing be upon him, was asked, 'By what did you know your Lord?' he replied that 'I knew everything by Him.'" *Sharḥ al-manẓūmah*, 2:60.

81. In the *Asfār*, Ṣadrā put the same point thus: "But the Necessary Being has no proof, no definition, and therefore no reason from a number of different points of view. It has no reason for existence, like an active [agent] and ultimate goal; no reason for constitution (*al-qiwām*), like matter and form; and no reason for quiddity, like genus and differentia. In spite of this, nothing is hidden from It, and It is the proof of everything and closest to everything. As He the Exalted said: 'And We are closer to you than your jugular vein' (Q. 50:16). And He said: 'And He is with you wherever you are' (Q. 57:4). And He is the proof of His own essence, as He said: 'God testifies that there is no god but He' (Q. 3:18). He also said: 'Is your Lord not sufficient [as a proof] that He is a witness to all things' (Q. 41:53), and 'Say: What is greater as witness? Say: Allah' (Q. 6:19)." *Asfār*, 1.3 (399–400).

82. In religious terms, this means that there cannot be more than one God. Two infinite beings cancel each other out because, as Ṣadrā said in the paragraph, this would imply sharing the qualities of infinitude, which would lead to imperfection. This is a commentary on the verse "al-Anbiyāʾ," 21:22: "If there were to be a deity other than God on [earth and heavens], they would certainly go corrupt." See also "al-Qaṣaṣ," 28:88; "al-Anbiyāʾ," 21:108; and "al-Nahl," 16:51.

83. Following the Platonic tradition, Muslim philosophers held that actuality signifies perfection, whereas potentiality implies privation and imperfection. Actuality is full realization because a substance *in actu* is not deprived of any real qualities it *may* possess. A potential substance, however, is marred by imperfection because it can be what it is only when it realizes its potentialities through the intervention of an external agent, a *more* actualized substance. See the *Asfār*, 1.3 (343–44).

84. "All points of view" is a reaffirmation of the fact that the Necessary Being is necessary by itself and in relation to everything else. Contingent beings are conditionally necessary when considered in relation to their concrete existence in the world. But they are contingent in relation to their source. This applies to all beings, from the detached intellects to material substances, with differing degrees of ontological intensity. The Necessary Being, however, is above such conditionalities; it is necessary in all regards and considerations. The Necessary Being cannot be necessary, one, or infinite from only one point of view; it must, by definition, be all these things in all respects. The confusion that some people have about the meaning of "all points of view" comes "from the contingent which is necessary by something else." *Sharḥ risālat al-mashāʿir*, 220.

85. Having established the absolute unity of "the essence of the Necessary Being" (*tawḥīd al-dhāt*), Ṣadrā moved to demonstrate the unity of "the act(s) of the Necessary Being" (*tawḥīd al-fiʿl*). The relation between essence and act is a key issue of metaphysics whereby a thing remains itself while exercising its agency in the world. When God carries out an action, He does not lose anything from His absolute oneness, the contrary of which would plunge Him into the multiplicities and contingencies of the world of creation. God's act of creation, or what Ṣadrā called the emanation of the Necessary Being upon all things, does not lead to multiplicity or indigence in His essence. To Ṣadrā, this was an important step toward seeing all things through the eyes of unity and thus recognizing the transcendent unity of being (*waḥdt al-wujūd*). For al-Ghazālī, the highest form of divine unity "is to see nothing but one in existence." Recognizing the reality of multiplicity, Ṣadrā hastened to add, "This [way of seeing] is the penultimate goal of the sciences of unveiling. Verily, what really exists is only one. The multiplicity [that you see] in it is only for the one who separates his vision. But the vision of the unifier (*al-muwaḥḥid*) is not separated [from oneness] by the multiplicity of the heavens, the earth, and other beings. He sees all things as one single thing. But the secrets of the sciences of unveiling cannot be jotted down in a book." *Asfār*, 1.2 (323–24). Ṣadrā also said: "The Necessary Being by itself is necessary from all points of view. There is no contingency in its all-inclusive essence. It is found with all beings, without any delimitation and multiplicity. Therefore, it is in everything and not in anything, at every moment and not in time, in every place and in no place; it is all things and not any one of them." *Asfār*, 3.2 (332). The same point is reiterated in the *Maẓāhir*: "His ipseity (*inniyyah*), the exalted, is His essence (*māhiyyah*), the exalted; and His existence, the exalted, is the existence of everything. His existence is the truth of existence without there being in it any stain of nonexistence and multiplicity." *Al-Maẓāhir*, 24–25.

86. Ṣadrā quoted this verse in the *Asfār* in the following context: "The essential contingency (*al-imkān al-dhātī*) comprising all contingent beings is pointed out in

His words, the exalted, 'All things are perishing save His face.' The perishing consists of the realization of *wujūd*. The exception is His face, and it is the aspect of necessity, which is the act of *wujūd*." *Asfār*, 1.1 (89).

87. As Lāhījī pointed out, this paragraph is concerned with "the manifestation of the penetration of the light of *wujūd* in all things, and the demonstration of unity in multiplicity (*al-waḥdah fī al-kathrah*)." *Sharḥ risālat al-mashāʿir*, 230.

88. This is one of the key elements of Ṣadrean metaphysics. "Ontological simplicity" is based on the premise that a simple, noncomposite being contains in itself multiple existential qualities without implying numerical multiplicity. A simple being cannot be divided into composites, and thus nothing can be "extracted" from it; otherwise, it would be composite, not simple. The Necessary Being is potentially "all things" because, as the source of all beings, nothing can be outside it. Cf. the *Asfār*, 1.3 (324–25); *Ittiḥād*, 93–94. In the *Asfār*, 1.2 (368); 1.3 (338); 2.2 (216–18), Ṣadrā traced the idea back to Plato. He also applied the principle of simplicity to God's Knowledge of things; cf. *Asfār*, 3.1 (110). Ṣadrā repeated the same principle for intellect when he said that "a simple intellect is all intelligibles" (*al-ʿaql al-basīṭ kull al-maʿqūlāt*). *Asfār*, 1.3 (377).

89. This section deals with the problem of God's knowledge of things—a problem with a long history among the Mutakallimūn, the philosophers, and the Sufis. Ṣadrā rejected the Peripatetic concept of knowledge as "representation" and "impression in the mind" (*irtisām*) for God, because it implies that God knows things as we know them. But since God is the creator of all things and precedes their existence, he must know them in a different way. God cannot know things through "abstraction" either, because there is nothing abstract or potential in God. Furthermore, God must know things in such a way that His knowledge does not cause change in His essence. In the *Asfār*, Ṣadrā provided a detailed summary of the views of previous philosophers on this subject all the way from Plato and Porphyry to al-Fārābī, Ibn Sīnā, Suhrawardī, and Ibn al-ʿArabī. See *Asfār*, 3.1 (180–81); 1.3 (387–95). He divided the various theories into two broad groups: those that consider God's knowledge separate from His essence and those that do not. He stated this point as follows: "In affirming God's knowledge of things, there are two possible ways: we say that it is either separate from His essence or not. Those who hold the view of separation either argue for the affirmation of nonexistents (*al-maʿdūmāt*) or [they do] not—that is, whether they are attributed to external existence, as in the case of the Muʿtazilites, or to the mind, as in the case of some Sufi masters such as the master sage and verifier (*al-muḥaqqiq*) Muḥyī al-Dīn ibn al-ʿArabī and the perfect master Ṣadr al-Dīn al-Qūnawī, from whose famous books benefits are derived. According to the second view, either we have to say that God's knowledge of external beings is forms that subsist by themselves and is separate from Him and other things—and these are the Platonic archetypes and separate forms—or we have to say that His knowledge of external beings is the things themselves. . . . As for those who argue for the nonseparation [of God's knowledge from His essence], either they have to say that it is other than His essence (which is the view of the two masters al-Fārābī and Ibn Sīnā), or they have to say that it is the same as His essence. In the second case, they either have to admit, like Porphyry and his followers among the Peripatetics, that His essence

is united with intellective forms, or [they must] say that His essence by itself has the summary knowledge of everything other than Himself and other than the first effect [the first created being] in the manner to which we have already alluded." *Asfār*, 3.1 (181–82).

90. The unification of the intellect and the intelligible (*ittiḥād al-ᶜaqil wa'l-maᶜqūl*) is one of the cornerstones of Ṣadrā's epistemology. It argues for a relation of unity between the intellect and its objects of intellection. Still, it is radically different from the representational theory of knowledge advocated by the Peripatetics. Ṣadrā devoted considerable space to this issue in his corpus and wrote a separate treatise, entitled *Ittiḥād al-ᶜāqil wa'l-maᶜqūl*, to defend it against Ibn Sīnā and his followers. For the English translation of the treatise and a detailed study, see Kalin, *Knowledge in Later Islamic Philosophy*.

91. This is the point Wittgenstein made concerning first-order propositions. When I say that "I am in pain," there is no difference between the I who utters this sentence and the I/person who is in pain. Cf. Wittgenstein, *Philosophical Investigations*, paragraph 246. For Ṣadrā, knowledge as representation, which places both an ontological and a cognitive distinction between the knower and the known, cannot account for self-knowledge and its modalities. See *Asfār*, 1.3 (288–89).

92. Reference to the Qur'anic verse, "All is perishing save His face" (28:88).

93. This is one of the clear statements of *waḥdat al-wujūd* in Ṣadrā. The transcendent unity of being, as formulated by Ibn al-ᶜArabī and his followers, is based on an ontological non-duality whereby all primary and secondary causes are reduced to *wujūd*. Just as God is the "Cause of all causes" and the "Principle of all principles" in theology, *wujūd* is the Source of all effects and qualities in ontology and cosmology. Ṣadrā also applied the principle of ontological simplicity to God's knowledge of things. See *Asfār*, 1.3 (399–400). God is the ultimate source of all existence, and *wujūd* is the proximate cause of contingent beings. As *wujūd* is God's face looking to the world of creation, all beings, small and big, are like rays and effusions from God through the modalities of *wujūd*. Ṣadrā said: "It is well-established and clear, in the view of the verifiers among the sages and the divine philosophers among the philosophers, that the *wujūd* of everything is nothing but an individual reality related to the *wujūd* of the True and Self-Subsisting One. . . . Existential ipseities are among the degrees of the manifestation of His essence and rays of His majesty and beauty." This principle of ontological simplicity-cum-relationality applies to the order of knowledge: "The perception of something is nothing but a consideration of the way in which this thing is related to the Necessary Being; [and] from this particular point of view, [the Necessary Being] is its existence and the state of its existing (*mawjudiyyah*)." This interplay between the order of existence and the order of knowledge led Ṣadrā to a conclusion that unites the two orders: "It is not possible to understand this [point] without understanding the essence of the True One." What Ṣadrā says here is extremely significant for his metaphysics of *wujūd*. Since, for Ṣadrā, *wujūd* is a single reality appearing as matter and form, substance and accident, actor and action, knower and known, all cognition is eventually an exercise in *wujūd*. All chains of causation return to the self-regulating and self-generating reality of *wujūd*. And since *wujūd* is nothing but an effusion from the infinite reality of God, "whoever has perceived

something of concrete beings, he has perceived God. People are ignorant of this except for the elite and the saints of God, the Exalted. As it is narrated from the Commander of the Believers (ᶜAlī ibn Abī Ṭālib), 'I saw nothing but God before it, with it, and in it.' It is clear and manifest that this simple perception of the True One, the Exalted, occurs for all of His servants. But this does not mean that one can perceive Him in the depth of His Essence." *Asfār,* 1.1 (116–17). To prove the eventual unity of being, Ṣadrā also used the argument from ontological simplicity, according to which "a simple being is all things" (*basiṭ al-ḥaqīqah kull al-ashyāʾ*). See the section entitled "The Necessary Being is all things and all beings, and all things return to Him" in *Asfār,* 3.1 (110–18).

94. Ṣadrā rejected both the Ashᶜarite and Muᶜtazilite positions by using again the argument from ontological simplicity. The Muᶜtazilites denied any names and attributes to God for fear of violating His absolute unity. Instead of saying that God has knowledge as an attribute, they said that He acts in a state of knowledge. By contrast, the Ashᶜarites affirmed the existence of divine names and qualities but pushed the argument to the point of intimating dualities and multiplicities in the divine essence. Al-Ashᶜarī's answer that "God's knowledge (*ᶜilm Allāh*) cannot be said to be either God himself or different from Him" is obviously not satisfactory. See his response to the Muᶜtazilites in his *Maqālāt al-islāmiyyīn*, 2:178. For a defense of the Ashᶜarite position by Fakhr al-Din al-Rāzī, see his *al-Maṭālib al-ᶜāliyah min al-ᶜilm al-ilāhī*, 3:141–79. Ṣadrā developed his concept of Divine names and attributes on the basis of the hierarchical simplicity of *wujūd*. God has names and qualities, but they exist neither apart from Him nor as part of His identity. He contains all such attributes because His *wujūd* is the most intense and simple of all beings. God can be said to have many names, but the real point is that "all of His qualities and attributes exist through a single *wujūd*, and it is the *wujūd* of the essence." *Asfār,* 3.1 (142). For more on this point, see Fazlur Rahman, *The Philosophy of Mulla Sadra*, 141–46.

95. As Lāhījī explained in his commentary, since God knows His own Self, He must also know all things because ultimately He is the "necessary cause" for all things. The difficult question is how God remains untainted by the knowledge of contingent and changing things. To avoid any confusion, the Muᶜtazilites postulated God's knowledge of things as separate from His essence. Some Sufis also subscribed to this view. Suhrawardī and Ṭūsī defined His knowledge as the very existence of things, therefore avoiding the assignment of a separate existence to things that God comes to know *a posteriori*. Some held that God knows things through the "Platonic forms," which are forms of knowledge existing by themselves. Lāhījī supported Suhrawardī's view as the "strongest argument." Cf. Lāhījī, *Sharḥ risālat al-mashāᶜir*, 273.

96. In epistemic terms, this means that knowledge of cause is more primary than knowledge of effect. This leads to a typical Aristotelian principle (*Posterior Analytics* 71b 10), according to which we have a full knowledge of an effect when we truly know its cause. The theological connotation of this principle is quite clear: it is only by knowing God that we can know the world. This conclusion can be seen as an intimation of Ṣadrā's defense of the *burhān al-ṣiddiqīn* (the argument of the veracious), which takes God's being, rather than that of the world, as the

starting point of a sound demonstration of the existence of God. Ṣadrā discussed the proofs for the existence of God in *Asfār*, 3.1 (1–118). See also Ayatollahy, *The Existence of God.* For Ibn Sīnā, see Mayer, "Ibn Sina's Burhān al-Ṣiddiqīn," 18–39.

97. Ṣadrā's conclusion was again based on the ontology of *wujūd*: just as pure *wujūd* is the source of all existents while remaining untainted by their deficiencies, God's knowledge of things does not bring any change, impermanence, and deficiency into the divine essence. See his discussion in *al-Mabda᾽ wa'l-maᶜad*, 121. Ṣadrā found all previous explanations of God's knowledge of things unsatisfactory because they take away something either from God's omnipresence (*al-qadir*) or from His omniscience (*al-ᶜalim*). For his detailed discussion, see *Asfār*, 3.1 (189–237); see also Rahman, *The Philosophy of Mullā Ṣadrā*, 146–50; Kalin, *Knowledge in Later Islamic Philosophy*, 173–80.

98. In other words, God's power is not an attribute separate from Himself, and His power encapsulates all forms of power. As a result, things have power because of their relation to God's power, not because they possess some essential properties.

99. Ṣadrā introduced two types of unity: numerical unity (*al-waḥdat al-ᶜadadiyyah*) and intellective oneness (*waḥdat al-ᶜaqliyyah*). The former refers to ordinary numerical order, whereby a thing is "one" as opposed to being "two," "three," etc. The latter denotes a state of ontological simplicity, whereby a being is single in its state of existence. As Ṣadrā put it: "The unity of expanding existence is not numerical (*ᶜadadī*), which is the beginning of numbers. It is a reality that expands in the temples (*hayākil*) of contingent beings and the tablets of quiddities," *Asfār*, 1.2 (328). In *Ittiḥād al-ᶜāqil wa'l-maᶜqūl*, 37–38, Ṣadrā provided a detailed description of the types of oneness. His analysis is worth quoting in full: "Oneness is of many modes, and the oneness of intellects is not numerical, which is the source of numbers, such as the oneness of body and blackness, movement, and so on among the material things. The oneness of the intellect is rather like the oneness that belongs to the species. The difference between numerical and other kinds of oneness is the following: oneness in material bodies, like their existence, accepts augmentation and diminution, and it is different from its like when it is considered to be [increased or decreased]. [In this way,] the sum total is greater and more than one. Therefore, two bodies are more than one of them [alone]. In the same way, the state of these two blacknesses, in their being two, is not like the state of one in its oneness; and this is in contradiction to intellective oneness. If we suppose, for instance, the existence of one thousand homogeneous intellective forms, the state of one [intellect] in its oneness would be like this one thousand in its multiplicity. An example of this is the man *qua* man. When you add to this meaning a meaning similar to it in terms of its specific reality after its being disembodied from [its] additional qualities (*al-zawā᾽id*), you would find neither it nor the whole [of man and the meaning added to it] in their second [state], except in the way you have found the first one in its oneness. For this reason, it is mentioned in discussions of quiddity that when additional qualities that individuate [a quiddity] are cut off from each meaning, which is related to its species with multiple members in the external world, an intellective form of it is inscribed in the soul. When it is cut off from another individual that distinguishes it [from others] in external existence, what is added to the shared quiddity does not affect the soul with a different effect

except the first [one]. The author of *Talwīḥāt* [Suhrawardī] pointed to this meaning when he said, 'Whenever you consider [the pure existence than which there is nothing more perfect] for the second time and look at it again, [you see that] it is what it is; thus, there is nothing that distinguishes (*mayyiz*) a pure thing [other than itself].'" For the full translation of *Risālah fī ittiḥād* . . . , see Kalin, *Knowledge in Later Islamic Philosophy*, 256–86.

100. This section is repeated almost verbatim in *al-Maẓāhir al-ilāhiyyah*, 62.

101. This is a reference to an old problem in Kalam discussions of divine speech. Is God's speech eternal or created? Since no temporality can be attributed to God, His speech must be eternal. But, then, does not this introduce change and multiplicity into the domain of the attributes of God, which, in turn, leads to change in the divine essence? To address this issue, some theologians argued that God's intended meaning is eternal (*qadīm*), whereas His words are temporal (*ḥadith*). In the discussion over the createdness of the Qurʾan, most Ashʿarites came to the conclusion that the meaning of the Qurʾan is eternal, whereas its words, letters, and sounds are created. Apart from the Ashʿarites, Ṣadrā criticized the Muʿtazilites for holding that God creates all "sounds and letters with a referent," because this theory collapses all speech into divine speech. Ṣadrā's solution is rooted in his ontology. God creates the "perfect words" which, according to Lāhījī, are the "beings of the world of the intellect and the world which subsists with the subsistence of God." *Sharḥ risālat al-mashāʿir*, 286.

102. The difference between *ʿālam al-amr*, translated here as "the world of the divine command," and *ʿālam al-khalq*, "the world of creation," is a key element of the Islamic metaphysics of creation. Throughout his writings, Ṣadrā described *ʿālam al-amr* as the abode of disembodied or "abstract" beings (*al-mujarradāt*) in which are to be found the intellects, the angels, the eternal souls, and other spiritual realities. This is the world that comes from the divine command and that also commands on lower levels of existence. In a sense, this is the world in which God acts directly and primarily before the effects of His command are manifested in the world of creation. In this regard, *ʿālam al-amr* is invisible, abstract, and absent to the naked eye. By contrast, the world of creation is visible, manifest, and concrete. It is where *wujūd* manifests itself as physical beings, sensate forms, corporeal entities, and so on. Everything in the world of the command is found in the form of principles, whereas the world of creation displays them as specific applications. That is why Ṣadrā made a distinction between *kalām* (word, speech, or speaking) and *kitāb* (the book). Word is the principle and is always more than its concrete form—namely, the book. The book, on the contrary, depends for its existence on the word. In another respect, the word is concise and condensed, whereas the book is detailed. Cf. *Asfār*, 3.2 (10–18). Another way of stating this is to say that the word is simple (*basiṭ*) and the book is composite (*murakkab*), in the philosophical senses of the terms. Cf. Lāhījī, *Sharḥ risālat al-mashāʿir*, 292.

103. Ṣadrā used the same analogy to explain the relationship between the Creator and the created. Since the world of creation is absolutely dependent upon its Creator for its existence, God's relation to the world is not like the relation of a building to its builder or the relation of a writing to its writer. Once a builder builds something, it continues to exist on its own, despite the fact that it bears the

imprint of its builder. Rather, the relation is more like the relation of a word to its speaker. The word exists as long as the speaker utters it; it ceases to exist when the speaker stops talking. Cf. *Asfār*, 1.2 (216).

104. Ṣadrā is playing here with the etymological connection between the words *qurʾān* and *furqān*. While *Qurʾān* is the name of the revealed book of Islam, it also means, among other things, that which can be compared and thus brought together. By contrast, *furqān*, which is also one of the names of the Qurʾan, means separating, putting apart, and discernment. Word, or speech, both unites and differentiates. The Qurʾan, as the scripture, differentiates truth from falsehood and then unites everything in the divine.

105. The expression "those who possess heart-knowledge" occurs sixteen times in the Qurʾan. In this passage, there is allusion to the verse "And no one remembers except those who possess heart-knowledge" (2:269; 3:7).

106. In the *Asfār*, 1.2 (220–24), Ṣadrā mentioned six types of action and omitted *tajallī* from the list. It is clear from this short discussion here, as well as from Ṣadrā's more extensive analyses of the subject in his other works, that the problem of action concerns three types of beings: humans, nature, and God. As the active and passive agents of action, humans occupy a central place in Ṣadrā's theory of action. But this is also true for divine action because all action, whether human or divine, voluntary or natural, is interrelated.

107. Ṣadrā equated the meaning of "the intellect," "the pen," and "My light" because their ultimate referent is the same: they are all pure, spiritual substances. The fact that the first existent that God has created is a spiritual substance is in tandem with Ṣadrā's ontocosmological hierarchy, which begins with pure being and then descends into lower levels of existence to the lowest rung of the great chain of being. It is clear that the intellect the philosophers talk about here is not human reason in the limited sense of the term, but intellect as a cosmological and ontological principle that unites the various orders of existence. Ṣadrā gave a philosophical exposition of this ḥadīth in his commentary on the famous Shiʿite Ḥadīth book *Uṣūl al-kāfī*, compiled by Abū Jaʿfar Kulaynī. Ṣadrā's commentary is subtitled *Kitāb al-ʿaql waʾl-jahl* ("The Book of Intellect and Ignorance"), which shows his concern for dealing with the concept of the intellect in a variety of ways.

108. Paragraphs 125–36 quote a number of sayings from Shiʿite sources. It is not uncommon to see Ṣadrā quoting verses and sayings of the Prophet Muḥammad and Shiʿite Imams in his discussions of dense philosophical and cosmological issues. As a matter of fact, Ṣadrā wrote a number of important works in the field of transmitted sciences (*al-ʿulūm al-naqliyyah*), including a philosophical commentary on the Qurʾan. Since in this part of the *Mashāʿir* he is dealing with the problem of cosmogenesis, he cites religious sources to explain the creation of the present order of existence. With this exercise, Ṣadrā also shows his desire and ability to dovetail rational and religious arguments in philosophical issues.

109. John 3:13.

110. *ʿIlliyyīn* is used in Qurʾan 83:18–19. According to most commentators, it refers to a sublime place where the book of deeds for the virtuous is preserved. Derived from the root word *ʿuluww* and from *ʿalā*, it signifies something high and

exalted and is contrasted with *sijjīn* (literally, prison or a prison-like place). Some ḥadīths describe *ʿIlliyyīn* as the seventh heaven. Ṣadrā used the word in *Iksīr al-ʿarifīn*, translated by Chittick as *The Elixir of the Gnostics*, 13. For the classical commentaries, see Ibn Kathīr, *Tafsīr al-Qurʾān al-ʿazīm*, 1693; al-Qurṭubī, *al-Jāmiʾ li'l-aḥkām al-Qurʾān*, 2:3277; see also the exposition given by the Sufi commentator Ibn ʿAjībah in *al-Baḥr al-madīd fī tafsīr al-Qurʾān al-majīd*, 263.

111. It is this impermanence that reveals the relative and ambiguous nature of things. In the *Asfār*, Ṣadrā stated this point as follows: "Motion, time, and the like belong to the category of things that have weak existence (*ḍaʿīfat al-wujūd*). Accordingly, their existence resembles their nonexistence, their actuality is similar to their potentiality, and their origination (*ḥudūthihā*) is nothing but their corruption (*zawālihā*). Each of these (qualities or attributes) requires the nonexistence of the other; in fact, their existence is their nonexistence. Therefore, motion is the very destruction of a thing itself after it (is established in the physical world) and its origination before it (is actualized in the external world). And this mode (of being) is comparable to the Absolute Being in the sense that all relational beings (*al-iḍāfat*) have some sort of existence. Likewise, the existence of motion displays ambiguity (*shukūk*) and similitude (*shabah*) (of being close to both being and non-being)." *Asfār*, 1.3 (37).

112. An allusion to the Qurʾanic verse "And every one of them will come to Him individually on the Day of Judgment" (19:95).

113. Nature as an inherent principle of change accounts for all primary and secondary motions, including external and forced motion. Ṣadrā reduced all change in things to their essential nature, which enables them from within, so to speak, to move. He summed up his position as follows: "And we are certain about the following conclusion on the basis of heart-knowledge (*al-wijdān*), rather than discursive proof (*al-burhān*): the cause that makes a thing yield and induces it to move from one place to another or from one state [of being] to another cannot but be an actual power inherent in that thing. This is called nature. Thus, the immediate cause of material [physical] motion (*al-ḥarakat al-jismiyyah*) is the substantial power that subsists in things, and all the accidents are subservient to the sustaining form (*al-ṣūrah al-muqawwimah*), which is nature. . . . The philosophers have shown conclusively that every (physical body) which accepts the act of yielding (*al-mayl*) from outside has to have a natural inclination (*mayl ṭibāʿī*) in itself. It is thus proved that the direct source of motion is something flowing with a continuously changing identity (*mutajaddid al-huwiyyah*). If this (substratum) were not to be something flowing and ever-changing, it would be impossible for these natural motions to emanate from it, on the basis of the principle that the ever-changing cannot emanate from the stable." *Asfār*, 1.3 (65).

114. Ṣadrā posited nature (*ṭabīʿah*) as the ultimate cause of motion or change in contingent beings because all other agents of change are secondary and come about under certain circumstances. Things change because it is in their very nature. Then the question arises as to how nature itself changes. Ṣadrā's answer went back to his concept of *wujūd*, which is self-renewing and self-generating without the need of external agents. In Ṣadrā's words: "The immediate cause of motion has to be something with a stable essence and continuously changing being (*thābitat*

al-māhiyyah mutajaddid al-wujūd). As you will see, the immediate cause of all kinds of motion is none other than nature. This nature is the substance by which things subsist and become actualized as a species [as a particular entity]. This refers to the first perfection of natural things insofar as they are actual beings (in the external world). Therefore, it is concluded and established from this (consideration) that every physical being is a continuously changing entity with a flowing identity (*sayyāl al-huwiyyah*), despite the fact that its quiddity is impervious to change." *Asfār*, 1.3 (62).

115. God is the source of all change and permanence in the world, but this does not introduce change into the divine essence. Ṣadrā reasoned as follows: God creates nature, and nature changes by itself. Therefore, change in the nature of things does not lead to change and multiplicity in God. Ṣadrā took motion in the ordinary philosophical sense to be a weak form of change and a unidirectional process. For him, nature, as the basic constitution of things, acts as a basis for both change and permanence. That is why he rejected motion as the best link between what is eternal and what is created and changing. Cf. *Asfār*, 1.3 (128ff.).

116. This and the preceding two paragraphs are a condensed summary of Ṣadrā's concept of the temporal origination of the world (*ḥudūth al-ᶜālam*) and substantial motion (*al-ḥarakat al-jawhariyyah*). Ṣadrā devoted considerable space in his writings to the first problem. See, for instance, *Risālah fī al-ḥudūth* (*Ḥudūth al-ᶜālam*) and *Asfār*, 1.3 (244–50). For the problem of motion/change as a cosmological principle and Ṣadrā's development of the concept of substantial motion, see *Asfār*, 1.3 (69–113). For an analysis, see Kalin, "Between Physics and Metaphysics, 65–93.

Bibliography

Ash^c^arī, Abū al-Ḥasan ^c^Alī ibn Ismā^c^īl al-. *Maqālāt al-islāmiyyīn*. 2 vols. Beirut: Maktabat al-^c^Asriyah, 1995.

Avicenna. *Al-Mubāḥathāt*. Edited by Muḥsin Bīdārfar. Qom, Iran: Intishārāt-i Bīdār, 1413/1992.

———. *Shifā': Ilāhiyyāt*. Edited by Ibrāhīm Madkour. Qom, Iran, n.d.

Ayatollahy, Hamidreza. *The Existence of God: Mulla Sadra's Seddiqin Argument versus Criticisms of Kant and Hume*. Tehran: Bunyād-i Ḥikmat-i Islāmī-yi Ṣadrā [Ṣadrā Islamic Philosophy Research Institute], 2005.

Babayan, Kathryn. *Mystics, Monarchs, and Messiahs: Cultural Landscapes of Early Modern Iran*. Harvard Middle Eastern Monographs. Cambridge, MA: Center for Middle Eastern Studies, Harvard University, 2002.

Bahmanyār ibn Marzubān, Abū al-Ḥasan. *Kitāb al-taḥṣīl*. Cairo, 1329/1911. New edition by Mortaża Moṭahharī, Tehran, 1349/1970.

Brockelmann, Carl. *Geschichte der arabischen Literatur and Geschichte der arabischen Literatur Supliment*. 2nd ed. 5 vols. Leiden: E. J. Brill, 1937–49.

Browne, Edward Granville. *A Literary History of Persia*. 4 vols. Cambridge: Cambridge University Press, 1951–53.

Chittick, William C. *The Self-Disclosure of God: Principles of Ibn al-^c^Arabī's Cosmology*. SUNY Series in Islam. Albany: State University of New York Press, 1998.

———. *The Sufi Path of Knowledge: Ibn al-^c^Arabī's Metaphysics of Imagination*. Albany: State University of New York Press, 1989.

Dihlawī, Walī Allāh al-. *The Conclusive Argument from God: Shāh Walī Allāh of Delhi's Ḥujjat Allāh al-Bāligha*. Translated by Marcia K. Hermansen. Leiden: E. J. Brill, 1996.

El-Cheikh, Nadia Maria. *Byzantium Viewed by the Arabs*. Harvard Middle Eastern Monographs. Cambridge, MA: Center for Middle Eastern Studies, Harvard University, 2004.

Fārābī, al-. *Jawābāt li-masā'il su'ila ^c^anhā*. In *Risālatān falsafiyatān*, edited by Ja'far Āl-i Yāsīn, 77–116. Beirut: Dār al-Manāhil, 1987.

Gleave, Robert. *Scripturalist Islam: The History and Doctrines of the Akhbārī Shī^c^ī School*. Leiden: E. J. Brill, 2007.

Goichon, Amélie-Marie. *Lexique de la langue philosophique d'Ibn Sīnā (Avicenne)*. Paris: Desclée de Brouwer, 1938.

Gutas, Dimitri. *Avicenna and the Aristotelian Tradition: Introduction to Reading Avicenna's Philosophical Works*. Leiden: E. J. Brill, 1988.

Halm, Heinz. *Shi^cism*. Translated by Janet Watson. Edinburgh: Edinburgh University Press, 1991.

Ibn ᶜAjībah. *Al-Baḥr al-madīd fī tafsīr al-Qur'an al-majīd*. Beirut: Dār al-Kutub al-ᶜIlmiyyah, 2005.

Ibn al-ᶜArabī. *Futūḥāt*. *See* Chittick, *The Sufi Path of Knowledge*.

Ibn Kathīr, Ismāᶜīl ibn ᶜUmar. *Tafsīr al-Qur'ān al-ᶜaẓīm*. Beirut: Dār al-Maᶜrifah, 2006.

Ibn Qayyim al-Jawziyyah. *Zād al-masīr fī ᶜilm al-tafsīr*. Beirut: Al-Maktab al-Islāmī, 2002.

Ibn Sīnā. *See* Avicenna.

Iqbal, Muḥammad. *The Development of Metaphysics in Persia: A Contribution to the History of Muslim Philosophy*. London: Luzac, 1908.

Izutsu, Toshihiko. *The Concept and Reality of Existence*. Studies in the Humanities and Social Relations 13. Tokyo: Keio Institute of Cultural and Linguistic Studies, 1971.

Jabre, Farīd. *Essai sur le lexique de Ghazali: Contribution à l'étude de la terminologie de Ghazali dans ses principaux ouvrages à l'exception du Tahafut*. Études philosophiques et sociales 5. Beirut: Publications de l'Université Libanaise, 1970.

Jāḥiẓ, Abū ᶜUthmān ᶜAmr ibn Baḥr al-. *Al-Radd ᶜalá al-naṣārā*. In *Rasā'il al-Jāḥiẓ: al-Rasā'il al-kalāmiyyah*, edited by ᶜAlī Abū Malḥim. Beirut: Dār al-Maktabat al-Hilāl and Dār al-Biḥār, 2004.

Jambet, Christian. *The Act of Being: The Philosophy of Revelation in Mullā Ṣadrā*. Translated by Jeff Fort. New York: Zone Books, 2006.

———. *Mort et résurrection en Islam: L'au-delà selon Mullâ Sadrâ*. Paris: Albin Michel, 2008.

Kalin, Ibrahim. "An Annotated Bibliography of the Works of Mullā Ṣadrā with a Brief Account of His Life." *Islamic Studies* 42, no. 1 (Spring 2003): 21–62.

———. "Between Physics and Metaphysics: Mulla Sadra on Nature and Motion." *Islam and Science* 1, no. 1 (June 2003): 65–93.

———. *Knowledge in Later Islamic Philosophy: Mullā Ṣadrā on Existence, Intellect, and Intuition*. New York: Oxford University Press, 2010.

———. "Will, Necessity, and Creation as Monistic Theophany in the Islamic Philosophical Tradition." In *Creation and the God of Abraham*, edited by David B. Burrell, Carlo Cogliati, Janet M. Soskice, and William R. Stoeger, 107–32. New York: Cambridge University Press, 2010.

Kāshānī, ᶜAbd al-Razzāq. *Iṣṭilāḥāt al-ṣūfiyyah*. Cairo: Dār al-Manār, 1992.

Kenney, John Peter. *Mystical Monotheism: A Study in Ancient Platonic Theology*. Providence, RI: Brown University Press, 1991.

Khamanei, Sayyid Muḥammad. *Mullā Ṣadrā: Zindagī, shakhṣiyyat wa maktab-i Ṣadr al-muta'allihīn*. Tehran: Bunyād-i Ḥikmat-i Islāmī-yi Ṣadrā [Ṣadrā Islamic Philosophy Research Institute], 1379/2000.

———. *Principles of Interpretation and Quranic Hermeneutics according to Mulla Sadra: Presented to the Conference of Qur'an, Text and Interpretation, SOAS (University of London), October 1999*. London: Islamic Studies Press, 1999.

Khwājawī, Muḥammad. *Lawāmiᶜ al-ᶜārifīn fī aḥwāl Ṣadr al-muta'allihīn*. Tehran: Ariyan Press, 1366/1987.

Lāhījī, Muḥammad Jaᶜfar. *Sharḥ risālat al-mashāᶜir*. Edited by Sayyid Jalāl al-Dīn Āshtiyānī. Tehran: Mu'assasat-yi Intishārāt-i Amīr Kabīr, 1376/1997.

Mayer, Toby. "Ibn Sina's 'Burhān al-Ṣiddīqīn.'" *Journal of Islamic Studies* 12, no. 1 (2001): 18–39.

Morgan, David. *Medieval Persia, 1040–1797*. A History of the Near East. Edited by Peter M. Holt. New York: Longman, 1988.

Mullā Ṣadrā. *See* Ṣadr al-Dīn Shīrāzī, Muḥammad ibn Ibrāhīm.

Naeem, Fuad S. "A Traditional Islamic Response to the Rise of Modernism." In *Islam, Fundamentalism, and the Betrayal of Tradition: Essays by Western Muslim Scholars*, edited by Joseph E. B. Lumbard, 79–116. Perennial Philosophy Series. Bloomington, IN: World Wisdom, 2004.

Nasr, Seyyed Hossein. "The Qur'ānic Commentaries of Mullā Sadrā." In *Being and Consciousness: Studies in Memory of Toshihiko Izutsu*, edited by S. J. Āshtiyānī, H. Matsubara, T. Iwami, and A. Matsumoto. Tokyo: Iwanami Shoten, 1998. Reprinted in Nasr, *Ṣadr al-Din Shīrāzī and His Transcendent Theosophy*, 123–35.

———. *Ṣadr al-Dīn Shīrāzī and His Transcendent Theosophy: Background, Life and Works.* 2nd ed. Tehran: Institute for Humanities and Cultural Studies, 1997.

———. "The School of Isfahan Revisited." In Nasr, *Islamic Philosophy from Its Origin to the Present: Philosophy in the Land of Prophecy*, 209–21. SUNY Series in Islam. Albany: State University of New York Press, 2006.

———. "The School of Iṣpahān." In *A History of Muslim Philosophy with Short Accounts of Other Disciplines and the Modern Renaissance in Muslim Lands*, edited by M. M. Sharif, 2:904–32. Wiesbaden, Germany: Otto Harrassowitz, 1966. Reprinted as "The School of Isfahan" in Nasr, *The Islamic Intellectual Tradition in Persia*, edited by Mehdi Amin Razavi, 239–70. Richmond, Surrey, England: Curzon Press, 1996.

———. "Spiritual Movements, Philosophy and Theology in the Safavid Period." In *The Cambridge History of Iran*, vol. 6, *The Timurid and Safavid Periods*, edited by Peter Jackson and Laurence Lockhart, 656–97. Cambridge: Cambridge University Press, 1986.

Newman, Andrew J. "The Nature of the Akhbārī/Uṣūlī Dispute in Late-Ṣafawid Iran. Part One: ʿAbdallāh al-Samāhijī's 'Munyat al-Mumārisīn,'" and "Part Two: The Conflict Reassessed." *Bulletin of the School of Oriental and African Studies* 55, no. 1 (1992): 22–51; 55, no. 2 (1992): 250–61.

———. "Towards a Reconsideration of the 'Isfahan School of Philosophy': Shaykh Baha'i and the Role of the Safawid Ulama." *Studia Iranica* [Paris] 15, no. 2 (1986): 165–99.

Peerwani, Latimah-Parvin. "Quranic Hermeneutics: The Views of Sadr al-Din Shirazi." *British Society for Middle East Studies Proceedings*, 1991, 468–77.

Qayṣarī, Dāwūd al-. *Al-Muqaddimāt.* In *Al-Rasā'il*, edited by Mehmet Bayraktar. Kayseri, Turkey: Kayseri Metropolitan Municipality, 1997.

Qurṭubī, Abū ʿAbdullah Muḥammad ibn Aḥmad al-Anṣārī al-. *Al-Jāmiʿ li'l-aḥkām al-Qur'ān.* Riyadh, Saudi Arabia: Dār al-ʿĀlam al-Kutub, 2003.

Rahman, Fazlur. *The Philosophy of Mullā Ṣadrā (Ṣadr al-Dīn al-Shīrāzī).* Studies in Islamic Philosophy and Science. Albany: State University of New York Press, 1975.

Rāzī, Fakhr al-Dīn al-. *Al-Mabāḥith al-mashriqiyyah.* Edited by Muḥammad al-Baghdādī. 2 vols. Beirut: Dār al-Kitāb al-ʿArabī, 1990.

———. *Al-Maṭālib al-ʿāliyah min al-ʿilm al-ilāhī.* Edited by Aḥmad Ḥijāzī al-Saqqā. 9 vols. Beirut: Dār al-Kitāb al-ʿArabī, 1987.

Rizvi, Sajjad H. *Mullā Ṣadrā and Metaphysics: Modulation of Being.* Culture and Civilization in the Middle East. New York: Routledge, 2009.

———. *Mullā Ṣadrā Shīrāzī: His Life and Works and the Sources for Safavid Philosophy.* Journal of Semitic Studies Supplement 18. Oxford: Oxford University Press, 2007.

Sabziwārī, al-Ḥājj Mullā Hādī al-. *Sharḥ al-manẓūmah.* 5 vols. Qom, Iran: Nāb, 1995.

Ṣadr al-Dīn Shīrāzī, Muḥammad ibn Ibrāhīm. *Aṣālat ja ʾl al-wujūd*. In *Majmūʿa-yi rasāʾil-i falsafī-yi Ṣadr al-Mutaʾallihīn*, edited by Ḥāmid Nājī Iṣfahānī. Tehran: Intishārāt-i Ḥikmat, AH 1375.

———. *The Elixir of the Gnostics* [Iksīr al-ʿārifīn]. Edited and translated by William C. Chittick. Provo, UT: Brigham Young University Press, 2003.

———. *Al-Ḥikmat al-ʿarshiyyah*. Edited by G. Āhanī. Isfahan: Irān, 1961.

———. *Al-Ḥikmat al-mutaʿāliyah fī al-asfār al-ʿaqliyyat al-ʿarbaʿah*. Edited by Muḥammad Riḍā al-Muẓaffar. 9 vols. Beirut: Dār Iḥyāʾ al-Turāth al-ʿArabī, 1981.

———. *Ḥudūth al-ʿālam*. Edited by S. H. Mūsawiyān. Tehran: Bunyād-i Ḥikmat-i Islāmī-yi Ṣadrā [Ṣadrā Islamic Philosophy Research Institute], AH 1378.

———. *Īqāẓ al-nāʾimīn*. Edited by Muḥammad Khwansārī. Tehran: Bunyād-i Ḥikmat-i Islāmī-yi Ṣadrā [Ṣadrā Islamic Philosophy Research Institute], AH 1384.

———. *Ittiḥād al-ʿāqil wa'l-maʿqūl*. In *Majmūʿa-yi rasāʾil-i falsafī-yi Ṣadr al-Mutaʾallihīn*, edited by Ḥāmid Nājī Iṣfahānī. Tehran: Intishārāt-i Ḥikmat, AH 1375.

———. *Kasr aṣnām al-jāhiliyyah*. Edited by N. Jahāngīrī. Tehran: Bunyād-i Ḥikmat-i Islāmī-yi Ṣadrā [Ṣadrā Islamic Philosophy Research Institute], AH 1381.

———. *Le Livre des pénétrations métaphysiques* [Kitāb al-mashāʿir]. Edited and translated by Henry Corbin. Tehran: Institut Français d'Iranologie de Téhéran, 1982.

———. *Al-Mabdaʾ wa'l-maʿād*. Edited by Muḥammad Dhabīhī and Jaʿfar Shāh Naẓari. 2 vols. Tehran: Bunyād-i Ḥikmat-i Islāmī-yi Ṣadrā [Ṣadrā Islamic Philosophy Research Institute], 2002–3.

———. *Mafātiḥ al-ghayb*. 2 vols. Beirut: Muʾassasat al-Tārīkh al-ʿArabī, 1999.

———. *Majmūʿa-yi rasāʾil-i falsafī-yi Ṣadr al-Mutaʾallihīn*. Edited by Ḥāmid Nājī Iṣfahānī. Tehran: Intishārāt-i Ḥikmat, AH 1375.

———. *Al-Masāʾil al-qudsiyyah*. In *Si risāla-yi falsafī*, edited by Sayyid Jalāl al-Dīn Āshtiyānī. Qom, Iran: Markaz-i Intishārāt-i Daftar-i Tablīghāt-i Islāmī, AH 1379.

———. *Al-Maẓāhir al-ilāhiyyah fī asrār al-ʿulūm al-kamāliyyah*. Edited by Sayyid Muḥammad Khamanei. Tehran: Bunyād-i Ḥikmat-i Islāmī-yi Ṣadrā [Ṣadrā Islamic Philosophy Research Institute], AH 1378.

———. *The Metaphysics of Mullā Ṣadrā*. Translated by Parviz Morewedge. Islamic Philosophy Translation Series. Binghamton, NY: Society for the Study of Islamic Philosophy and Science, 1992.

———. *Al-Risālah fī al-ḥudūth (Ḥudūth al-ʿālam)*. Edited by S. H. Mūsawiyān. Tehran: Bunyād-i Ḥikmat-i Islāmī-yi Ṣadrā [Ṣadrā Islamic Philosophy Research Institute], AH 1378.

———. *Risālat al-ḥashr*. Edited with Persian translation by Muḥammad Khwājawī. Tehran: Intishārāt-i Mawlawī, 1988.

———. *Se rendre immortel, suivi du Traité de la résurrection* [Risālat al-ḥashr]. Translated by Christian Jambet. Paris: Fata Morgana, 2000.

———. *Sharḥ al-hidāyah al-athiriyyah*. Tehran: Lithograph edition, 1313/1895.

———. *Sharḥ-i ilāhiyyāt-i shifāʾ*. Edited by Najafqulī Ḥabībī. 2 vols. Tehran: Bunyād-i Ḥikmat-i Islāmī-yi Ṣadrā [Ṣadrā Islamic Philosophy Research Institute], AH 1382.

———. *Sharḥ uṣūl al-kāfī*. Edited by Muḥammad Khwājawī. 5 vols. Tehran, AH 1366.

———. *Al-Shawāhid al-rubūbiyyah*. Edited by Sayyid Jalāl al-Dīn Āshtiyānī. 2nd ed. 2 vols. Mashhad, Iran: Al-Markaz al-Jāmiʿ liʾl-Nashr, 1981.

———. *Si aṣl.* Edited by Seyyed Hossein Nasr. Tehran: Tehran University Press, 1340/1961; reprint, Tehran: Intishārāt-i Rawzanah, 1377/1998.

———. *Tafsīr al-Qurʾān al-karīm.* Edited by Muḥammad Khwājawī. 7 vols. Qom, Iran: Intishārāt-i Bīdār, 1366–69/1987–90.

———. *The Wisdom of the Throne* [Al-Ḥikmat al-ʿarshiyyah]*: An Introduction to the Philosophy of Mullā Ṣadrā.* Translated by James Winston Morris. Princeton Library of Asian Translations. Princeton, NJ: Princeton University Press, 1981.

Salih, Muhsin. "The Verse of Light: A Study of Mullā Ṣadrā's Philosophical Qurʾān Exegesis." PhD diss., Temple University, 1993.

Shboul, Ahmad M. H. "Byzantium and the Arabs: The Image of the Byzantines as Mirrored in Arabic Literature." In *Arab-Byzantine Relations in Early Islamic Times*, edited by Michael Bonner, 235–60. New York: Ashgate, 2004.

Sorabji, Richard. *Animal Minds and Human Morals: The Origins of the Western Debate.* Cornell Studies in Classical Philology–Townsend Lectures 54. Ithaca, NY: Cornell University Press, 1993.

Walbridge, John. *The Leaven of the Ancients: Suhrawardī and the Heritage of the Greeks.* SUNY Series in Islam. Albany: State University of New York Press, 2000.

Wittgenstein, Ludwig. *Philosophical Investigations.* Translated by Gertrude Elizabeth Margaret Anscombe. New York: Macmillan, 1968.

Yazdi, Mehdi Haʾiri. *The Principles of Epistemology in Islamic Philosophy: Knowledge by Presence.* SUNY Series in Islam. Albany: State University of New York Press, 1992.

Ziai, Hossein. *Knowledge and Illumination: A Study of Suhrawardī's Ḥikmat al-Ishrāq.* Brown University Judaic Studies 97. Atlanta: Scholars Press, 1990.

Index

Index of Qur'ānic Citations

About the Editors and Translators

A prominent Islamic philosopher, SEYYED HOSSEIN NASR (PhD, Harvard University) is professor of Islamic Studies at The George Washington University. He writes and lectures widely in the fields of Islamic esoterism, Sufism, philosophy of science, and metaphysics. He is author of numerous books and articles, including Knowledge and the Sacred (SUNY Press, 1989), The Heart of Islam: Enduring Values for Humanity (HarperOne, 2004), Islamic Philosophy from Its Origin to the Present: Philosophy in the Land of Prophecy (SUNY Press, 2006), and The Garden of Truth: The Vision and Promise of Sufism, Islam's Mystical Tradition (HarperOne, reprint edition, 2008).

A broadly trained scholar of Islamic studies, Dr. IBRAHIM KALIN concentrates on post-Avicennan Islamic philosophy with research interests in comparative philosophy, Muslim-Christian relations, and modern Turkish history. Professor Kalin (PhD, The George Washington University) has published widely on Islamic philosophy and the relations between Islam and the West. He is the author of Knowledge in Later Islamic Philosophy: Mulla Sadra on Existence, Intellect, and Intuition (Oxford University Press, 2010) and editor, together with John Esposito, of Islamophobia: The Challenge of Pluralism in the 21st Century (Oxford University Press, 2011). A fellow at the Prince Alwaleed Center for Muslim-Christian Understanding, Georgetown University, he also serves as deputy undersecretary, Turkish Prime Ministry.